BIZ TALK·2

MORE AMERICAN BUSINESS SLANG & JARGON

BIZ TALK·2

MORE AMERICAN BUSINESS SLANG & JARGON

David Burke

Optima Books

Publisher: Optima Books
Editor: Robert Graul
Editing, Design, and Production: Optima Books
Front Cover Illustration: Ty Semaka
Inside Illustrations: Ty Semaka

The persons, entities and events in this book are fictitious. Any similarities to actual persons or entities, past and present, are purely coincidental.

ISBN 1-879440-19-9
Printed in the United States of America
97 10 9 8 7 6 5 4 3 2 1

This book is dedicated to my wonderful and adorable friend, cohort, and fellow conniver, Chelita Lupita Powell (aka *Chellie*).

Introduction

BIZ TALK -2, the second book in the *Biz Talk* series, is an entertaining step-by-step approach to more of the actual spoken language used in American business and international trade. Many of these business terms have found their way into the home, movies, books, magazines, television, and day-to-day life.

BIZ TALK -2 is a companion volume to *Biz Talk -1* and presents additional popular slang and jargon used in the general office, the computer world (essential terms for today's information age), international trade (plus commonly used initials), bureaucracy, management, politics, and more.

This easy-to-use textbook/workbook is divided into five parts:

- **DIALOGUE**

  Approximately twenty new slang terms and expressions (indicated in boldface) are presented as they might be heard in an actual conversation. A translation of the dialogue in standard English is given on the opposite page followed by an important phonetic version of the dialogue as it would actually be spoken by a native-born American. This page will prove instructive to any non-native speaker since Americans tend to rely heavily on contractions and shortcuts in pronunciation.

  NOTE -1: On occasion, some of the words used in *Biz Talk 1* will be repeated here due to their frequent usage.

  NOTE -2: See *Colloquial Pronunciation Used in Biz Talk -2* on page xi.

- **VOCABULARY**

  This section spotlights all of the slang words and expressions used in the dialogue and offers more examples of usage, synonyms and antonyms, as well as special notes.

- **PRACTICE THE VOCABULARY**

  These word games include all of the terms and idioms presented in the vocabulary section and will help to test the reader's comprehension. *(The pages providing the answers to all the drills are indicated at the beginning of this section.)*

- **A CLOSER LOOK**
  This section offers an in-depth look at common words used in slang expressions pertaining to that chapter's theme.

- **EXERCISES**
  These exercises help to familiarize the reader with the terms just encountered in the *A CLOSER LOOK* section.

BIZ TALK -2 will guide the reader through some of the most popular slang terms, jargon, and expressions used today in American business and international trade. Any business reader, from the twenty-year veteran of the English language, to the beginning student, is sure to find the following terms informative, helpful, and perhaps, even essential.

David Burke
Author

Acknowledgments

I can't thank Janet Graul enough for her invaluable assistance as copy editor of this book. Once again, she made this phase of production wonderfully enjoyable and effortless.

I'm forever grateful for finding Ty Semaka, a gifted illustrator who never ceases to amaze me with drawings that are clever, hilarious, and exciting.

Legend

verb

a term or expression opposite in meaning of the main entry in boldface

bend (to) *v.* to be flexible.
ANTONYM: give an inch (not to) *exp.* (usually used in the negative) to be very inflexible.

boldface words in parentheses are used before the main entry — they appear after the main entry for alphabetization purposes only i.e. *to get booted.*

literal translation

a common variation of the main entry in boldface

booted (to get) *exp.* to get fired · (lit.): to get kicked out by someone in uniform (who typically wears boots).
VARIATION: get the boot (to) *exp.*

noun

additional information about the main entry in boldface

reserved note (black on white) - useful information about the entry directly above

poll *n.* the place where voting takes place (usually in the plural: *polls*).
ALSO: straw poll *n.* a random sampling of opinion.
NOTE: This comes from drawing straws which is used to insure that participants are chosen at random.

adjective

dysfunctional *adj.* ineffective.

expression

a term or expression equivalent in meaning to the main entry in boldface

get to the bottom of something (to) *exp.* to identify something.
SYNONYM: zero in on something (to) *exp.*

useful information about the main entry

gubernatorial race *exp.* a contest for the election of governor.
NOTE: gubernatorial *adj.* having to do with a governor.

COLLOQUIAL PRONUNCIATION USED IN BIZ TALK -2

As Written	Colloquial Pronunciation	Notes / Examples
and	*n' / an'*	The reduction **'n** is used when the next word is quickly connected: *That's Steve* ***'n*** *Michael.* However, if the speaker takes a brief pause before reducing the conjunction *and,* **an'** is commonly used: *Yesterday I went to an amusement park...* ***an'*** *tomorrow I'm spending the day at the beach.*
because	'cuz	I don't like Steve ***'cuz*** *he's mean.*
can	*c'n*	*I* ***c'n*** *be ready to leave in two minutes.*
did you	*didja / didju*	Although these reductions may be used interchangeably, ***didja*** is commonly followed by a consonant, and ***didju*** is usually followed by a vowel: ***Didja*** *see Nancy at the party?* ***Didju*** *invite him for dinner?*
for	*fer*	*Steve gave me a great present* ***fer*** *my birthday.*
forget / forgot	*ferget / fergot*	*I always* ***ferget*** *where I put my car keys.*
going to	gonna	*If you don't hurry, you're* ***gonna*** *be late!*
have to	*hafta*	*I* ***hafta*** *leave in a minute.*
he	'e	*Who does* ***'e*** *think* ***'e*** *is?!*
her	'er	*What's* ***'er*** *problem now?*
him	'im	*Look at* ***'im*** *run!*

COLLOQUIAL PRONUNCIATION USED IN BIZ TALK -2		
As Written	**Colloquial Pronunciation**	**Notes / Examples**
his	*'is*	*That's* ***'is*** *mother.*
look at	*look 'it*	*Look* ***'it*** *what you've done!*
of	*'a / 'ev*	Although these reductions may be used interchangeably, ***'a*** is commonly followed by a consonant, and ***'ev*** is usually followed by a vowel: *Karen has a lot* ***'a*** *children.* *(pronounced: a lodda)* *I have an account with Bank* ***'ev*** *America.*
or	*'r*	*Which dress do you prefer? The green one* ***'r*** *the black one?*
ought to	*odda*	*You* ***odda*** *put on a sweater. It's cold outside.*
our	*'ar*	*Do you like* ***'ar*** *new house?*
should have	*should 'a*	*I* ***should 'a*** *listened to Connie when she warned me not to buy a used car.*
some	*s'm*	*I need* ***s'm*** *more time to finish this work.*
than	*th'n*	*Jim is a year older* ***th'n*** *you.*
them	*'em / th'm*	Athough both reductions may be used interchangeably, ***th'm*** is often used to make a distinction from ***'im*** (a reduction of "him") when the context is not clear: *I haven't met* ***'em*** *before.* *I haven't met* ***th'm*** *before.*

COLLOQUIAL PRONUNCIATION USED IN BIZ TALK -2		
As Written	**Colloquial Pronunciation**	**Notes / Examples**
to	*ta / da*	When followed by a vowel, ***ta*** becomes ***da***: *Did you give a birthday gift* ***ta*** *Rob?* *I'll go* ***da*** *the store later.*
would have	*would 'a*	*I* ***would 'a*** *called you but I lost your telephone number.*
you	*ya*	*How are* ***ya****?*
you're	*y'r*	***Y'r*** *a very hard worker.*
your	*yer*	***Yer*** *work has improved a lot.*

SPECIAL NOTE

In the *as spoken* sections of this book, when the letter "t" is preceded by an "n," the "t" is often in parenthesis. This is because many Americans tend not to articulate the "t" in these cases. Example: *During the tour of the movie studio, we visited the en***(t)***ertainment cen***(t)***er.*

TABLE OF CONTENTS

Introduction vii
Acknowledgments ix
Legend x

Lesson 1 **1**

General Business Slang & Jargon
(Part A)

Dialogue 2
Vocabulary 5
Practice the Vocabulary 11
A Closer Look: *General Business Slang & Jargon (Part A)* 17

Lesson 2 **29**

General Business Slang & Jargon
(Part B)

Dialogue 30
Vocabulary 33
Practice the Vocabulary 42
A Closer Look: *General Business Slang & Jargon (Part B)* 46

Lesson 3 **55**

International Trade Slang & Jargon
(Part A)

Dialogue 56
Vocabulary 59
Practice the Vocabulary 63
A Closer Look: *International Trade Slang & Jargon (Part A)* 66

Lesson 4 **79**

International Trade Slang & Jargon
(Part B)

Dialogue 80
Vocabulary 83
Practice the Vocabulary 88
A Closer Look: 91
International Trade Slang & Jargon (Part B)

Lesson 5 **107**

Initials Used in International Trade

Dialogue 108
Vocabulary 111
Practice the Vocabulary 116
A Closer Look: 121
Initials Used in International Trade

Lesson 6 **135**

MORE Computer Slang
(Common slang and jargon used in the world of computers)

Dialogue 136
Vocabulary 139
Practice the Vocabulary 145
A Closer Look: 149
More Computer Slang

Lesson 7 **165**

Bureaucratese
(Useful terms for anyone living in the United States)

Dialogue 166
Vocabulary 169
Practice the Vocabulary 173
A Closer Look: 176
Popular Bureaucratese

Lesson 8 183

Political Slang & Jargon
(Popular political terms, particularly during elections)

Dialogue 184
Vocabulary 187
Practice the Vocabulary 195
A Closer Look: 200
Common Political Slang & Jargon

Lesson 9 211

Management Slang & Jargon
(Part A)

Dialogue 212
Vocabulary 215
Practice the Vocabulary 222
A Closer Look: 225
Management Slang & Jargon (Part A)

Lesson 10 239

Management Slang & Jargon
(Part B)

Dialogue 240
Vocabulary 243
Practice the Vocabulary 250
A Closer Look: 254
Management Slang & Jargon(Part B)

Answers To Lessons 1-10 268

Glossary 282

LESSON ONE

General Business Slang & Jargon (Part A)

Janet and David enjoy working ***hand in hand.***

Lesson One

Dialogue in slang

Janet: Were you able **to smooth everything out** with our distributors? Did you **get to the bottom of** our poor **sales performance**?

David: **All in all**, it went pretty well. **In a nutshell**, we had an **in-depth** discussion about the importance of **working hand in hand**. Since our success **hinges on** their efforts **to push** our products, we renegotiated our contract. After a lot of **give-and-take**, and **back-and-forth**, we **reached an agreement**. It only took an hour **or so** to **thrash it all out** and while there are still some **loose ends**, I think it'll all work out **in the long run**.

Janet: They certainly do know **the ins and outs** of distribution. It sounds like **all systems are go**.

David: Everything should **run smoothly** now. I predict that sales will **pick up** in a month **at the outside**.

Lesson One

Translation of dialogue in standard English

General Business Slang & Jargon (Part A)

Janet: Were you able **to rectify the situation** with our distributors? Did you **investigate** the reasons for our poor **sales efficiency**?

David: **Considering all the elements**, it went pretty well. **To be brief**, we had a **detailed** discussion about the importance of **working together**. Since our success **depends on** their efforts **to promote** our products, we renegotiated our contract. After a lot of **compromise**, and **lenthy discussion**, we **arrived at an agreement**. It took an hour **approximately** to **discuss every point** and while there are still some **unresolved issues**, I think it'll all work out **over a long period of time**.

Janet: They certainly do know **the particulars** of distribution. It sounds like **everything is ready**.

David: Everything should **operate without problems** now. I predict that sales will **increase** in a month **at the most**.

Lesson One

Dialogue in slang as it would be heard

General Business Slang & Jargon (Part A)

Janet: Were ya able **ta smooth ev'rything out** with 'r distribyaders? Didja **get ta the boddom of** 'r poor **sales performance**?

David: **All 'n all**, it went preddy well. **In a nutshell**, we had an **in-depth** discussion about thee importance of **working hand in hand**. Since our success **hinges on** their efferts **ta push** 'r products, we renegoshiaded 'r contract. After a lod 'a **give 'n take**, 'n **back 'n forth**, we **reached an agreement**. Id only took an hour **'r so** da **thrash id all out** an' while there'er still s'm **loose ends**, I think id'll all work oud **in the long run**.

Janet: They certainly do know **thee ins 'n outs** of distribution. It sounds like **all systems'er go**.

David: Ev'rything should **run smoothly** now. I predict that sales'll **pick up** in a month **at thee outside**.

Vocabulary

all in all *exp.* considering all the elements, all things considered.

example: **All in all**, I think your ideas are very good.

translation: **Considering all the elements**, I think your ideas are very good.

as spoken: **All in all**, I think yer ideaz'er very good.

all systems are go *exp.* everything is ready.

example: **All systems are go**. The photocopy machine is plugged in, it has new toner and it's full of paper.

translation: **Everything is ready**. The photocopy machine is plugged in, it has new toner and it's full of paper.

as spoken: **All systems are go**. The phodocopy machine's plugged in, it has new toner and it's full of paper.

at the outside *exp.* at the most.

example: The publisher said it will take four weeks **at the outside** to print the books.

translation: The publisher said it will take four weeks **at the most** to print the books.

as spoken: The publisher said id'll take four weeks **at thee outside** ta print the books.

back-and-forth *n.* lengthy discussion between two people (or two groups).

example: After a lot of **back-and-forth**, we agreed on the terms of the contract.

translation: After a lot of **lengthy discussion**, we agreed on the terms of the contract.

as spoken: After a lotta **back-'n- forth**, we agreed on the terms 'a the contract.

ALSO: **back-and-forth (to go)** *exp.* to discuss something at length.

get to the bottom (to) *exp.* to investigate, to begin an investigation.

example: We need **to get to the bottom** of the problems we're having with international sales.

translation: We need **to investigate** the problems we're having with international sales.

as spoken: We need **ta get ta the boddom** 'a the problems w'r having with in(t)ernational sales.

give-and-take *exp.* compromise.

example: Before you begin negotiations, just remember that there's going to be a lot of **give-and-take**.

translation: Before you begin negotiations, just remember that there's going to be a lot of **compromise**.

as spoken: Before ya b'gin negotiations, just ramember that there's gonna be a lod of **give-'n-take**.

ALSO: **meet half way (to)** *exp.*

hinge (to) *v.* to depend on.

example: The success of this product **hinges** on our ability to buy television advertising by tomorrow.

translation: The success of this product **depends** on our ability to buy television advertising by tomorrow.

as spoken: The success of this product **hinges** on our abilidy ta buy TV advertising by d'morrow.

in-depth • **1.** *adv.* in detail • **2.** *adj.* detailed.

example (1): Before we can begin this project, we need to look at it **in-depth**. Let's make sure that nothing will go wrong.

translation: Before we can begin this project, we need to look at it **in detail**. Let's make sure that nothing will go wrong.

as spoken: Before we c'n b'gin this project, we need ta look ad id **in-depth**. Let's make sher th't nothing'll go wrong.

example (2): We need to have an **in depth** discussion about your work.

translation: We need to have a **detailed** discussion about your work.

as spoken: We need ta have 'n **in depth** discussion about ch'r work.

in the long run *exp.* over a long period of time.

example: The money we're spending on publicity may not help right away, but **in the long run**, should improve our sales.

translation: The money we're spending on publicity may not help right away, but **over a long period of time**, should improve our sales.

as spoken: The money w'r spending on publicidy may not help ride away, but **in the long run**, should improve 'ar sales.

loose ends *n.* unresolved issues, unfinished business.

example: We've decided that we're going to merge our two companies to form one large organization. We still have some **loose ends** to tie up, but all of the most important points have been settled.

translation: We've decided that we're going to merge our two companies to form one large organization. We still have some **unresolved issues** to tie up, but all of the most important points have been settled.

as spoken: We've decided that w'r gonna merge 'ar two companies ta form one large organization. We still have s'm **loose ends** ta tie up, bud all 'a the most important points've been settled.

NOTE: **tie up (to)** *v.* to resolve.

nutshell (in a) *n.* in summation.

example: I could take an hour explaining all the reasons why we should publish more books about science-fiction. **In a nutshell**, it's a subject that's in high demand right now.

translation: I could take an hour explaining all the reasons why we should publish more books about science-fiction. **In summation**, it's a subject that's in high demand right now.

as spoken: I could take 'n hour explaining all the reasons why we should publish more books about science-fiction. **In a nutshell**, it's a subject that's in high demand right now.

SYNONYM: **the long and the short of it** *exp.*

or so *exp.* approximately.

example: Richard said he'll be five minutes **or so** late to our meeting.

translation: Richard said he'll be **approximately** five minutes late to our meeting.

as spoken: Richard said e'll be five minutes **'r so** late ta 'ar meeding.

pick up (to) *v.* to increase.

example: Sales usually **pick up** dramatically in December.

translation: Sales usually **increase** dramatically in December.

as spoken: Sales ujally **pick up** dramadic'lly in D'cember.

push (to) *v.* to promote.

example: If we want to improve our sales, we need to **push** our products in the local magazines.

translation: If we want to improve our sales, we need to **promote** our products in the local magazines.

as spoken: If we wanna improve 'ar sales, we need ta **push** 'ar produc's in the local magazines.

reach an agreement (to) *v.* to agree, to make a mutual arrangement.

example: After negotiating for months, our two companies finally **reached an agreement**.

translation: After negotiating for months, our two companies finally **made a mutual arrangement**.

as spoken: After negoshiading fer months, 'ar two companies fin'lly **reached 'n agreement**.

run smoothly (to) *v.* to operate without problems.

example: Our business has been **running smoothly** since we got a new manager.

translation: Our business has been **operating without problems** since we got a new manager.

as spoken: 'Ar business iz been **running smoothly** since we god a new manager.

sales performance *n.* rating of a salesperson's efficiency (such as good or bad).

example: My boss gave me a raise for my **sales performance** last month!

translation: My boss gave me a raise for my (good) **sales efficiency** last month!

as spoken: My boss gave me a raise fer my **sales performance** las' month!

smooth everything out (to) *v.* to rectify a situation.

example: Our distributor is angry with our sales representative. I'd better meet with them and try **to smooth everything out**.

translation: Our distributor is angry with our sales representative. I'd better meet with them and try **to rectify the situation**.

as spoken: 'Ar distribuder's angry with 'ar sales reprezen'adive. I bedder meet with 'em 'n try **da smooth everything out**.

SYNONYM: **iron everything out (to)** *exp.*

the ins and outs *n.* the particulars, the details.

example: Bob knows all **the ins-and-outs** of the business.

translation: Bob knows all **the particulars** of the business.

as spoken: Bob knows all **thee ins-'n-outs** of the business.

thrash out (to) *exp.* to discuss in detail.

example: I don't have time to argue with you right now. Why don't you come to my office first thing tomorrow morning and we can **thrash this out**?

translation: I don't have time to argue with you right now. Why don't you come to my office first thing tomorrow morning and we can **discuss this in detail**?

as spoken: I don't have time ta argue with you right now. Why donchu come ta my office firs' thing tomorrow morning 'n we c'n **thrash this out**?

SYNONYM -1: **hash over (to)** *v.*

SYNONYM -2: **hash out (to)** *v.*

work hand in hand (to) *exp.* to work together as a team.

example: We're **working hand-in-hand** with our distributor to promote the books in Japan.

translation: We're **working as a team** with our distributor to promote the books in Japan.

as spoken: W'r **working hand-in-hand** with 'ar distribyader ta promote the books in Japan.

Practice the Vocabulary

(Answers to Lesson 1, p. 268)

A. Choose the correct phrase that completes the sentence or thought.

1. **I'm sure sales will pick up in a month.**
   ☐ We'll be making less money soon.
   ☐ We'll be making more money soon.

2. **In a nutshell, tell me what happened.**
   ☐ I want you to be as concise as possible.
   ☐ Take as long as you need.

3. **We had an in-depth conversation.**
   ☐ We didn't talk in great detail.
   ☐ We talked in great detail.

4. **Our business is running very smoothly.**
   ☐ We don't have any problems at all!
   ☐ We have nothing but problems!

5. **Our meeting took an hour or so.**
   ☐ It started at 2 o'clock and ended at exactly 3 o'clock.
   ☐ It started at 2 o'clock and ended around 3 o'clock.

6. **All systems are go!**
   ☐ We're all ready!
   ☐ We're not ready yet!

7. **The boss was angry, but I smoothed everything out.**
   ☐ Now he's angrier than ever.
   ☐ He feels much better now.

8. **Everyone in our company works hand in hand.**
   ☐ Each employee is completely independent.
   ☐ Each employee cooperates with the other.

9. **You really know the ins and outs of the business.**
   ☐ I didn't realize you were so inexperienced.
   ☐ I didn't realize you were so knowledgeable!

10. **I'm glad our two companies finally reached an agreement.**
    ☐ Let's celebrate our future together!
    ☐ I guess we won't be working together.

11. **It will take a month, at the outside, to complete this report.**
    ☐ In fact, I'll give it to you in two months.
    ☐ In fact, I'll give it to you in a few weeks.

12. **We need to push our products more.**
    ☐ It's going to be difficult because they're so heavy.
    ☐ We need to increase our advertising.

B. CONTEXT EXERCISE
Choose the idiom from the right column that follows the phrase in the left column.

☐ 1. We made twice as much money this year as we made last year.

☐ 2. Let me tell you exactly what happened during my meeting with the boss.

☐ 3. I need you to develop some new designs that will make our products more attractive.

☐ 4. Our negotiations took weeks.

☐ 5. We're all ready to begin operation of our new company.

☐ 6. It shouldn't take too long to finish this project.

☐ 7. I can't wait to go on vacation next week.

☐ 8. We had some trouble in the beginning.

☐ 9. There seems to be a real team effort among your employees.

☐ 10. Steven was late again this morning. He claims he was stuck in traffic.

A. Our success **hinges on** your creativitiy!

B. But after a lot of **give and take**, we finally agreed on a fee.

C. I have a few **loose ends** to tie up and then I'll be ready to leave!

D. **All systems are go!**

E. Fortunately, everything is **running smoothly** now.

F. **In a nutshell**, everything went great! I'm getting a raise!

G. I'm glad sales have finally **picked up**!

H. I'd say that I'll be done in a week **at the outside**.

I. I'm going to **get to the bottom of this** right now. Our employees need to be punctual!

J. It's nice to see people **working hand in hand**.

C. CROSSWORD

Fill in the crossword puzzle on the opposite page by choosing the correct word(s) from the list below. (Note: "run" is used twice.)

all	**nutshell**	**reached**
bottom	**outs**	**run**
depth	**outside**	**smooth**
give-and-take	**performance**	**so**
hand	**pick**	**systems**
hinges	**push**	**thrash**

ACROSS

1. Advertising will cost a lot of money, but in the long ____ , it will be worth it.

13. We had an in- ____ conversation and discussed all the details.

21. Because your sales ____ has been so good, I'm giving you a raise!

23. I won't go into every detail, but all in____ , the meeting went very well.

27. After two weeks, both sides finally ____ an agreement.

33. The sucess of our company ____ on next year's sales.

43. I'm sorry to be late. I should be there by 3 o'clock at the ____ .

DOWN

3. In a ____ , I'm firing you because of your attitutde.

6. We're all ready. All ____ are go!

12. Something is wrong here. I'm going to get to the ____ of it.

16. In any negotiation, there has to be a lot of ____ .

19. It's a lot easier to work hand in____ than working all by yourself.

34. I've heard that Jim and Earl are having a big disagreement. I'd better go ____ everything out.

35. Bob really knows the ins and____ of publishing.

ACROSS (con't)

44. We don't have any more problems. Everything should ____ smoothly from now on.

45. It should take me an hour or ____ to finish this report.

51. Our meeting took three hours. We had a lot to ____ out.

DOWN (con't)

40. Business is really starting to ____ up. Look at all these sales!

42. We need to ____ our products if we want sales to increase.

CROSSWORD PUZZLE

D. Complete the opening dialogue using the appropriate idioms from the list below.

all	**ins**	**run**
bottom	**loose**	**sales**
depth	**nutshell**	**smooth**
forth	**outside**	**smoothly**
go	**pick**	**so**
hand	**push**	**take**
hinges	**reached**	**thrash**

Janet: Were you able **to** *(1)* ___________ **everything out** with our distributors? Did you **get to the** *(2)* _____________ **of** our poor *(3)* ______________________ **performance**?

David: **All in** *(4)* ________, it went pretty well. **In a** *(5)* _____________, we had an **in-** *(6)* _________ **discussion** about the importance of **working hand in** *(7)* _________. Because our success *(8)* __________ **on** their efforts **to** *(9)* __________ our products, we renegotiated our contract. After a lot of **give-and-** *(10)* _________ and **back-and-** *(11)* _____________, we *(12)* ______________ **an agreement**. It only took an hour **or** *(13)* _____________ to *(14)* _________________ **it all out** and while there are still some *(15)* ______________ **ends**, I think it'll all work out **in the long** *(16)* _____________.

Janet: They certainly do know **the** *(17)* ________ **and outs** of distribution. It sounds like **all systems are** (18) ____ .

David: Everything should **run** *(19)* _______ now. I predict that sales will *(20)* _______ **up** in a month **at the** *(21)* ___________.

A CLOSER LOOK:
General Business Slang & Jargon (Part A)

A common complaint from non-native speakers is that they consider themselves to be fluent in English, yet can't seem to fully understand a conversation between two native born Americans. The reason is quite simple. Native speakers commonly use contractions and reductions in their every day speech, plus an enormous amount of slang, jargon and idioms.

The non-native speaker has an added burden in the workplace since there is a vast array of additional idioms and slang common in the world of business.

Biz Talk -1 introduced you to hundreds of popular business terms. The following list is a continuation designed to help you integrate quickly into any business situation.

above all *adj.* most importantly.

example: When you meet Mr. Yamamoto, be sure you bow to show your respect. **Above all**, don't hug him! It's not the custom in Japan.

translation: When you meet Mr. Yamamoto, be sure you bow to show your respect. **Most importantly**, don't hug him! It's not the custom in Japan.

as spoken: When ya meet Mr. Yamamodo, be sher ya bow ta show yer r'spect. **Above all**, don't hug 'im! It's not the custom in Japan.

SYNONYM: first and foremost *exp.*

agree up to a point (to) *exp.* to agree partially.

example: "Our company isn't producing as well as it should. I think we need to fire everyone and start over."
"I **agree up to a point**. The company certainly needs to start producing more efficiently. But I think we can encourage our current employees to work harder!"

translation: "Our company isn't producing as well as it should. I think we need to fire everyone and start over."
"I **agree partially**. The company certainly needs to start producing more efficiently. But I think we can encourage

our current employees to work harder!"

as spoken: 'Ar company isn't praducing 'ez well 'ez it should. I think we need ta fire ev'ryone 'n stard over."
"I **agree up to a point**. The company certainly needs ta start producing more efficiently. Bud I think we c'n encourage 'ar current employees ta work harder!"

ahead of schedule (to be) *exp.* to complete or arrive earlier than planned (said of a product or a person).

example: I have good news for you. The books were printed **ahead of schedule** and that means we'll be able to get them into the bookstores early.

translation: I have good news for you. The books were printed **earlier than planned** and that means we'll be able to get them into the bookstores early.

as spoken: I have good news fer you. The books were printed **ahead of schedule** and that means we'll be able da get th'm inta the bookstores early.

ANTONYM: **behind schedule** *exp.* later than planned.

arrange for *exp.* to set up (something), to organize, to coordinate.

example: You need to be at the airport in an hour. Let me **arrange for** a taxi.

translation: You need to be at the airport in an hour. Let me **set up the arrival of** a taxi.

as spoken: Ya need ta be at thee airpord in 'n hour. Lemme **arrange fer** a taxi.

as a rule *exp.* usually, typically.

example: **As a rule**, we send out all orders within 24 hours.

translation: **Usually**, we send out all orders within 24 hours.

as spoken: **As a rule**, we send oud all orders within 24 hours.

as to *prep.* in regard to.

example: The books will be printed in two weeks. **As to** shipping instructions, please let us know where you would like the books sent.

translation: The books will be printed in two weeks. **In regard to** shipping instructions, please let us know where you would like the books sent.

as spoken: The books'll be printed in two weeks. **Az ta** shipping instructions, please led us know where you'd like the books sent.

back down (to) *v.* to concede.

example: The managers and union officials have been negotiating for three weeks. Eventually, one side will have **to back down**!

translation: The managers and union officials have been negotiating for three weeks. Eventually, one side will have **concede**!

as spoken: The managers 'n union officials'ev been negotiating fer three weeks. Evenchally, one sides'll haf **ta back down**!

better safe than sorry *exp.* it's better to be cautious than to regret being hasty.

example: I'm sure our new client will pay us, but we should check his references before we send him all his merchandise. **Better safe than sorry**.

translation: I'm sure our new client will pay us, but we should check his references before we send him all his merchandise. **It's better to be cautious than to regret being hasty**.

as spoken: I'm sher 'ar new client'll pay us, but we should check 'iz references before we send 'im all 'iz merchandise. **Bedder safe th'n sorry**.

breakthrough *n.* innovation.

example: The new diet pill is an exciting **breakthrough** for people who suffer from obesity.

translation: The new diet pill is an exciting **innovation** for people who suffer from obesity.

as spoken: The new diet pill'z 'n exciding **breakthrough** fer people who suffer fr'm obesity.

break new ground (to) *exp.* to make new discoveries (in medicine, science, product development, etc.).

example: Our company has **broken new ground** with the invention of its electronic vacuum cleaner.

translation: Our company has **made new discoveries** with the invention of its electronic vacuum cleaner.

as spoken: Our company's **broken new ground** with thee invention of its electronic vacuum cleaner.

bring about (to) *v.* to produce or generate, to facilitate.

example: We need **to bring about** higher sales this month.

translation: We need **to generate** higher sales this month.

as spoken: We need **ta bring about** higher sales this month.

carry out (to) *v.* to follow, to implement.

example: Did the messenger **carry out** my instructions to deliver the package to the customer's back entrance?

translation: Did the messenger **follow** my instructions to deliver the package to the customer's back entrance?

as spoken: Did the messenger **carry out** my instructions ta deliver the package ta the customer's back entrance?

catch (to) *v.* to understand or hear something.

example: I'm sorry, I didn't **catch** that. When will you be able to ship our products to us?

translation: I'm sorry, I didn't **understand** that. When will you be able to ship our products to us?

as spoken: I'm sorry, I didn' **catch** that. When'll you be able da ship 'ar produc's to us?

check it over (to) *v.* to examine something (for errors or appropriateness).

example: When you're done typing that letter, I'd like **to check it over** before you send it.

translation: When you're done typing that letter, I'd like to **examine it for errors** before you send it.

as spoken: When y'r done typing that ledder, I'd like **ta check id over** before you send it.

come up with (to) *v.* **1.** to gather information • **2.** to invent.

example (1): I **came up with** some information about our competitor that you may find interesting.

translation: I **gathered** some information about our competitor that you may find interesting.

as spoken: I **came up with** s'm inf'rmation aboud 'ar compedider tha'chu may find in'tristing.

example (2): Arnold thinks he **came up with** a cure for the common cold!

translation: Arnold thinks he **invented** a cure for the common cold!

as spoken: Arnold thinks 'e **came up with** a cure fer the common cold!

cut corners (to) *v.* to use less expensive means to produce something.

example: We want to be known as a company that doesn't **cut corners**... a company that produces a quality product.

translation: We want to be known as a company that doesn't **use less expensive means to produce something**... a company that produces a quality product.

as spoken: We wanna be known 'ez a company th't duzn' **cut corners**... a company th't praduces a qualidy product.

cut one's losses (to) *exp.* to get out of a bad financial situation (before it gets worse).

example: The expensive advertising we've been doing doesn't seem to be working. We need **to cut our losses** and rethink our strategy.

translation: The expensive advertising we've been doing doesn't seem to be working. We need **to get out of this bad financial situation before it gets worse** and rethink our strategy.

as spoken: Thee expensive advertising we've been doing doesn't seem da be working. We need **ta cud 'ar loses** 'n rethink 'ar stradegy.

do lunch (to) *exp.* to have lunch (very popular, yet pretentious, since this was originally coined by phoney Hollywood agents).

example: Let's **do lunch** some time.

translation: Let's **have lunch together** some time.

as spoken: [no change]

VARIATION: **do a lunch thing (to)** *exp.*

drawback *n.* obstacle, problem, barrier.

example: I was invited to be on a national television show where I'm going to promote my new book! The only **drawback** is that I've only printed 1,000 books and 40 million people watch the show.

translation: I was invited to be on a national television show where I'm going to promote my new book! The only **problem** is that I've only printed 1,000 books and 40 million people watch the show.

as spoken: I was invided ta be on a national TV show where I'm gonna pramote my new book! Thee only **drawback** is thad I've only printed 1,000 books 'n 40 million people watch the show.

dud *n.* failure.

example: The last book we published was a real **dud**. We only sold ten in a year!

translation: The last book we published was a real **failure**. We only sold ten in a year!

as spoken: The las' book we published was a real **dud**. We only sold ten in a year!

end product *n.* the final result.

example: We had a lot of disagreements during development but the **end product** is sensational.

translation: We had a lot of disagreements during development but the **final result** is sensational.

as spoken: We had a lod of disagreements during development but thee **en' product**'s sensation'l.

end user *n.* the targeted customer.

example: The **end users** of these books will be teachers.

translation: The **targeted customers** of these books will be teachers.

as spoken: Thee **end users** of these books'll be teachers.

final analysis (in the) *exp.* when everything has been carefully examined.

example: There are many reasons we're losing sales. But **in the final analysis**, the products themselves are just not attractive.

translation: There are many reasons we're losing sales. But **when everything has been carefully examined**, the products themselves are just not attractive.

as spoken: There'er many reasons w'r losing sales. Bud **in the final analysis**, the produc's th'mselves'er jus' nod attractive.

focus (to) *v.* to direct one's energy toward; to concentrate.

example: We have hundreds of products that need to be sold. Starting now, we need **to focus** on publicity.

translation: We have hundreds of products that need to be sold. Starting now, we need **to concentrate** on publicity.

as spoken: We have hundreds of produc's that need ta be sold. Starding now, we need **ta focus** on publicidy.

from the outset *exp.* from the beginning.

example: We've had trouble with this client **from the outset**. Frankly, I don't think we should work with him anymore.

translation: We've had trouble with this client **from the beginning**. Frankly, I don't think we should work with him anymore.

as spoken: We've had trouble with this client **fr'm thee outset**. Frankly, I don' think we should work with 'im anymore.

game plan *n.* strategy.

example: We need to increase our sales substantially this year. Steve, as our marketing expert, what do you think our **game plan** should be?

translation: We need to increase our sales substantially this year. Steve, as our marketing expert, what do you think our **strategy** should be?

as spoken: We need ta increase 'ar sales substantially this year. Steve, as 'ar markeding expert, whaddy'a think 'ar **game plan** should be?

get down to business (to) *exp.* to begin working, to concentrate on business matters.

example: I'd like to hear about your vacation, but we really need **to get down to business** right now.

translation: I'd like to hear about your vacation, but we really need **to concentrate on business matters** right now.

as spoken: I'd like to hear abou' cher vacation, but we really need **ta get down ta business** right now.

give or take *exp.* approximately.

example: This shipment weighs a ton, **give or take** 100 pounds.

translation: This shipment weighs **approximately** a ton.

as spoken: This shipment weighs a ton, **give 'r take** 100 poun's.

hard facts *exp.* the undisputable truths.

example: I know you don't want to fire Mark, but the **hard facts** are that he's lazy, rude, usually dishonest, and late.

translation: I know you don't want to fire Mark, but the **undisputable truths** are that he's lazy, rude, dishonest, and usually late.

as spoken: I know you don't wanna fire Mark, but the **hard facts**'er thad 'e's lazy, rude, dishonest, 'n usually late.

in accordance with *exp.* following the guidelines of.

example: **In accordance with** our contract, you must pay us in ninety days.

translation: **Following the guidelines of** our contract, you must pay us in ninety days.

as spoken: **In accordance with** 'ar contract, you must pay us in ninedy days.

in full *exp.* complete (in reference to a payment).

example: You'll have to pay your last invoice **in full** before we can send you more merchandise.

translation: You'll have to pay your last invoice **completely** before we can send you more merchandise.

as spoken: You'll hafta pay yer last invoice **in full** before we c'n sen'ju more merchandise.

in order *exp.* said of something that is free of problems.

example: We just received your shipment and everything seems to be **in order**.

translation: We just received your shipment and everything seems **free of problems**.

as spoken: We just received yer shipment an' ev'rything seems ta be **'n order**.

insofar as *conj.* to the extent that.

example: Optima Books is different from other publishers **insofar as** it specializes in books on slang and idioms.

translation: Optima Books is different from other publishers **to the extent that** it specializes in books on slang and idioms.

as spoken: Optima Books'z different fr'm other publishers **insofar 'ez** it specializes in books on slang 'n idioms.

in terms of *exp.* in regard to.

example: **In terms of** design, the book covers have a modern look.

translation: **In regard** to design, the book covers have a modern look.

as spoken: **In terms of** design, the book covers have a modern look.

in the meantime *exp.* for the moment, for now.

example: We'll be receiving our new computers in about a week. **In the meantime**, we'll have to keep using the old ones.

translation: We'll be receiving our new computers in about a week. **For the moment**, we'll have to keep using the old ones.

as spoken: We'll be receiving 'ar new c'mpuders in aboud a week. **In the meantime**, we'll have to keep using thee old ones.

in time *exp.* during a scheduled period of time.

example: I'm sorry I didn't arrive **in time** for the meeting.

translation: I'm sorry I didn't arrive **as scheduled** for the meeting.

as spoken: I'm sorry I didn' arrive **in time** fer the meeting.

in touch (to be) *exp.* to be in contact .

example: I'll be **in touch** with you next week.

translation: I'll be **in contact** with you next week.

as spoken: A'll be **in touch** with you next week.

in turn *exp.* in return.

example: We would be happy to send you the merchandise right away. **In turn**, we require that you pay us a 50 percent deposit.

translation: We would be happy to send you the merchandise right away. **In return**, we require that you pay us a 50 percent deposit.

as spoken: We'd be happy da send you the merchandise ri' daway. **In turn**, we r'quire that chu pay us a 50 percent deposit.

knock-off *n.* a cheap imitation of an expensive product.

example: Look at this beautiful sofa! It's a **knock-off** of an original Burke design.

translation: Look at this beautiful sofa! It's a **cheap imitation** of an original Burke design.

as spoken: Look 'it this beaudiful sofa! It's a **knock-off** of 'n origin'l Burke design.

ALSO: **knock off (to)** *v.* to stop working.

example: Since it's Friday and we've all worked extra hard, let's **knock off** early today.

translation: Since it's Friday and we've all worked extra hard, let's **stop work** early today.

as spoken: Since it's Friday 'n we've all worked extra hard, let's **knock off** early today.

Practice Using General Business Slang & Jargon (Part A)

(Answers, p. 269)

A. Underline the word that best completes the phrase.

1. Your advertising plan sounds good, except for one (**game plan**, **safe bet**, **drawback**). It would be so expensive to implement that we'd go out of business!

2. This medical discovery is an exciting (**dud**, **drawback**, **breakthrough**) for people who suffer from allergies!

3. I agree with you up to a (**line**, **dot**, **point**). Some of what you say is true but I don't think that you've looked at all the facts.

4. Our competitor just went out of business. It seems he was cutting (**edges**, **corners**, **curves**) in the manufacturing of his products and it showed.

5. The last car we produced was a real (**drawback**, **hit**, **dud**). I'm glad our new one is a success.

6. I'll arrive at noon, give or (**get**, **take**, **lend**) ten minutes.

7. We require payment in (**full**, **empty**, **so far as**) on all orders made by new customers.

8. The (**end**, **beginning**, **middle**) user of our products will be students of English.

B. Circle the letter of the correct definition of the word(s) in boldface.

1. **breakthrough:**
   a. innovation
   b. loss of sales
   c. expensive item

2. **dud:**
   a. success
   b. failure
   c. any new product

3. **above all:**
   a. expensive
   b. least importantly
   c. most importantly

4. **as a rule:**
   a. usually
   b. rarely
   c. never

5. **cut corners (to):**
   a. to gather information
   b. break new ground
   c. to use less expensive means to produce something

6. **back down (to):**
   a. to reduce
   b. to be aggressive
   c. to concede

7. **cut one's losses (to):**
   a. to use less expensive means to produce something
   b. to get out of a bad financial situation (before it gets worse)
   c. to lower one's prices

8. **give or take:**
   a. approximately
   b. exactly
   c. said of an expensive product

9. **carry out (to):**
   a. to work hard
   b. to leave work early
   c. to implement

10. **in touch with (to be):**
    a. to be an expert in one's field
    b. to work very hard
    c. to be in contact with

LESSON TWO

General Business Slang & Jargon (Part B)

Sometimes Ernie just won't ***bend****!*

Lesson Two

Dialogue in slang

Nick: This is **off the record**, but I've decided **to take steps** to get Ernie **booted**.

Anne: I wouldn't **make a snap decision** like that if I were you. Maybe you should **sleep on it**. After all, he really is a great guy outside of work…at least **on the surface**.

Nick: I've **taken that into account**. But **the facts speak for themselves**. He **slacks off** all the time and that's just **the tip of the iceberg**. He always **punches in** late, usually **goes over budget** and never **meets his deadlines**. **What's more,** he **calls it quits** early almost every day, while I end up **plugging away** every night **after hours**. But **the crux of the matter** is that he does everything his own way and won't work with me. He's not a **team player**.

Anne: Nick, you've **pointed** all this out to me before. Maybe you just need to **take a hard line** with him.

Nick: I've tried but he just won't **bend**. The problem is that shortly after he **came on board**, he was **bumped up** to a supervisory position. Now he won't listen to anyone or **meet you halfway** on anything! I'm tired of **going above his head** on everything. It's time for him **to shape up or ship out**!

Lesson Two

Translation of Dialogue

General Business Slang & Jargon (Part B)

Nick: This is **unofficial**, but I've decided **to take the appropriate action** to get Ernie **fired**.

Anne: I wouldn't **make a hasty decision** like that if I were you. Maybe you should **get a good nights' sleep in order to think more clearly**. After all, he really is a great guy outside of work...at least **at first glance**.

Nick: I've **considered that**. But **the facts are clear**. He **performs his work in a substandard way** all the time and that's just **the beginning**. He always **arrives at work** late, usually **exceeds the allocated spending-money** and **never gets his work finished on time**. **Additionally**, he **leaves work early** almost every day, while I end up **working hard** every night **after normal business hours**. **But the main problem** is that he does everything his own way and won't work with me. He's not a **person who can work with others**.

Anne: Nick, you've **made me aware** of all this before. Maybe you just need to **be firm** with him.

Nick: I've tried but he just won't be **flexible**. The problem is that shortly after he **was hired**, he was **promoted** to a supervisory position. Now he won't doesn't listen to anyone or **compromise** on anything! I'm tired of **going to his superiors** on everything. It's time for him **to improve his job performance or leave**!

Dialogue in slang as it would be heard

General Business Slang & Jargon (Part B)

Nick: This'z **off the record**, bud I've decided **ta take steps** ta ged Ernie **booded**.

Anne: I wouldn't **make a snap decision** like thad if I were you. Maybe you should **sleep on it**. After all, he really is a great guy outside of work...at least **on the surface**.

Nick: I've **taken thad into account**. But **the fac's speak fer th'mselves**. He **slacks off** all the time an that's just **the tip 'a the iceberg**. He always **punches in** late, usually goes **over budget** and never **meets 'is deadlines**. **What's more**, he **calls it quits early** almost ev'ry day, while I end up **plugging away** ev'ry nide **after hours**. But **the crux 'a the madder** is that 'e does ev'rything 'is own way 'n won't work with me. He's nod a **team player**.

Anne: Nick, you've **poin'ed all this out ta me** before. Maybe you just need ta **take a hard line** with 'im.

Nick: I've tried bud 'e just won't **bend**. The problem is that shortly after 'e **came on board**, he was **bumped up** to a supervisery position. Now 'e won't listen ta anyone or **meet chu halfway** on anything! I'm tired of **going above 'is head** on ev'rything. It's time fer him **ta shape up 'r ship out**!

Vocabulary

after hours *adj.* after the close of business.

example: I just don't have time to help you with your project during the day. We'll have to stay **after hours** to work on it.

translation: I just don't have time to help you with your project during the day. We'll have to stay **after the close of business** to work on it.

as spoken: I jus' don't have time ta help you with yer project during the day. We'll hafta stay **after hours** ta work on it.

bend (to) *v.* to be flexible, to adjust.

example: I asked the boss if I could take my vacation a little earlier, but she just won't **bend**.

translation: I asked the boss if I could take my vacation a little earlier, but she just won't **be flexible**.

as spoken: I asked the boss if I could take my vacation a liddle earlier, but she jus' won't **bend**.

ANTONYM: **give an inch (not to)** *exp.* (used in the negative) to be inflexible and uncompromising.

example: You can try and discuss it with him, but I'm warning you: he **won't give an inch**.

translation: You can try and discuss it with him, but I'm warning you: he **won't compromise**.

as spoken: You c'n try 'n discuss it with 'm, bud I'm warning you: he **won't give 'n inch**.

booted *exp.* to get fired • (lit); to be kicked by someone.

example: You're going to **get booted** if you keep making personal phone calls at work.

translation: You're going to **get fired** if you keep making personal phone calls at work.

as spoken: Y'r gonna **get booded** if ya keep making personal phone calls at work.

VARIATION: **get the boot (to)** *exp.*

bumped up *exp.* to get promoted.

example: Did you hear the news? Jill just got **bumped up** to supervisor!

translation: Did you hear the news? Jill just got **promoted** to supervisor!

as spoken: Didja hear the news? Jill jus' got **bumped up** ta superviser!

NOTE: This expression is also commonly used in the tourism industry to mean "to get upgraded from one class of travel to the next."

> example: I've been flying with the same airline for so many years, that I automatically got **bumped up** from coach to first class!
>
> translation: I've been flying with the same airline for so many years, that I automatically got **upgraded** from coach to first class!
>
> as spoken: I been flying with the same airline fer so many years, thad I audamadic'ly got **bumped up** fr'm coach ta first class!

call it quits (to) *exp.* to stop working for the day or to quit one's job permanently (depending on the context).

example: I'm exhausted. I'm going to **call it quits**. See you tomorrow.

translation: I'm exhausted. I'm going to **stop working for the day**. See you tomorrow.

as spoken: I'm exhausted. I'm gonna **call it quits**. See ya damorrow.

VARIATION: **call it a day (to)** *exp.* to stop working for the day.

crux of the matter (the) *n.* the main issue or reason.

example: The company may have to close soon. **The crux of the matter** is declining sales.

translation: The company may have to close soon. **The main reason** is declining sales.

as spoken: The company may hafta close soon. **The crux 'a the matter** is declining sales.

deadline *n.* the time when a project must be completed.

example: You'd better hurry. Your **deadline** is in two hours!

translation: You'd better hurry. Your **project is due** in two hours!

as spoken: Ya bedder hurry. Yer **deadline**'s in two hours!

NOTE: On occasion, you may hear the expression **drop dead date**, meaning "the absolute latest a project must be completed."

meet halfway (to) *v.* to compromise.

example: I know you want to leave work early tomorrow, but we have a lot of work to do. I'll **meet you halfway**. You can leave two hours early if you come in early in the morning.

translation: I know you want to leave work early tomorrow, but we have a lot of work to do. I'll **compromise with you**. You can leave two hours early if you come in early in the morning.

as spoken: I know ya wanna leave work early tamorrow, but we have a lotta work ta do. A'll **meet cha halfway**. You c'n leave two hours early if ya come in early in the morning.

off-the-record *adj.* unofficially.

example: I'm going to tell you something **off-the-record**. Your competitor is about to close his business.

translation: I'm going to tell you something **unofficially**. Your competitor is about to close his business.

as spoken: I'm gonna tell you something **off-the-record**. Yer compedider's about ta close 'is business.

on board (to) *exp.* hired, appointed.

example: We just brought a new employee **on board**. I think you're going to like her.

translation: We just **hired** a new employee. I think you're going to like her.

as spoken: We jus' brought a new employee **on board**. I think y'r gonna like 'er.

ORIGIN: Originally a nautical term referring to the boards that make up the main deck of a ship.

on the surface *exp.* at first glance, apparently.

example: **On the surface**, this looks like a product that will be tremendously successful overseas. But before we spend the money for marketing and advertising, we should research the customs of the people in each country to make sure this product will be popular.

translation: **At first glance**, this looks like a product that will be tremendously successful overseas. But before we spend the money for marketing and advertising, we should research the customs of the people in each country to make sure this product will be popular.

as spoken: **On the surface**, this looks like a product that'll be tremendously successful overseas. But before we spen' the money fer markeding 'n advertising, we should research the customs of the people in each country da make sure this product'll be populer.

over-budget *adj., adv.* said of a project whose costs exceed the allocated amount of spending-money.

example: If we are to make a ten-thousand-dollar profit on this event, we can't afford to go **over budget** on expenses.

translation: If we are to make a ten-thousand-dollar profit on this event, we can't afford to **exceed the allocated amount of spending-money** on expenses.

as spoken: If we're ta make a ten-thousan'-doller profid on this event, we can' afford ta **go over budged** on expenses.

ANTONYM: **meet one's budget (to)** *exp.*

example: The boss gave us all bonuses for **meeting this year's budget**!

translation: The boss gave us all bonuses for **completing the project without exceeding the allocated amount of money**!

as spoken: The boss gave us all bonuses fer **meeding this year's budget**!

over (someone's) head *exp.* to go to someone's superior to demand action, report behavior, or request that a decision be overruled.

example: My supervisor wouldn't let me take my vacation next week. So I **went over his head** and got approval.

translation: My supervisor wouldn't let me take my vacation next week. So I **went to his superior** and got approval.

as spoken: My supervisor wouldn' lemme take my vacation next week. So I **wen' over 'is head** 'n god approval.

plug (to) *v.* to work hard.

example: You've been **plugging** away at your desk for hours. What are you working on?

translation: You've been **working hard** at your desk for hours. What are you working on?

as spoken: You've been **plugging** away at cher desk fer hours. What cha workin' on?

point (to) *v.* to indicate, direct attention to.

example: I'd like **to point** out some of the problems we're having in the company.

translation: I'd like **to indicate** some of the problems we're having in the company.

as spoken: I'd like **ta poin'** out some 'a the problems w'r having in the company.

punch in (to) *v.* to insert one's timecard into a timeclock which stamps or punches the time and date of arrival.

example: I hope the boss doesn't get angry when he sees that I **punched in** ten minutes late today.

translation: I hope the boss doesn't get angry when he sees that I **stamped my timecard** ten minutes late today.

as spoken: I hope the boss doesn' ged angry when 'e sees thad I **punched in** ten minutes late today.

VARIATION: **clock in (to)** *exp.*

shape up or ship out (to) *exp.* to improve one's job performance or lose his/her job.

example: This is the last time I'm warning you. Either you **shape up or ship out**!

translation: This is the last time I'm warning you. Either you **improve your job performance or leave**!

as spoken: This is the las' time I'm warning you. Either you **shape up 'r ship out**!

slack off (to) *exp.* to neglect one's responsibilities, to perform one's work in a substandard way.

example: You should be at your desk working! If you don't stop **slacking off**, you're going to get yourself fired.

translation: You should be at your desk working! If you don't stop **neglecting your responsibilities**, you're going to get yourself fired.

as spoken: You should be at cher desk working! If you don't stop **slacking off**, y'r gonna get cherself fired.

NOTE: **slacker** *n.* one who is negligent in his responsibilities.

sleep on it (to) *exp.* to get a good night's sleep to reach a clear decision about something.

example: Let me **sleep on it**. I'll give you my answer in the morning.

translation: Let me **get a good night's sleep to reach a clear decision**. I'll give you my answer in the morning.

as spoken: Lemme **sleep on it**. A'll give you my answer in the morning.

snap decision *n.* an impulsive determination made without taking the time to consider all of the consequences.

example: I only had two minutes to find a reporter to cover the news story downtown. I made a **snap decision** and assigned Jimmy. I know he's not very experienced, but at least he has a lot of enthusiasm.

translation: I only had two minutes to find a reporter to cover the news story downtown. I made **an impulsive decision** and assigned Jimmy. I know he's not very experienced, but at least he has a lot of enthusiasm.

as spoken: I only had two minutes ta find a reporder ta cover the news story downtown. I made a **snap decision** and assign' Jimmy. I know 'e's not very experienced, bud at least 'e has a lod of enthusiasm.

take a hard line (to) *exp.* to be uncompromising.

example: Since you've failed to pay your bills on time, I have no choice but **to take a hard line**. We now require that you pay us in advance for all merchandise.

translation: Since you've failed to pay your bills on time, I have no choice but **to be uncompromising**. We now require that you pay us in advance for all merchandise.

as spoken: Since you've failed ta pay yer bills on time, I've no choice but **ta take a hard line**. We now r'quire that chu pay us in advance fer all merchandise.

take into account (to) *v.* to make allowance for, to consider.

example: Before I accept the promotion, I have **to take** everything **into account**. I'm not sure that I'm willing to work such long hours.

translation: Before I accept the promotion, I have **to consider everything**. I'm not sure that I'm willing to work such long hours.

as spoken: Before I accept the promotion, I haf**ta take** ev'rything **inta account**. I'm not sh'r th'd I'm willing ta work such long hours.

take steps (to) *exp.* to take appropriate action.

example: We are **taking steps** to increase the company's productivity.

translation: We are **taking appropriate actions to** increase the company's productivity.

as spoken: We're **taking steps** ta increase the company's productividy.

team player *n.* one who works well with others.

example: In our company, everyone works well together. We're all **team players**.

translation: In our company, everyone works well together. We're all **part of a team**.

as spoken: In 'ar company, ev'ryone works well t'gether. W'r all **team players**.

the facts speak for themselves *exp.* the facts are obvious and don't need explaining.

example: I don't need to tell you that our products are superior to those of our competitors. Just look at this report. **The facts speak for themselves**.

translation: I don't need to tell you that our products are superior to those of our competitors. Just look at this report. **The facts are obvious and don't need explaining**.

as spoken: I don't need ta tell you th'd 'ar produc's'er superier ta those of 'ar c'mpediders. Just look at this report. **The fac's speak fer th'mselves**.

tip of the iceberg (the) *n.* the seemingly small part of a larger situation, the beginning of something formidable and usually undesirable.

example: The new market they built behind my house is just the **tip of the iceberg**. Next month they're putting in an entire mall!

translation: The new market they built behind my house is just **the beginning of a larger and undesirable situation**. Next month they're putting in an entire mall!

as spoken: The new market they built behind my house is jus' **the tip 'a thee iceberg**. Next month they're pudding in 'n entire mall!

what's more *exp.* additionally.

example: Steve is a very hard worker. **What's more**, he's always honest.

translation: Steve is a very hard worker. **Additionally**, he's always honest.

as spoken: Steve's a very hard worker. **What's more**, he's always honest.

Practice the Vocabulary

(Answers to Lesson 2, p. 270)

A. Circle the letter corresponding to the correct definition of the words in boldface.

1. **point out (to):**
   a. to indicate
   b. to criticize
   c. to argue

2. **bend (to):**
   a. to reduce the price of a product
   b. to argue
   c. to compromise

3. **booted (to get):**
   a. to get promoted
   b. to get fired
   c. to get busy

4. **meet half way (to):**
   a. to fire someone
   b. to compromise
   c. to leave work early

5. **plug away (to):**
   a. to work hard
   b. to leave work early
   c. to get promoted

6. **take into account (to):**
   a. to make a lot of money
   b. to make a hasty decision
   c. to consider something

7. **sleep on it (to):**
   a. to be negligent at work
   b. not to pay attention to one's work
   c. to get a good night's sleep in order to reach a clear decision.

8. **crux of the matter (the):**
   a. the least important part
   b. the most important part
   c. exceptionally high sales

9. **bumped up (to get):**
   a. to get fired
   b. to get promoted
   c. to get reprimanded

10. **after hours:**
    a. the time when a company opens for business
    b. the time after a company closes for the day
    c. break time

B. FIND-THE-WORD GRID

Step 1: Fill in the blanks with the most appropriate word using the list below.

Step 2: Find and circle the word(s) in the grid on the opposite page. Words may be spelled vertically or horizontally.

bend	**quits**
booted	**record**
bumped	**slacks**
crux	**snap**
line	**surface**

1. I need to tell you something off the ________________. This is just between us!

2. Ed got ________________ today for drinking at work.

3. Congratulations! I heard you got __________________ up to vice president today!

4. Greg isn't a very good worker. He ________________ off too much.

5. I need to be at the airport by five o'clock, so I'm going to call it __________ early today.

6. The ____________ of the matter is that our company isn't making enough money this year.

7. Karen is taking advantage of you. You need to take a hard _______ and tell that her behavior won't be tolerated.

8. I've asked the boss a thousand times to get me a secretary but he just won't ______________ because it will cost too much.

9. Since this is an emergency, I'll have to make a _________ decision. Let's hire another ten people immediately.

10. On the ________________, it looks like a good product. But the quality of materials used in manufacture is not very good.

FIND-THE-WORD GRID

N	A	R	K	O	W	T	O	W	S	A	S	A	A
B	E	N	D	U	B	B	L	T	B	T	L	B	K
U	U	C	S	R	C	H	C	A	S	N	A	P	I
M	C	O	U	X	D	A	R	W	C	D	C	D	S
P	K	R	R	W	T	E	U	I	E	A	K	E	S
E	L	E	F	N	Y	F	X	G	B	F	S	F	F
D	E	C	A	G	G	L	F	G	C	G	K	U	P
E	L	O	C	Q	U	I	T	S	H	K	E	E	L
F	P	R	E	C	J	N	T	B	O	O	T	E	D
E	R	D	J	P	U	E	H	E	R	J	L	P	J

C. Replace the boldfaced word(s) in the left column with the appropriate slang terms on the right.

☐ 1. This is **unofficial,** but I heard that the president of our company is going to retire next year.

☐ 2. We're going to have **to take the appropriate action** to get this project done as soon as possible if we want to beat our competition.

☐ 3. We need to produce more products this year. **In addition,** we'll need to hire about thirty new employees since we're growing so quickly.

☐ 4. I noticed that Steve sometimes takes office supplies home with him. But that was just **the seemingly small part of a large situation**. I just learned that Steve has been stealing expensive products from the company for the past three years!

☐ 5. This is the first year we didn't **spend more money than was allocated.**

☐ 6. The boss said that if I don't **finish this project by the due date,** I'll have to look for another job!

☐ 7. Let me **direct your attention to** some of the rules this company follows.

☐ 8. **Improve your job performance or leave!**

☐ 9. Steve **was hired** last November.

☐ 10. Since you've failed to pay your bills on time, I have no choice but **to be uncompromising**. We now require that you pay us for all merchandise in advance.

A. **take a hard line**

B. **what's more**

C. **the tip of the iceberg**

D. **came on board**

E. **point out**

F. **go over budget**

G. **to take steps**

H. **meet the deadline**

I. **off the record**

J. **shape up or ship out**

A CLOSER LOOK:
General Business Slang & Jargon (Part B)

last, but not least *exp.* following all the rest, but not the least important.

example: Thank you for your applause for our new Board of Directors. And now, **last, but not least**, please welcome the new president of our company, Joe Dover.

translation: Thank you for your applause for our new Board of Directors. And now, **following all the rest, but not the least important**, please welcome the new president of our company, Joe Dover.

as spoken: Thank you fer yer applause fer 'ar new Board 'ev Directers. An'now, **last, b't not least**, please welcome the new president 'ev 'ar company, Joe Dover.

long shot *n.* something that is not likely to succeed.

example: I'm going to ask the boss to give me a week off. I'll even tell him that I'll work at night. It's a **long shot** but I'm going to try.

translation: I'm going to ask the boss to give me a week off. I'll even tell him that I'll work at night. It's **not likely to succeed** but I'm going to try.

as spoken: I'm gonna ask the boss ta gimme a week off. A'll even tell 'im th'd a'll work 'it night. It's **a long shot** bud I'm gonna try.

look into (to) *exp.* to investigate .

example: I can't understand why your shipment hasn't arrived yet. I'll **look into** it and call you right back.

translation: I can't understand why your shipment hasn't arrived yet. I'll **investigate** it and call you right back.

as spoken: I can' understand why yer shipment hasn' arrived yet. A'll **look into** id 'n call you right back.

make do (to) *v.* to make the best use of something that is not adequate.

example: I was hoping that we'd get a new photocopy machine but I'm afraid we can't afford it. We'll just have **to make do** with the old one for now.

translation: I was hoping that we'd get a new photocopy machine but I'm afraid we can't afford it. We'll just have **to do the best we can** with the old one for now.

as spoken: I was hoping that we'd ged a new phodocopy machine bud I'm afraid we can' afford it. W'll jus' haf**ta make do** with thee old one fer now.

make headway (to) *v.* to make progress.

example: Science is **making headway** toward finding a cure for cancer.

translation: Science is **making progress** toward finding a cure for cancer.

as spoken: Science'ez **making headway** tord finding a cure fer cancer.

make or break (to) *exp.* to allow no middle ground between success and failure.

example: After spending millions of dollars on this new product, it's finally ready to be introduced. Depending on the public's reaction, this could **make or break** our company.

translation: After spending millions of dollars on this new product, it's finally ready to be introduced to the public. Depending on the public's reaction, our company will **either succeed or fai**l.

as spoken: After spending millions 'a dollars on this new product, it's fin'ly ready da be intraduced ta the public. Depending on the public's reaction, this could **make or break** 'ar company.

mark-up *n.* a price increase attached to a piece of merchandise before it is sold, as a way of making a profit.

example: We'll buy each dress from you for $50. Then, we'll add a 20% **mark-up** in order to make a profit of $10 for each dress sold.

translation: We'll buy each dress from you for $50. Then, we'll add a 20% **price increase** in order to make a profit of $10 for each dress sold.

as spoken: W'll buy each dress fr'm you fer $50. Then, w'll add a 20% **mark-up** in order da make a profit of $10 fer each dress sold.

ALSO: **mark (something) up (to)** *v.* to increase the price of merchandise in order to make a profit.

on behalf of *exp.* as a representative of.

example: **On behalf of** our company, I'd like to thank you for your continued interest in our products.

translation: **As a representative of** our company, I'd like to thank you for your continued interest in our products.

as spoken: **On behalf of** our company, I'd like ta thank you fer yer continued int'rest in 'ar products.

play ball (to) *v.* cooperate.

example: If our distributor isn't going **to play ball** with us, let's find a new one.

translation: If our distributor isn't going to **cooperate** with us, let's find a new one.

as spoken: If 'ar distribyader isn't gonna **play ball** with us, let's find a new one.

pros and cons *exp.* good points and bad points, pluses and minuses.

example: There are lots of **pros and cons** about my promotion. I'll earn more money, but I'll have to travel a lot and be away from my family.

translation: There are lots of **good points and bad points** about my promotion. I'll earn more money, but I'll have to travel a lot and be away from my family.

as spoken: There'er lotz 'a **pros 'n cons** about my pramotion. A'll earn more money, bud a'll hafta travel a lot 'n be away fr'm my family.

put pressure on (to) *exp.* to be firm (with someone.)

example: We have three customers who are over thirty days late in paying us. I guess I'll have **to put** some **pressure on** them.

translation: We have three customers who are over thirty days late in paying us. I guess I'll have **to be firm with** them.

as spoken: We 'ave three custamers who'er over thirdy days lade in paying us. I guess a'll haf**ta put** s'm **pressure on** 'em.

put/set the record straight (to) *exp.* to correct a wrong impression, to establish the facts.

example: I'd like **to put/set the record straight** before I leave. I've never stolen any money from this company or any other company.

translation: I'd like **to establish the facts** before I leave. I've never stolen any money from this company or any other company.

as spoken: I'd like **ta put/set the record straight** before I leave. I've never stolen any money fr'm this company 'r any other company.

rule out (to) *v.* to eliminate.

example: We need to find a larger building since our company is growing. We can **rule-out** New York. The rents there are too expensive.

translation: We need to find a larger building since our company is growing. We can **eliminate** New York. The rents there are too expensive.

as spoken: We need ta find a larger building since 'ar company is growing. We c'n **rule out** New York. The rents there'er too expensive.

run out (to) *v.* to be depleted of one's merchandise.

example: I couldn't find milk at the market today. They **ran out**!

translation: I couldn't find milk at the market today. They **are depleted of their merchandise**!

as spoken: I couldn' fin' milk at the market today. They **ran out**!

run the risk (to) *exp.* to take a chance.

example: If we change the look of our product to attract new customers, we **run the risk** of losing our current customers.

translation: If we change the look of our product to attract new customers, we **take the chance** of losing our current customers.

as spoken: If we change the look of 'ar product ta attract new custamers, we **run the risk** of losing 'ar current custamers.

safe bet *n.* to be risk-free, assured, or "a sure thing."

example: My broker assures me that investments in technology stocks are a **safe bet**.

translation: My broker assures me that investments in technology stocks are **risk free**.

as spoken: My broker assures me thad investments in technalagy stocks 'er a **safe bet**.

split hairs (to) *v.* to argue about something trivial.

example: It seems that all our attorney does is **split hairs**. With a good negotiator, we could have settled our contract dispute weeks ago.

translation: It seems that all our attorney does is **argue about trivial points**. With a good negotiator, we could have settled our contract dispute weeks ago.

as spoken: It seems th'd all 'ar attorney does is ta **split hairs**. With a good negochiader, we could've seddled 'ar contract dispute weeks ago.

stand (to) *v.* to be likely (to accomplish something).

example: Our company **stands** to make a lot of money in the next couple of years.

translation: Our company **is likely** to make a lot of money in the next couple of years.

as spoken: 'Ar company **stanz** ta make a lotta money in the next couple 'a years.

stem (to) *v.* to result from, to be caused by.

example: Our displeasure with our foreign distributor probably **stems** from a language barrier.

translation: Our displeasure with our foreign distributor probably **results from** a language barrier.

as spoken: 'Ar displeasure with 'ar forin distribuder prob'ly **stems** fr'm a language barrier.

take shape (to) *v.* to assume a definite form.

example: Your new office is really **taking shape**.

translation: Your new office is really **assuming a definite form**.

as spoken: Yer new office'ez really **taking shape**.

that is [to say] *exp.* in other words.

example: All the employees think you're unreasonable. **That is [to say]**, you expect more out of them than they can possibly give.

translation: All the employees think you're unreasonable. **In other words**, you expect more out of them than they can possibly give.

as spoken: All thee employees think y'r unreasonable. **That is [ta say]**, you expect more oud of th'm th'n they c'n possibly give.

the ball's in your court *exp.* It's up to you to decide how to continue.

example: If you don't start performing your job properly, I'll have no choice but to let you go. **The ball's in your court**.

translation: If you don't start performing your job properly, I'll have no choice but to let you go. **It's up to you to decide how to continue**.

as spoken: If ya don't start performing yer job properly, a'll have no choice but ta let chu go. **The ball's in yer court**.

the fact of the matter *exp.* the most important issue, the truth.

example: I know you want to continue using him as our distributor, but **the fact of the matter** is that he hasn't been paying his bills.

translation: I know you want to continue using him as our distributor, but **the truth** is that he hasn't been paying his bills.

as spoken: I know ya wanna continue using 'im as 'ar distribuder, but **the fact 'a the madder** is that 'e hasn't been paying 'is bills.

think through (to) *exp.* to evaluate, strategize, plan.

example: Before we spend a lot of money producing our new product, we need **to think through** how we're going to publicize it.

translation: Before we spend a lot of money producing our new product, we need to **evaluate** how we're going to publicize it.

as spoken: Before we spend a lod 'a money producing 'ar new product, we need **ta think through** how w'r gonna publicize it.

trigger (to) *v.* to cause, set off.

example: When the new diet pill was announced on television, it **triggered** a buying *frenzy* at all the stores.

translation: When the new diet pill was announced on television, it **caused** a buying *frenzy* at all the stores.

as spoken: When the new diet pill was announced on TV, it **triggered** a buying *frenzy* ad all the stores.

NOTE: **frenzy** *n.* an outburst or explosion. Therefore the expression buying *frenzy* (as used in the previous example) refers to a sudden explosion of buyers attacking the stores at the same time.

SYNONYM (1): **spark (to)** *v.*

SYNONYM (2): **touch off (to)** *v.*

twofold *adj.* that which contains two parts.

example: The company's problems are **two-fold**: first, employees are not motivated to perform better and secondly, we can't afford to pay them more money.

translation: The company's problem is **composed of two parts**: first, employees are not motivated to perform better and secondly, we can't afford to pay them more money.

as spoken: The company's problems'er **two-fold**: first, employees aren't modivaded ta perform bedder 'n secon'ly, we can' afford ta pay th'm more money.

unit price *exp.* cost for each item.

example: The **unit price** of the book is $18. If you want to buy three of them, the total is $54.

translation: The **cost for each** book is $18. If you want to buy three of them, the total is $54.

as spoken: The **unit price** of the book is $18. If ya wanna buy three of 'em, the total's $54.

without further ado *exp.* without further bother or fuss.

example: **Without further ado**, I'd like to present the new president of our company.

translation: **Without further bother or fuss**, I'd like to present the new president of our company.

as spoken: **Without further ado**, I'd like ta present the new president of 'ar company.

Practice Using General Business Slang & Jargon (Part B)

(Answers, p. 271)

A. Circle the letter of the correct definition of the word(s) in boldface.

1. **last but not least:**
   a. following all the rest, but not the least expensive
   b. following all the rest, but not the least important
   c. following all the rest, but not the slowest

2. **to run out:**
   a. to be depleted of one's merchandise
   b. to argue about something trivial
   c. to make the best use of something that is inadequate

3. **long shot:**
   a. a long and difficult work day
   b. a difficult problem to solve
   c. something that is not likely to succeed

4. **to take shape:**
   a. to think something over
   b. to assume a definite form
   c. to allow no middle ground between success and failure

5. **to make headway:**
   a. to make progress
   b. to compromise
   c. to be likely to do something

6. **to rule out:**
   a. to be firm with someone
   b. to come close to being completed
   c. to eliminate.

7. **without further ado:**
   a. without further work
   b. without further bother or fuss
   c. without further business

8. **to put/set the record straight:**
   a. to do financial reports
   b. to correct a wrong impression, to establish the facts
   c. to organize an office

9. **a mark-up:**
   a. a failure
   b. a price increase attached to a piece of merchandise before it is sold to someone else as a way of making a profit
   c. said of something that is not likey to succeed

10. **to split hairs:**
   a. to be firm with someone
   b. to be in the process of doing something
   c. to argue about something trivial

11. **to take someone on board:**
   a. to fire someone
   b. to hire someone
   c. to reprimand someone

LESSON THREE

International Trade
(Part A)

*Our **freight forwarder** always gets our shipments delivered on time.*

Lesson Three

Dialogue in slang

Earl: I just heard from the **freight forwarder** that our **container** is going to be picked up tomorrow. We'd better make sure everything is ready to go.

Ted: Let's see…our **general export license** is current and the **destination control statement** has been filed.

Earl: ...and the shipping container has the proper **markings**. We also have the **certificate of inspection**.

Ted: We already calculated the weight of the shipment and we know the **tare weight**. Now we just need to subtract it from the **gross weight** to get the correct **net weight**.

Earl: We inspected the shipment and know that it's in good condition, so we should receive a **clean bill of lading** from the shipping line.

Ted: Well, that sounds like everything. As soon as we receive a copy of the **dock receipt** we can submit our **collection papers**.

Lesson Three

Translation of dialogue in standard English

International Trade (Part A)

Earl: I just heard from the **company which prepares shipping and insurance documents, and arranges cargo deliveries for domestic manufacturers** that our **shipping crate** is going to be picked up tomorrow. We'd better make sure everything is ready to go.

Ted: Let's see…our **export license covering certain export commodities** is current and the **statement required by the U.S. government listing the authorized export destination for the cargo** has been filed.

Earl: …and the shipping container has the proper **letters, numbers, and symbols for identification purposes**. We also have the **document which certifies that the merchandise was in acceptable condition before being shipped**.

Ted: We already calculated the weight of the shipment and we know the **weight of the container**. Now we just need to substract it from the **entire weight of the shipment which includes the contents and container** to get the correct **weight of the contents only**.

Earl: We inspected the shipment and know that it's in good condition, so we should receive a **declaration indicating that all cargo accepted for transporation was in good condition when received** from the shipping line.

Ted: Well, that sounds like everything. As soon as we receive a copy of the **receipt issued by the ocean carrier to acknowledge arrival of the cargo at the carrier's warehouse or dock facilities**, we can submit our **documents (including bills of lading, invoices, etc.) to the buyer in order to get paid for the shipment**.

Lesson Three

Dialogue as spoken

International Trade
(Part A)

Earl: I just heard fr'm the **freight forwerder** that 'ar **c'ntainer**'s gonna be picked up tomorrow. We bedder make sher ev'rything's ready da go.

Ted: Let's see…'ar **general export license** is current an' the **destination c'ntrol statement**'s been filed.

Earl: ...an' the shipping c'ntainer has the proper **markings**. We also have the **certificad 'ev inspection**.

Ted: We already calculaded the wade 'a the shipment, and we know the **tare weight**. Now we jus' need ta subtract it from the **gross weight** ta get the correct **net weight**.

Earl: We inspected the shipment an' know th'd it's in good c'ndition, so we should receive a **clean bill of lading** fr'm the shipping line.

Ted: Well, that soun'z like ev'rything. As soon 'ez we receive a copy 'a the **dock receipt** we c'n submid 'ar **collection papers**.

Vocabulary

certificate of inspection *n.* a document which certifies that goods or merchandise are in acceptable condition before being shipped.

example: If the supplier doesn't send us a **certificate of inspection**, we won't accept delivery of the goods.

translation: If the supplier doesn't send us a **document which certifies that the goods are in acceptable condition before they were shipped**, we won't accept delivery of the goods.

as spoken: If the supplier doesn' send us a **certificade of inspection**, we won't accept delivery of the goods.

clean bill of lading *n.* a declaration for goods issued by a common carrier indicating that all cargo accepted for transporation was in good condition when received.

example: Since all of our merchandise was carefully crated and inspected, the shipper issued a **clean bill of lading**.

translation: Since all of our merchandise was carefully crated and inspected, the shipper issued a **declaration indicating that all cargo accepted for transportation was in good condition**.

as spoken: Since all 'ev 'ar merchandise was carefully craded and inspected, the shipper issued a **clean bill of lading**.

collection papers *n.* any documents (including *bills of lading*, invoices, etc.) presented to a buyer to receive payment for a shipment.

example: I've just received notification that our shipment has arrived. Let's schedule the invoice for payment as soon as we receive the **collection papers**.

translation: I've just received notification that our shipment has arrived. Let's schedule the invoice for payment as soon as we receive **any documents, including bills of lading, invoices, etc. presented to receive payment**.

as spoken: I just received nodification thad 'ar shipment arrived. Let's schedule the invoice fer payment as soon as we receive the **collection papers**.

SEE: **clean bill of lading**, *p. 59*.

container *n.* a large rectangular shipping crate (usually made of steel) designed to be loaded and unloaded from transport vehicles without being unpacked.

example: The *freight forwarder* is sending out a truck to pick up our **container** this afternoon.

translation: The *freight forwarder* is sending out a truck to pick up our **large rectangular shipping crate** this afternoon.

as spoken: The *freight forwarder's* sending oud a truck ta pick up 'ar **c'ntainer** this afternoon.

SEE: **freight forwarder**, *p. 61*.

destination control statement *n.* a statement required by the U.S. government to prevent diversion of U.S. exports to unauthorized destinations.

example: Shipments of certain cargo to particular countries may need a **destination control statement**.

translation: Shipments of certain cargo to particular countries may need a **statement required by the U.S. government to prevent diversion to unauthorized destinations.**

as spoken: Shipments of certain cargo ta particular countries may need a **destination c'ntrol statement**.

dock receipt *n.* a receipt issued by an ocean carrier to acknowledge arrival of cargo at the carrier's warehouse or dock facilities.

example: The **dock receipt** shows that we're short by one cargo *container*.

translation: The **receipt which acknowledges arrival of cargo** shows that we're short by one cargo *container*.

as spoken: The **dock receipt** shows that w'r short by one cargo *c'ntainer*.

SEE: **container**, *p. 60*.

freight forwarder *n.* company that prepares shipping and insurance documents, and arranges cargo deliveries for domestic manufacturers.

example: For this shipment to Taiwan, contact the **freight forwarder**.

translation: For this shipment to Taiwan, contact the **company that prepares shipping and insurance documents, and arranges cargo deliveries for domestic manufacturers**.

as spoken: Fer this shipment ta Taiwan, contact the **freight forwarder**.

general export license *n.* an export license covering certain export commodities when no formal or written application is needed.

example: A list of products covered by a **general export license** is published by the U.S. Department of Commerce.

translation: A list of products covered by an **export license which includes certain export commodities when no formal or written application is needed** is published by the U.S. Department of Commerce.

as spoken: A list of produc's covered by a **general export license** is published by the U.S. Department of Commerce.

gross weight *n.* the entire weight of a shipment, including packaging and containers.

example: The weight of the packing crate will be included in the **gross weight**.

translation: The weight of the packing crate will be included in the **entire weight of the shipment, including packing and containers**.

as spoken: The wade of the packing crate'll be included in the **gross weight**.

SEE: **tare weight**, *p. 62*.

markings (or marks) *n.* letters, numbers, or symbols, attached to a *bill of lading* or cargo to expedite identification.

example: Make sure we have the correct **markings** on our shipment so that it passes through customs without any trouble.

translation: Make sure we have the correct **letters, numbers, or symbols for identification** on our shipment so that it passes through customs without any trouble.

as spoken: Make sher we have the correct **markings** on 'ar shipment so th'd it passes through customs withoud any trouble.

SEE: **clean bill of lading**, *p. 59.*

net weight *n.* the weight of the contents of a shipment excluding the weight of the container, pallet, skid, or crate.

example: To calculate the **net weight**, we'll take the total weight, 600 lbs., subtract the weight of the pallet, 50 lbs., for a net weight of 550 lbs.

translation: To calculate **only the weight of the merchandise itself**, we'll take the total weight, 600 lbs., subtract the weight of the pallet, 50 lbs., for a net weight of 550 lbs.

as spoken: Ta calculate the **net weight**, we'll take the todal weight, 600 lbs., subtract the wade of the pallet, 50 lbs., fer a net wade of 550 lbs.

SEE -1: **gross weight**, *p. 61.*

SEE -2: **tare weight**, *next entry.*

tare weight *n.* the weight of an empty shipping container or packing crate.

example: The total weight of our shipment includes the **tare weight** of the container in addition to the weight of the merchandise and packing.

translation: The total weight of our shipment includes the **weight of the empty container** in addition to the weight of the merchandise and packing.

as spoken: The todel wade 'ev 'ar shipment includes the **tare waid** 'ev the c'ntainer in addition ta the waid 'ev the merchandise 'n packing.

SEE -1: **gross weight**, *p. 61.*

SEE -2: **net weight**, *p. 62.*

Practice the Vocabulary

(Answers to Lesson 3, p. 271)

A. Fill in the blank with the corresponding letter of the word that best completes the phrase.

1. Our ______ receipt shows that our shipment is short.
   a. **markings** b. **tare weight** c. **dock**

2. Because all of our merchandise was carefully crated and inspected, the shipper issued a ______ bill of lading.
   a. **clean** b. **foreign** c. **standard**

3. If we don't receive a certificate of ______ from the supplier, we won't accept delivery of the merchandise.
   a. **collection** b. **lading** c. **inspection**

4. I was just notified that our shipment has arrived. Let's schedule the invoice for payment as soon as we receive the ______ papers.
   a. **collection** b. **dock** c. **inspection**

5. Make sure that we have the correct ______ on our shipment so that it passes through customs without any trouble.
   a. **export license** b. **markings** c. **container**

6. The ______ weight is the weight of a shipment which excludes the weight of the container, pallet, skid, or crate.
   a. **tare** b. **commercial** c. **net**

7. The ______ weight is the weight of an empty shipping container or packing crate.
   a. **tare** b. **tear** c. **net**

8. A ______ export license is an export license covering certain export commodities when no formal or written application is needed.
   a. **standard** b. **clean** c. **general**

B. Complete the phrases by choosing the appropriate word(s) from the list below.

certificate of inspection	**control statement**
clean bill of lading	**dock receipt**
collection papers	**general export license**
container	**markings**

1. A destination ______________________________ is a statement required by the U.S. government that is displayed on export shipments and lists the authorized export destination for the shipment.

2. A ______________________________ is a document which certifies that goods or merchandise were in acceptable condition before being shipped.

3. A ___________________________ is a declaration for goods issued by a common carrier indicating that all cargo accepted for transportation was in good condition when received.

4. A __________________ is a large rectangular shipping crate (usually made of steel) designed to be loaded and unloaded from transport vehicles without being unpacked.

5. ________________________ refers to any documents (including bills of lading, invoices, etc.) presented to a buyer for the purpose of receiving payment for a shipment.

6. A ________________________ is an export license covering certain export commodities when no formal or written application is needed.

7. Letters, numbers, or symbols, attached to bills of lading or cargo to expedite identification are called _________________.

8. A ______________________ is a receipt issued by an ocean carrier to acknowledge arrival of cargo at the carrier's warehouse or dock facilities.

C. Complete the opening dialogue using the list below.

bill	**forwarder**
certificate	**markings**
collection	**net**
container	**receipt**
control	**weight**
export	

Earl: I just heard from the **freight** *(1)* ____________________ that our *(2)* ______________ is going to be picked up tomorrow. We'd better make sure everything is ready to go.

Ted: Let's see...our **general** *(3)* ____________ **license** is current and the **destination** *(4)* ____________ **statement** has been filed.

Earl: ...and the shipping container has the proper *(5)* ______________. We also have the *(6)* ________________ **of inspection**.

Ted: We verified the **tare** *(7)* ____________ of our container so we have the correct *(8)* _________ **weight** for the shipment.

Earl: We inspected the shipment and know that it's in good condition. So we should receive a **clean** *(9)* ______________ **of lading** from the shipping line.

Ted: Well, that sounds like everything. As soon as we receive a copy of the **dock** *(10)* ________________________, we can submit our *(11)* _______________**papers**.

A CLOSER LOOK:
International Trade Slang & Jargon (Part A)

alongside *exp.* refers to goods which are to be delivered "alongside" a ship within reach of the transport ship's tackle.

example: Our sea freight arrangement with the shipping line specifies that we deliver our goods **alongside**.

translation: Our sea freight arrangement with the shipping line specifies that we deliver our goods **within reach of the transport ship's tackle**.

as spoken: 'Ar sea freight arrangement with the shipping line specifies th't we deliver 'ar goods **alongside**.

antidiversion clause *n.*

SEE: **destination control statement**, *p. 60.*

arbitrage *n.* the practice of purchasing stocks, bonds, foreign exchange, and other commodities in one market and immediately reselling them for a profit in another market.

example: Jack has always been a risk-taker. Now he's going to experiment with **arbitrage**.

translation: Jack has always been a risk-taker. Now he's going to experiment with **purchasing stocks, bonds, foreign exchange, and other commodities in one market and immediately reselling them for a profit in another market**.

as spoken: Jack's always been a risk-taker. Now 'e's gonna experiment with **arbitrage**.

authority to purchase *n.* authorization from a seller's bank to an importer's bank to draw a draft against the buyer's account to cover a specified shipment of merchandise.

example: Notify our customer that we cannot release the shipment until we have received notification of **authority to purchase**.

translation: Notify our customer that we cannot release the shipment until we have received notification of **authorization from the seller's bank to the importer's bank to draw a draft against the buyer's account to cover a specified shipment of merchandise**.

as spoken: Nodify 'ar custamer th't we can't r'lease the shipment until we've r'ceived nodification of **authoridy ta purchase**.

bilateral trade agreement *n.* a reciprocal commerce arrangement between two governments that specifies tradeable goods, categories, and quantities; and contains provisions for remittance of balances due.

example: We're not allowed to ship this particular commodity to Zamboanga because it's prohibited by a **bilateral trade agreement**.

translation: We're not allowed to ship this particular commodity to Zamboanga because it's prohibited by a **reciprocal commerce arrangement between our two governments**.

as spoken: W'r nod allowed ta ship this perticular commodidy ta Zamboanga 'cuz it's prahibided by a **biladeral trade agreement**.

bill of lading *n.* a document that specifies the terms of a shipping contract betweeen a shipper and transportation company. It serves three main functions: **1.** a document of title; **2.** a contract of carriage; **3.** and a receipt for goods.

example: Let's prepare a **bill of lading** for the pallets we are shipping.

translation: Let's prepare a **document that details the terms of our shipping contract** for the pallets we are shipping.

as spoken: Let's prepare a **bill of lading** fer the pallets w'r shipping.

NOTE -1: **air waybill** *n.* a bill of lading which covers domestic and international air transportation of goods to a specified destination.

NOTE -2: **inland bill of lading** *n.* a bill of lading used when moving cargo via truck or train to an exporter's international shipper.

NOTE -3: **ocean bill of lading** *n.* a bill of lading indicating that an exporter transfers title of cargo to an ocean-going carrier for transportation to a specified foreign destination.

NOTE -4: **through bill of lading** *n.* a single *bill of lading* used when transporting cargo through intermediate domestic or foreign ports.

Bloc *n.* the members of the European Monetary System, formed to stabilize exchange rate fluctuations. When the values of the bloc countries exceed an agreed upon value, there is a currency devaluation (The deutsche mark is the bloc's primary currency).

example: Germany, Holland, Denmark, Norway, Belgium, and Luxembourg are all members of the **Bloc**.

translation: Germany, Holland, Denmark, Norway, Belgium, and Luxembourg are all members of the **European Monetary System**.

as spoken: Germany, Holland, Denmark, Norway, Belgium, and Luxembourg'er all members of the **Bloc**.

blocked currency *n.* a currency that a particular government prohibits from being converted on the foreign exchange market.

example: We can't accept this payment because it has been made in a **blocked currency**.

translation: We can't accept this payment because it has been made in a **currency that a government prohibits from being converted on the foreign exchange market**.

as spoken: We can't accept this payment 'cuz it's been made in a **blocked currency**.

blocked exchange *n.* a currency that cannot be easily converted into other currencies.

example: Our transfer of Russian rubles to U.S. dollars is a **blocked exchange**.

translation: Our transfer of Russian rubles to U.S. dollars is a **currency that cannot be easily converted into other currencies**.

as spoken: 'Ar transfer 'ev Russian rubles ta U.S. dollers is a **blocked exchange**.

bonded warehouse *n.* a facility approved by customs authorities for storage of goods upon which payment of *duties* is deferred until the goods are withdrawn.

example: If we want to delay the payment of *duties* on this merchandise, regulations will require that we store it in a **bonded warehouse**.

translation: If we want to delay the payment of *duties* on this merchandise, regulations will require that we store it in a **facility approved by customs authorities for storage of goods upon which payment of duties is deferred until the goods are withdrawn**.

as spoken: If we wanna delay the payment of dudies on this merchandise, regulations will require that we store id in a **bonded warehouse**.

SEE: **duty**, *p. 74.*

buying agent *n.*

SEE: **purchasing agent**, *p. 87.*

Common Market *n.* (also referred to as "The European Economic Community" or "EEC") an economic arrangement between Western and European nations that facilitates trade.

example: Since our two countries are members of the **Common Market**, our tariff and regulatory barriers will be lowered.

translation: Since our two countries are members of the **European Economic Community**, our tariff and regulatory barriers will be lowered.

as spoken: Since 'ar two countries'er members of the **Common Market**, 'ar tariff 'n regulatory barriers'll be lowered.

confirmed letter of credit *n.* a letter of credit that guarantees payment to the beneficiary, even if the buyer defaults and his bank fails to pay.

example: Payment for our shipment of books to Korea is ensured by our requirement for a **confirmed letter of credit**.

translation: Payment for our shipment of books to Korea is ensured by our requirement for a **letter of credit that guarantees payment even if the buyer defaults and his bank fails to pay**.

as spoken: Payment fer 'ar shipment 'ev books ta Korea is ensured by 'ar requirement fer a **c'nfirmed ledder 'ev credit**.

SEE: **LC**, an abbreviation for *"letter of credit", p. 113.*

consignment *n.* delivery of goods from the owner to a dealer. The owner retains title to the goods until the dealer has sold them. Upon sale of the goods, the dealer retains his commission, and sends the net proceeds to the owner.

example: Since this shipment is a **consignment**, we will continue to list it in our inventory until the goods are sold.

translation: Since this shipment is a **delivery of goods from the owner to a dealer in which the owner retains title**, we will continue to list it in our inventory until the goods are sold.

as spoken: Since this shipment's a **c'nsignment**, we will c'ntinue ta list id in 'ar inv'ntory until the goods'er sold.

consular declaration *n.* a formal statement describing goods to be shipped, made to the consul of a foreign country.

example: Before we call our *freight forwarder,* let's find out if a **consular declaration** is needed.

translation: Before we call our *freight forwarder,* let's find out if a **formal statement describing goods to be shipped made to the consul of a foreign country** is needed.

as spoken: Before we call 'ar *freight forwarder,* let's find oud if a **consular declaration** is needed.

SEE: **freight forwarder**, *p. 61.*

consular invoice *n.* a document describing a shipment of goods, listing such information as the consignor, consignee, and value of the shipment. It is verified by the consular official and used by the receiving country's *customs* officials to confirm the shipment specifications.

example: Some foreign countries require **Consular Invoices** for all goods shipped to them.

translation: Some foreign countries require **a document describing a shipment of goods, used by the country's customs officials to confirm shipment specifications** for all goods shipped to them.

as spoken: Some forin countries require **Consular Invoices** fer all goods shipped ta th'm.

SEE: **customs**, *p. 84*.

convertibility *n.* the ease with which a particular currency may be exchanged for another in foreign exchange markets.

example: The dollar is a *hard currency* and has excellent **convertibility**.

translation: The dollar is a *hard currency* and is **easy to exchange for another currency in a foreign exchange market**.

as spoken: The dollar's a *hard currency* an' has excellent **c'nverdabilidy**.

SEE: **hard currency**, *p. 86*.

countertrade *n.* goods traded for other goods rather than for cash; also known as "barter."

example: Since there is no exchange for the Russian ruble, **countertrade** might be our best option when doing business with Russian manufacturers.

translation: Since there is no exchange for the Russian ruble, **barter** might be our best option when doing business with Russian manufacturers.

as spoken: Since there's no exchange fer the Russian ruble, **coun'ertrade** might be 'ar best option when doing bizness with Russian manufacturers.

country manager *n.* an individual in charge of a multinational company's operations in a particular foreign country.

example: For shipments to Saudi Arabia, you'll have to talk to Ted. He's the **country manager**.

translation: For shipments to Saudi Arabia, you'll have to talk to Ted. He's the **individual in charge of operations in that particular foreign country**.

as spoken: Fer shipments ta Saudi Arabia, you'll hafta talk ta Ted. He's the **country manager**.

credit risk insurance *n.* insurance designed to cover losses resulting from nonpayment of an obligation.

example: With **credit risk insurance**, shipments to developing nations are less problematic.

translation: With **insurance designed to cover losses resulting from nonpayment of an obligation**, shipments to developing nations are less problematic.

as spoken: With **credit risk insurance**, shipments ta developing nations'er less problemadic.

currency depreciation *n.* the process of a nation's money decreasing in value compared to the currency of other nations or compared to its own previous value. The opposing process is called **currency appreciation**.

example: The dollar continues to fall relative to the yen due to **currency depreciation**.

translation: The dollar continues to fall relative to the yen due to **the decrease in value of a nation's money compared to the currency of other nations**.

as spoken: The dollar continues ta fall reladive ta the yen due da **currency depreciation**.

currency devaluation *n.* the process that occurs when a government purposely reduces the value of its money relative to that of other countries.

example: The Japanese **currency devaluation** will make it easier for U.S. customers to buy Japanese products.

translation: The Japanese **reduction of the value of the Yen relative to the Dollar** will make it easier for U.S. customers to buy Japanese products.

as spoken: The Japenese **currency devaluation**'ll make id easier fer U.S. custamers ta buy Japanese produc's.

currency exposure *n.* the amount of investments a country or business has placed overseas that is subject to changes in value as a result of fluctuations in currency valuations.

example: Due to instability in foreign exchange rates, let's try to minimize our **currency exposure**.

translation: Due to instability in foreign exchange rates, let's try to minimize our **investments overseas that are subject to changes in value as a result of fluctuations in currency valuations**.

as spoken: Due to instabilidy in forin exchange rates, let's try da minimize 'ar **currency exposure**.

domicile *n.* • **1.** the principle place of business, or where the governing power of an enterprise is exercised • **2.** a place where a *draft* or acceptance is made payable.

example (1): For tax purposes, the **domicile** is considered to be where the address of an establishment is maintained.

translation: For tax purposes, the **principle place of business** is considered to be where the address of an establishment is maintained.

as spoken: Fer tax purposes, the **domicile**'s considered ta be where thee address of 'n establishment is maintained.

example (2): Check the draft contained in our shipping documents. Its **domicile** is the port of entry.

translation: Check the draft contained in our shipping documents. Its **location where a draft or acceptance is made payable** is the port of entry.

as spoken: Check the draft c'ntained in 'ar shipping docyam'nts. Its **domicile**'s the pord of entry.

SEE: **draft**, *(next entry)*.

draft *n.* an order, in writing, directing a person (other than the maker) to pay a specified sum to a named person.

example: We will need a bank **draft** to move money to our offshore company.

translation: We will need an **order, in writing, directing a person (other than the maker) to pay a specified sum to a named person** to move money to our offshore company.

as spoken: We'll need a bank **draft** ta move money ta 'ar offshore company.

SYNONYM: **Bill of Exchange**.

drawee *n.* a firm or individual in whose name a *draft* is drawn and who is responsible for the specified amount.

example: Let's make sure that this draft lists the proper **drawee** before we authorize release of the shipment.

translation: Let's make sure that this draft lists the proper **individual in whose name a draft is drawn and who is responsible for the specified amount** before we authorize release of the shipment.

as spoken: Let's make sher th't this draft lists the proper **drawee** before we autherize release of the shipment.

SEE: **draft**, *p. 73*.

drawer *n.* the firm or individual that signs or issues a *draft* and receives payment of the specified amount from the *drawee*.

example: We need your signature on this *draft* because it specifies you as the **drawer**.

translation: We need your signature on this *draft* because it specifies you as the **individual that signs or issues a draft and receives payment of the specified amount from the drawee**.

as spoken: We nee'jer signature on this *draft* 'cuz it specifies you as the **drawer**.

SEE -1: **draft**, *p. 73*.

SEE -2: **drawee**, *p. 73*.

dumping *n.* the practice of selling goods overseas below their cost of production as a means of competing with foreign producers.

example: Some domestic manufacturers have cited **dumping** by foreign competitors as one reason for their poor sales performance.

translation: Some domestic manufacturers have cited **the practice of selling goods abroad below their cost of production** by foreign competitors as one reason for their poor sales performance.

as spoken: Some damestic manufacturers have cided **dumping** by forin compediders 'ez one reason fer their poor sales performance.

duty *n.* a tax imposed on the importation, exportation, or consumption of goods. Duties may be based on the value, weight, or quantity of goods, or a combination of value and other factors.

example: **Duty** on our import shipment of books will be based on their value.

translation: **Tax imposed on the importation, exportation, or consumption of goods** on our import shipment of books will be based on their value.

as spoken: **Dudy** on 'ar import shipment of books'll be based on their value.

duty drawback *n.* a *customs* law which refunds *duties* on imported components used to manufacture *exports*.

example: Since these imported components are going to be used to manufacture products for export, they may qualify for a **duty drawback**.

translation: Since these imported components are going to be used to manufacture products for export, they may qualify for a **refund of duties on imported components used to manufacture exports**.

as spoken: Since these imporded c'mponents'er gonna be used ta manufacture produc's fer export, they may qualify fer a **doody drawback**.

SEE -1: **customs**, *p. 84.*

SEE -2: **duty**, *p. 74.*

SEE -3: **export**, *(next entry).*

export • **1.** *n.* a domestic product or service sold in a foreign market • **2.** *v.* to send or transport products or services out of the country for sale in a foreign market.

example (1): This computer will be a foreign **export**. Make sure the instructions are translated into Chinese.

translation: This computer will be a **domestic product sold in a foreign market**. Make sure the instructions are translated into Chinese.

as spoken: This c'mpuder will be a forin **export**. Make sher thee instructions 'er transladed inta Chinese.

example (2): Let's see if we can **export** our cellular telephone technology to Korea.

translation: Let's see if we can **send** our cellular telephone technology to Korea.

as spoken: Let's see if we c'n **expord** 'ar cellular telephone technalagy ta Korea.

export broker *n.* an individual or company, generally paid on a commission basis, who arranges contacts between sellers and importers.

example: The **export broker** has located a new Japanese distributor for our line of business books.

translation: The **individual who arranges contacts between sellers and importers** has located a new Japanese distributor for our line of business books.

as spoken: The **export broker**'s locaded a new Japanese distribuder fer 'ar line of business books.

export license *n.* a government permit which enables the holder to *export* certain goods to specific destinations.

example: Since our shipment contains pharmaceuticals, we will require an **export license**.

translation: Since our shipment contains pharmaceuticals, we will require a **permit which enables the holder to export certain goods to specific destinations**.

as spoken: Since 'ar shipment c'ntains pharmaceudicles, w'll require 'n **export license**.

SEE: **export**, *p. 75*.

export merchant *n.* a company which *imports* directly from an overseas manufacturer, then resells the merchandise under its own name.

example: As an **export merchant**, we will substantially reduce our manufacturing costs.

translation: As a **company which imports directly from an overseas manufacturer, then resells the merchandise under its own name**, we'll substantially reduce our manufacturing costs.

as spoken: As 'n **export merchant**, w'll substantially reduce 'ar manufacturing costs.

SEE: **import**, *p. 94*.

export trade certificate of review *n.* a document which grants partial immunity from antitrust regulations. It is issued by the Justice Department in conjunction with the Department of Commerce and is based on ETCA (Export Trading Company Affairs) legislation.

example: A company which holds an **export trade certificate of review** and whose activity does not adversely effect the U.S. domestic economy, is generally immune from prosecution under antitrust regulations.

translation: A company which holds a **document granting partial immunity from antitrust regulations** and whose activity does not adversely effect the U.S. domestic economy, is generally immune from prosecution under antitrust regulations.

as spoken: A company which holds 'n **export trade certificad of review** an' whose actividy doesn' adversely effect the U.S. d'mestic econamy, is generally immune fr'm prosecution under antitrust regulations.

Practice Using International Trade Slang & Jargon (Part A)

(Answers, p. 272)

A. Choose the correct international trade term of the definition in boldface. Write the letter of the corresponding answer in the box.

A) **bilateral trade agreement**
B) **bill of lading**
C) **blocked exchange**
D) **consignment**
E) **countertrade**
F) **currency depreciation**
G) **domicile**
H) **draft**
I) **dumping**
J) **duty**

☐ 1. The Dollar continues to fall relative to the Yen due to **the process of a nation's money decreasing in value relative to the currency of other nations.**

☐ 2. Some domestic manufacturers have cited **the practice of selling goods abroad below the cost of their production by foreign competitors** as one reason for their poor sales performance.

☐ 3. **Tax imposed on the importation, exportation, or consumption of goods** on our import shipment of books will probably be based on their value.

☐ 4. We're not allowed to ship this particular commodity to Zamboanga because it's covered by a **reciprocal commerce arrangement between two governments.**

☐ 5. Let's prepare a **document specifying the terms of our shipping contract** for this shipment.

☐ 6. For tax purposes, the **principle place of business** is considered to be where the address of the establishment is maintained.

☐ 7. Since there is no exchange for the Russian ruble, **barter** might be our best option when doing business with them.

☐ 8. Since this shipment is a **delivery of goods from the owner to a dealer in which the owner retains title,** we will continue to list it in our inventory until the goods are sold.

☐ 9. Our transfer of U.S. dollars to Russia is **an exchange which is prohibited.**

☐ 10. We will need a bank **order in writing directing a person (other than the maker) to pay a specified sum to a named person** to move money to our offshore company.

LESSON FOUR

International Trade
(Part B)

Our shipment was sent
to a port known for ***dock wallopers****!*

Lesson Four

Dialogue in slang

Earl: Today I heard from our **foreign sales agent**. It seems that our cargo was sent through a port known for **dock wallopers**. To make matters worse, he arranged a **booking** with a sea freight line that's had several cases of **barratry** this year.

Ted: Well, I'm not too concerned because I'm sure that our **marine insurance** will cover us for any losses due to negligence of the crew.

Earl: What about damage or theft if the shipment is delayed while awaiting clearance through **customs**?

Ted: The shipment won't be in customs very long because we paid the proper fees to the **customs broker**. Actually, I'm more concerned that the **purchasing agent** won't pay.

Earl: I don't think that will be a problem. Our payment terms are **demand draft** with payment **at sight** and secured by an **irrevocable letter of credit**.

Ted: I feel better. We'll be paid in **hard currency**.

Lesson Four

Translation of dialogue in standard English

International Trade (Part B)

Earl: Today I heard from our **foreign representative**. It seems that our cargo was sent through a port known for **thieves who steal cargo**. To make matters worse, he arranged a **reservation** with a sea freight line that's had several cases of **fraud or negligence** this year.

Ted: Well, I'm not too concerned because I'm sure that our **insurance that covers loss or damage of our ship's cargo** will cover us for any losses due to negligence of the crew.

Earl: What about damage or theft if the shipment is delayed while awaiting clearance through **the government agency responsible for collecting duties levied on imports and exports**?

Ted: The shipment won't be in customs very long because we paid the proper fees to the **person licensed to enter and clear goods through customs**. Actually, I'm more concerned that the **agent who purchases goods on the organization's behalf** won't pay.

Earl: I don't think that will be a problem. Our payment terms are **a draft payable upon presentation rather than on a specified date** with payment **due upon presentation** and secured by **a letter of credit which guarantees a specified payment if the seller meets the stipulated terms and which cannot be cancelled**.

Ted: I feel better. We'll be paid in **currency which is stable and acceptable for international transactions.**

Lesson Four

Dialogue as spoken

International Trade (Part B)

Earl: Today I heard fr'm 'ar **forin sales agent**. It seems thad 'ar cargo was sent through a port known fer **dock wallopers**. Ta make madders worse, he arranged a **booking** with a sea freight line th't's had sev'ral cases of **barratry** this year.

Ted: Well, I'm not too c'ncerned 'cuz I'm sher thad 'ar **marine insurance**'ll cover us fer any losses due da negligence of the crew.

Earl: What about damage 'r theft if the shipment's delayed while awaiding clearance through **customs**?

Ted: The shipment won't be in customs very long 'cuz we paid the proper fees ta the **customs broker**. Ackshelly, I'm more c'ncerned that the **purchasing agent** won't pay.

Earl: I don' think that'll be a problem. 'Ar payment terms'er **deman' draft** with payment **at sight** 'n secured by 'n **irrevocable ledder of credit**.

Ted: I feel bedder. We'll be paid in **hard currency**.

Vocabulary

at sight *exp.* a term stipulating that payment on a draft or other negotiable instrument is due upon presentation.

example: Please note that the payment terms on our freight bill are **at sight**.

translation: Please note that the payment terms on our freight bill are **payment due upon presentation**.

as spoken: Please note that the payment terms on 'ar freight bill'er **at sight**.

barratry *n.* fraud or negligence on the part of ship's officers or crew resulting in loss or injury to the owners of the ship.

example: The shipping line we've been using has experienced several cases of **barratry**. We should locate a more dependable carrier.

translation: The shipping line we've been using has experienced several cases of **fraud or negligence**. We should locate a more dependable carrier.

as spoken: The shipping line we've been using has experienced sev'ral cases of **barratry**. We should locade a more dependable carrier.

booking *n.* a reservation with a sea freight company for the acceptance and transportation of cargo.

example: If we want those *containers* to go out next month, we'll need a **booking** as soon as possible.

translation: If we want those *containers* to go out next month, we'll need a **reservation with a sea freight company** as soon as possible.

as spoken: If we want those *c'ntainers* ta go out nex' month, w'll need a **booking** ez soon ez possible.

NOTE: **container** *n.* a large rectangular shipping crate (usually made of steel) designed to be loaded and unloaded from transport vehicles without unpacking.

customs *n.* • **1.** a government agency responsible for collecting duties levied on imports and exports • **2.** the actual tariff, tax, or duty levied on imports and exports.

example (1): The shipment will have to pass through **customs** on its way to Canada.

translation: The shipment will have to pass through **the government agency responsible for collecting duties levied on imports and exports** on its way to Canada.

as spoken: The shipment'll hafta pass through **customs** on its way da Canada.

example (2): You'll have to pay some **customs** on the Japanese camera you bought when we arrive at the airport in San Francisco.

translation: You'll have to pay some **duty** on the Japanese camera you bought when we arrive at the airport in San Francisco.

as spoken: You'll hafta pay s'm **customs** on the Japanese camera you bought when we arrive at the airpord in San Francisco.

customs broker *n.* an individual or business licensed to enter and clear goods through customs.

example: All of our shipments to Japan go through a **customs broker**.

translation: All of our shipments to Japan go through a **business licensed to enter and clear goods through customs**.

as spoken: All 'ar shipments ta Japan go through a **cusdoms broker**.

demand draft *n.* a draft payable upon presentation rather than on a specified date.

example: We will need sufficient money in our account to pay for this shipment because terms are **demand draft**.

translation: We will need sufficient money in our account to pay for this shipment because terms are **draft payable upon presentation**.

as spoken: We'll need sufficient money in 'ar account ta pay fer this shipment 'cuz terms'er **deman' draft**.

dock walloper *n.* a thief who steals cargo before it has received customs clearance or has been unloaded.

example: Tell our security guard to keep his eyes open. Last month we had a loss due to a **dock walloper**.

translation: Tell our security guard to keep his eyes open. Last month we had a loss due to an **individual who steals cargo before it has received customs clearance or has been unloaded**.

as spoken: Tell 'ar securidy guard ta keep 'iz eyes open. Las' month we had a loss due do a **dock wallaper**.

foreign sales agent *n.* an individual or firm which acts as the foreign representative of a domestic manufacturer and sells goods on a commission basis.

example: To minimize the risk to our sales campaign in South Africa, we will need to contract with a **foreign sales agent**.

translation: To minimize the risk to our sales campaign in South Africa, we will need to contract with an **individual or firm which acts as our foreign representative and sells goods on a commission basis**.

as spoken: Ta minimize the risk to 'ar sales campaign in South Africa, we'll need ta contract with a **forin sales agent**.

hard currency *n.* a currency that is stable and acceptable for international transactions.

example: The U.S. dollar is accepted worldwide and is considered a **hard currency**.

translation: The United States dollar is accepted worldwide and is considered a **currency which is stable and acceptable for international transactions.**

as spoken: The U.S. doller is accepted worldwide an' is c'nsidered a **hard currency**.

irrevocable letter of credit *n.* a letter of credit which guarantees a specified payment if the seller meets the stipulated terms. It cannot be revoked.

example: If the shipment arrives according to the terms of our agreement, the buyer cannot void the **irrevocable letter of credit**.

translation: If the shipment arrives according to the terms of our agreement, the buyer cannot void the **letter of credit which guarantees a specified payment if the seller meets the stipulated terms**.

as spoken: If the shipment arrives according ta the terms of 'ar agreement, the buyer can't void thee **irrevocable ledder of credit**.

marine insurance *n.* insurance that covers loss or damage of a ship's cargo.

example: **Marine insurance** now covers cargo during transportation overland in addition to transit at sea.

translation: **Insurance that covers loss or damage of a ship's cargo** now covers cargo during transportation overland in addition to transit at sea.

as spoken: **Marine insurance** now covers cargo during transpertation overland in addition ta transid 'it sea.

purchasing agent *n.* an agent, either an individual or private firm, who purchases goods on behalf of an organization.

example: We're not allowed to purchase computers directly from a supplier. We have to go through the **purchasing agent**.

translation: We're not allowed to purchase computers directly from a supplier. We have to go through the **firm who purchases goods on our behalf**.

as spoken: W'r nod allowed ta purchase c'mpuders directly from a supplier. We hafta go through the **purchasing agent**.

Practice the Vocabulary

(Answers to Lesson 4, p. 272)

A. Fill in the blank with word(s) that best complete(s) the phrase.

agent	**demand**
at sight	**hard**
barratry	**irrevocable**
booking	**marine**
broker	**purchasing**
customs	**walloper**

1. ____________________ *n.* fraud or negligence on the part of ship's officers or crew resulting in loss or injury to the owners of a ship.

2. ____________________ *exp.* an expression stipulating that payment on a draft or other negotiable instrument is due upon presentation.

3. ____________________ *n.* • **1.** a government agency responsible for collecting duties levied on imports and exports • **2.** the actual tariff, tax, or duty levied on imports and exports.

4. **customs** ____________________ *n.* an individual or business licensed to enter and clear goods through customs.

5. ____________________ *n.* a reservation with a sea freight company for the acceptance and transportation of cargo.

6. **dock** ____________________ *n.* a thief who steals cargo before it has received customs clearance or has been unloaded.

7. **foreign sales** ____________________ *n.* an individual or firm who acts as the foreign representative of a domestic manufacturer and sells goods on a commission basis.

8. ____________________ **agent** *n.* an agent, either an individual or private firm, that purchases goods on behalf of an organization.

9. ________________ **currency** *n.* a currency that is stable and acceptable for international transactionsl.

10. __________________________ **letter of credit** *n.* a letter of credit which guarantees a specified payment if the seller meets the stipulated terms, and which cannot be canceled.

11. ___________________ **insurance** *n.* insurance that covers loss or damage of a ship's cargo.

12. ___________________ **draft** *n.* a draft payable upon presentation rather than on a specified date.

B. Underline the appropriate word that best completes the phrase.

1. This time we're going to be paid in (**hard**, **soft**, **purchasing**) currency.

2. Our (**booking**, **freight**, **marine**) insurance policy will cover us for any losses due to negligence of the crew.

3. To minimize the risk of our sales campaign in France, we will need to contract with a foreign sales (**delegate**, **agent**, **deputy**).

4. I hope our shipment is going to be safe. This port has had numerous problems with (**barratry**, **barraging**, **bartering**).

5. The shipment will have to pass through (**customs**, **customers**, **customhouses**) on its way to South America.

6. Tell our security guard to keep his eyes open. Last month we had a loss due to a (**customs**, **marine**, **dock**) walloper.

7. We will need sufficient money in our account to cover this shipment because terms are (**demand**, **at sight**, **purchase**) draft.

8. The payment terms on our freight bill are at (**dock**, **sight**, **walloper**).

9. If the shipment arrives according to the terms of our agreement, the buyer cannot void the irrevocable letter of (**credit**, **credentials**, **credibility**).

10. We're not allowed to purchase computers directly from a supplier. We have to go through our (**purchasing**, **selling**, **bartering**) agent.

C. Are the following true or false?

1. **Marine insurance** covers loss or damage to the ship itself.
☐ True ☐ False

2. A **purchasing agent** is an agent, either an individual or private firm, that purchases goods on behalf of an organization.
☐ True ☐ False

3. **Customs** is a government agency responsible for collecting duties levied on imports and exports
☐ True ☐ False

4. An **irrevocable letter of credit** is a letter of credit that guarantees a specified payment if the seller does not meet the stipulated terms.
☐ True ☐ False

5. A **demand draft** is currency that is easily converted into the currency of another country.
☐ True ☐ False

6. A **dock walloper** is an individual or firm who acts as the foreign representative of a domestic manufacturer and sells goods on a commission basis.
☐ True ☐ False

7. A **customs broker** is an individual or business licensed to enter and clear goods through customs.
☐ True ☐ False

8. **Barratry** refers to fraud or negligence on the part of a ship's officers or crew resulting in loss or injury to the owners of a ship.
☐ True ☐ False

9. A **booking** is a reservation with a sea freight company for the acceptance and transportation of cargo.
☐ True ☐ False

10. **At sight** is an expression stipulating that payment on a draft or other negotiable instrument is due upon presentation.
☐ True ☐ False

A CLOSER LOOK:
International Trade Slang & Jargon (Part B)

foreign exchange *n.* *(also known as "FOREX" or "FX")* in a given country; the currency of another country.

example: **Foreign exchange** is a means of making payment overseas.

translation: **FOREX** is a means of making payment overseas.

as spoken: [no change]

foul bill of lading *n.* a *bill of lading* indicating that goods were damaged when delivered to a carrier.

example: Along with the shipment that just arrived, we received a **foul bill of lading**. Don't pay the invoice until we've inspected the goods carefully.

translation: Along with the shipment that just arrived, we received a **bill of lading indicating that goods were damaged when delivered to the carrier**. Don't pay the invoice until we've inspected the goods carefully.

as spoken: Along w'th the shipment th't just arrived, we raceived a **foul bill of lading**. Don't pay the invoice 'til we've inspected the goods carefully.

SEE (1): **bill of lading**, *p. 67.*

SEE (2): **clean bill of lading**, *p. 59.*

free port *n.* a port available to all traders in which imported goods may be held while awaiting re-export, without the need to pay duties.

example: We can simplify our customs paperwork for this cargo if we ship it through a **free port**.

translation: We can simplify our customs paperwork for this cargo if we ship it through a **port available to all traders in which imported goods may be held while awaiting re-export, without the need to pay duties**.

as spoken: We c'n simplify 'ar cust'ms paperwork fer this cargo if we ship it through a **free port**.

free trade *n.* commerce without trade or tax barriers.

example: Since there are no import duties on this shipment, we could consider it a good example of **free trade**.

translation: Since there are no import duties on this shipment, we could consider it a good example of **commerce which occurs without trade or tax barriers**.

as spoken: Since there'er no import dudies on this shipment, we could c'nsider id a good example of **free trade**.

futures market *n.* (also known as *forward market*) the purchasing and selling of contracts for commodities at a price set at the time of purchase, but not to be delivered or paid for until a specified time in the future.

example: Jack decided to take a chance on farm commodities in the hope of making a profit if the price of corn increases in the future. This is the first time he's invested in the **futures market**.

translation: Jack decided to take a chance on farm commodities in the hope of making a profit if the price of corn increases in the future. This is the first time he's invested in the **purchasing and selling of contracts for commodities at a price set at the time of purchase, but not to be delivered or paid for until a specified time in the future**.

as spoken: Jack decided ta take a chance on farm commodidies in the hope of making a profid if the price of corn increases in the future. This is the firs' time 'e's invested in the **futures market**.

NOTE: The contract for the commodity is known as a *future*.

gross weight *n.* the entire weight of a shipment, including packing and containers.

example: The weight of the packing crate will be included in the **gross weight**.

translation: The weight of the packing crate will be included in the **entire weight of the shipment, including packing and containers**.

as spoken: The wade of the packing crate'll be included in the **gross weight**.

SEE: **tare weight**, *p. 62*.

guest workers *n.* foreign laborers admitted to a country to work at certain jobs for a specific period of time.

example: Mexican farm laborers working in agricultural fields in California are an example of **guest workers**.

translation: Mexican farm laborers working in agricultural fields in California are an example of **foreign laborers admitted to a country to work at certain jobs for a specific period of time**.

as spoken: Mexic'n farm laberers working in agricultural fields in California are 'n example of **guest workers**.

hedging *n.* the purchase of a foreign currency to sell at a future date as a means of protecting against variations in the exchange rate.

example: **Hedging** is one technique for shifting speculative foreign exchange rate risk to banks.

translation: **The purchase of a foreign currency to sell at a future date as a means of protecting against variations in the exchange rate** is one technique for shifting speculative foreign exchange rate risk to banks.

as spoken: **Hedging**'s one technique fer shifding speculadive forin exchange rate risk ta banks.

import • **1.** *n.* a good or service produced in one country and brought into another country for the purposes of sale • **2.** *v.* to bring a good or service produced in one country into another country for the purposes of sale.

example (1): Nice car! Is that an **import**?

translation: Nice car! Is that a **good or service produced in one country and brought into another country for the purposes of sale**?

as spoken: Nice car! Izzat'n **import**?

example (2): Repair parts for this equipment are not available in the United States. We have no choice but to **import**.

translation: Repair parts for this equipment are not available in the United States. We have no choice but to **bring a good or service produced in one country into another country for the purposes of sale**.

as spoken: Repair parts fer this equipment are nod available in the U.S. We have no choice but to **import**.

SEE: **export**, *p. 75*.

inland bill of lading *n.* a *bill of lading* used when moving cargo via truck or train to an exporter's international shipper.

example: We will need an **inland bill of lading** in addition to our *ocean bill of lading* for this shipment.

translation: We will need **a bill of lading used when moving cargo via truck or train to an exporter's international shipper** in addition to our *ocean bill of lading* for this shipment.

as spoken: We'll need 'n **inl'nd bill of lading** in addition ta 'ar ocean bill of lading fer this shipment.

SEE (1): **bill of lading**, *p. 67.*

SEE (2): **ocean bill of lading**, NOTE (3), *p. 68.*

SEE (3): **through bill of lading**, NOTE (4), *p. 68.*

International Monetary Fund *n.*

SEE: **IMF**, *p. 127.*

inward investment *n.* a *multinational corporation's* investment in projects in its home country.

example: A large corporation may use an **inward investment** as a means of improving its image domestically.

translation: A large corporation may **invest in projects in its home country** as a means of improving its image domestically.

as spoken: A large corperation may use 'n **inward investment** as a means of improving its image d'mestic'ly.

SEE: **MNC**, *p. 128.*

irrevocable letter of credit *n.* a letter of credit which cannot be modified or canceled by the drawee (buyer) after it has been issued by the drawee's bank.

example: Before we ship this merchandise to our foreign distributor, he must present us with an **irrevocable letter of credit**.

translation: Before we ship this merchandise to our foreign distributor, he must present us with a **letter of credit which cannot be modified or canceled by the buyer**.

as spoken: Before we ship this merchandise ta 'ar forin distribuder, he must present us with 'n **irrevocable ledder of credit**.

SEE: **revocable letter of credit**, *p. 99.*

joint venture *n.* an agreement between firms to share expenses, profits, and losses from a commercial undertaking.

example: A **joint venture** to develop a new multimedia CD would reduce our risk and help us to bring the product to market earlier.

translation: An **agreement between firms** to develop a new multimedia compact disc would reduce our risk and help us to bring the product to market earlier.

as spoken: A **joint venture** ta develop a new multimedia CD would r'duce 'ar risk 'n help us bring the product ta marked earlier.

lighter *n.* an open or covered flat-bottomed boat, motorized or towed by a tugboat, and used primarily on inland waterways and harbors.

example: Cargo from ships at deep water ports will be carried by **lighter** to shallow inland ports.

translation: Cargo from ships at deep water ports will be carried by an **open or covered flat-bottomed boat** to shallow inland ports.

as spoken: Cargo fr'm ships at deep wader ports'll be carried by **lider** ta shallow inl'nd ports.

mule *n.* low-level, often unsuspecting, smuggler of contraband.

example: When it comes to the illegal drug trade, the **mule** takes most of the risk while others make all the profit.

translation: When it comes to the illegal drug trade, the **smuggler of contraband** takes most of the risk while others make most of the profit.

as spoken: When it comes ta the illegal drug trade, the **mule** takes most 'a the risk while other make most of the profit.

multinational corporation *n.*

SEE: **MNC**, *p. 128.*

offshore financing *n.* raising money in foreign countries for domestic business operations.

example: Domestic banks won't help us with our third world investments. We'll have to investigate **offshore financing**.

translation: Domestic banks won't help us with our third world investments. We'll have to investigate **raising money in foreign countries for our domestic business operations**.

as spoken: D'mestic banks won't help us with 'ar third world investments. W'll hafta investigade **offshore financing**.

NOTE: **third world** *n.* a synonym for "LDC" or "less-developed country."

open account *n.* a credit method for financing trade transactions in which goods are shipped to a buyer without guarantee of payment.

example: Our new customer wants to be on **open account**, so he'll need to supply us with three trade references.

translation: Our new customer wants to be on a **credit method for financing trade transactions in which goods are shipped to him without guarantee of payment**, so he'll need to supply us with three trade references.

as spoken: 'Ar new custamer wants ta be on **open account**, so he'll need to supply us with three trade references.

open insurance policy *n.* a marine insurance policy that covers all shipments made by an exporter during a specified period of time.

example: If the insurance value of the policy is not exceeded, our **open insurance policy** will cover all of our exports, even if they're not declared.

translation: If the insurance value of the policy is not exceeded, our **marine insurance, which covers all shipments made by an exporter during a specified period of time**, will cover all of our exports, even if they're not declared.

as spoken: If the insurance value of the policy's nod exceeded, 'ar **open insurance policy**'ll cover all of 'ar exports, even if they're not daclared.

Organization for Economic Cooperation and Development *n.*

SEE: OECD, *p. 128.*

Organization of Petroleum-Exporting Countries *n.*

SEE: OPEC, *p. 129.*

Overseas Private Investment Corporation *n.*

SEE: OPIC, *p. 129.*

phytosanitary inspection certificate *n.* a certificate issued by the U.S. Department of Agriculture certifying that U.S. agricultural exports have been inspected and are free from insects or plant diseases.

example: Before we can release this shipment of rice, we'll need a **phytosanitary inspection certificate**.

translation: Before we can release this shipment of rice, we'll need a **certificate issued by the USDA certifying that the export has been inspected and is free from insects or plant diseases**.

as spoken: Before we c'n r'lease this shipment of rice, we'll need a **phydosanitary inspection certificate**.

pro forma invoice *n.* a facsimile of an invoice describing the type, quantities, and value of the goods to be sent, specifications such as weight or size and shipping and/or handling costs. Payment terms of a pro forma invoice are generally "payment in advance" or "collect on delivery."

example: This customer doesn't have a credit record with us so we'd better issue a **pro forma invoice**.

translation: This customer doesn't have a credit record with us so we'd better issue a **an invoice whose payment terms are payment in advance or collect on delivery**.

as spoken: This custamer doesn't have a credit rec'rd with us so we bedder issue a **pro forma invoice**.

procuring agent *n.*

SEE: **purchasing agent**, *p. 87*.

protectionism *n.* a government policy to protect domestic producers from foreign competition.

example: It is difficult for United States manufacturers to sell in Japan because of Japanese **protectionism**.

translation: It is difficult for United States manufacturers to sell in Japan because of a **government policy to protect domestic producers from foreign competition**.

as spoken: It's difficult fer U.S. manufacturers ta sell in Japan 'cuz 'ev Japanese **protectionism**.

quotation *n.* an offer to sell merchandise at a specified price and under named conditions.

example: Our purchasing department requires that we get three **quotations** before we decide on a supplier for our air conditioners.

translation: Our purchasing department requires that we get three **offers to sell merchandise at a specified price** before we decide on a supplier for our air conditioners.

as spoken: 'Ar purchasing department r'quires that we get three **quotations** before we decide on a supplier fer 'ar air c'nditioners.

reserve assets *n.* a country's holdings in convertible foreign currencies or precious metals as a final means of making payment overseas.

example: Many third world countries have little or no **reserve assets**.

translation: Many third world countries have little or no **holdings in convertible foreign currencies or precious metals as a final means of making payment overseas**.

as spoken: Many third world countries have liddle'r no **reserve assets**.

revaluation *n.*

SEE: **currency devaluation**, *p. 72.*

revocable letter of credit *n.* a letter of credit that can be modified or cancelled by the buyer after it has been issued by the buyer's bank.

example: This is not acceptable. Our customer sent us a **revocable letter of credit** that he can void at any time.

translation: This is not acceptable. Our customer sent us a **letter of credit that he can modify or cancel** at any time.

as spoken: This isn' acceptable. 'Ar customer sen(t) us a **revocable ledder 'ev credit** that 'e c'n void id any time.

SEE: **irrevocable letter of credit**, *p. 95.*

soft currency *n.* a currency that cannot be easily converted into gold or other foreign currency.

example: Currencies of many third world nations are **soft currencies** as a consequence of their balance of payments situation.

translation: Currencies of many third world nations **cannot be easily converted into gold or other foreign currency** as a consequence of their balance of payments situation.

as spoken: Currencies of many third world nations'er **soft currencies** as a consequence of their balance of payments situation.

SEE: **hard currency**, *p. 86.*

spot exchange *n.* a foreign currency purchased or sold at its current market price.

example: Our conversion of Deutschemarks into U.S. dollars was a **spot exchange** so today's exchange rate will apply to the transaction.

translation: Our conversion of Deutschemarks into United States dollars was a **foreign currency purchased at its current market price** so today's exchange rate will apply to the transaction.

as spoken: 'Ar c'nversion of Deutschemarks inta U.S. dollars was a **spod exchange** so today's exchange rade'll apply da the transaction.

spot market *n.* the market for cash purchases of foreign currencies or other commodities where delivery occurs within two days of the transaction.

example: Let's see if we can quickly convert these French francs into dollars on the **spot market**.

translation: Let's see if we can quickly convert these French francs into dollars on the **market for cash purchases of foreign currencies where delivery occurs within two days of the transaction**.

as spoken: Let's see if we c'n quickly c'nvert these French francs inta dollars on the **spot market**.

state-controlled trading company *n.* an authorized trading monopoly; often a primary *purchasing agent* for basic commodities.

example: Since we are selling to a nonmarket-economy country, we will probably need to deal with their **state- controlled trading company**.

translation: Since we are selling to a nonmarket- economy country, we will probably need to deal with their **authorized trading monopoly**.

as spoken: Since w'r selling to a nonmarked-economy country, w'll pro'bly need ta deal with their **state- controlled trading company**.

SEE: **purchasing agent**, *p. 87.*

steamship conference *n.* a shipping association composed of several ocean carriers operating over the same trade routes and setting uniform freight and service standards for their members.

example: If we agree to ship all of our cargo with one of their members, we will get better rates from the **steamship conference**.

translation: If we agree to ship all of our cargo with one of their members, we will get better rates from the **shipping association, composed of several ocean carriers operating over the same trade routes and setting uniform freight and service standards for their members**.

as spoken: If we agree da ship all 'ev 'ar cargo with one 'a their members, w'll get bedder rates fr'm the **steamship conference**.

tramp steamer *n.* a ship without regular routes or port schedules.

example: We can get a really good freight discount on this **tramp steamer**. The only problem is that they can't guarantee a delivery date.

translation: We can get a really good freight discount on this **ship that doesn't have regular routes or port schedules**. The only problem is that they can't guarantee a delivery date.

as spoken: We c'n ged a real good freight discount on this **tramp steamer**. Thee only problem's that they can't guarantee a delivery date.

trust receipt *n.* a document used when financing by *letter of credit* in which a buyer pledges goods as collateral for the credit. After disposal of the goods, the buyer must place the sales proceeds in trust for the financing bank.

example: **Trust receipts** cover certain merchandise that must be held distinct from the buyer's remaining assets.

translation: **Documents used when financing by letter of credit where a buyer pledges goods as collateral for the credit** cover certain merchandise that must be held distinct from the buyer's remaining assets.

as spoken: **Trust receets** cover certain merchandise that must be held distinct fr'm the buyer's remaining assets.

SEE: **LC**, *p. 113.*

turnkey *n.* a method of construction or manufacturing in which a prime contractor assumes responsibility for all phases of the project.

example: Even though the installation of our new merchandising computer system is very complex, the contractor has guanteed that it will be a **turnkey**.

translation: Even though the installation of our new merchandising computer system is very complex, the contractor has **assumed responsibility for all phases of the project**.

as spoken: Even though the installation of 'ar new merchandising c'mpuder system'z very c'mplex, the contracter's guanteed thad it'll be a **turnkey**.

without reserve *exp.* a term describing the unconditional authority granted to a shipper's agent to alter the terms of a transaction without consulting a principal.

example: Our agent will be operating **without reserve** in an effort to close this deal.

translation: Our agent will be operating **with unconditional authority** in an effort to close this deal.

as spoken: 'Ar agent'll be operading **without reserve** in 'n effort ta close this deal.

World Bank *n.* an autonomous agency composed of the International Bank for Reconstruction and Development and the International Development Association. The World Bank makes low-cost, long-term loans to limited-development countries for infrastructure projects (such as drinking water systems, irrigation systems, etc.).

example: The **World Bank** is funded through capital subscriptions of member countries and is based in Washington, DC.

translation: The **agency composed of the International Bank for Reconstruction and Development and the International Development Association** is funded through capital subscriptions of member countries and is based in Washington, DC.

as spoken: The **World Bank** is funded through capidal subscriptions of member countries and is based in Washington, DC.

Practice Using International Trade Slang & Jargon (Part B)

(Answers, p. 273)

A. CROSSWORD

Fill in the crossword puzzle on the opposite page by choosing the correct word from the list below.

forma	**hedging**	**quotation**
free	**irrevocable**	**soft**
futures	**joint**	**spot**
gross	**lading**	**turnkey**

ACROSS

2. ________ **weight** *n.* the entire weight of a shipment, including packing and containers.

14. ________ **port** *n.* a port available to all traders where imported goods may be held while awaiting re-export, without the need to pay duties.

15. ________ **exchange** *n.* a foreign currency purchased or sold at its current market price.

24. ________ **venture** *n.* an agreement between firms to share expenses, profits, and losses from a commercial undertaking.

35. ________ **letter of credit** *n.* a letter of credit that cannot be modified or canceled by the drawee (buyer) after it has been issued by the drawee's bank.

DOWN

6. ________ **currency** *exp.* a currency that cannot be easily converted into gold or other foreign currency.

12. ________ *n.* the purchase of a foreign currency to sell at a future date as a means of protecting against variations in the exchange rate.

18. ________ *n.* an offer to sell merchandise at a specified price and under named conditions.

23. ________ **market** *exp.* (also known as the *forward market*) the purchasing and selling of contracts for commodities at a price set at the time of purchase, but not to be delivered or paid for until a specified time in the future.

25. ________ *n.* a method of construction or manufacturing in which a prime contractor assumes responsibility for all phases of the project.

32. **pro** ________ **invoice** *n.* a facsimile of an invoice describing the type, quantities, and value of the goods to be sent, specifications such as weight or size and shipping and/or handling costs.

33. **foul bill of** ________ *n.* a bill of lading indicating that goods were damaged when delivered to a carrier.

CROSSWORD PUZZLE

LESSON FIVE

Initials Used in International Trade

Lesson Five

Dialogue in slang

Larry: Since this is your first day at Apex Computer Company, there are a few simple things you need to know. We concentrate our export effort on those countries with **MFN** status. While there are always some **NTB**s to deal with, a **CVD** or **VAT** is unlikely. Don't worry about routing through **FTZ**s; we leave that to the importer. I'm sure you understand exactly what I'm talking about.

George: Well, actually I…

Larry: Now, before you contact our **EMC**, pick up a copy of the **SITC** and look up the **SIC** for all products in the shipment. Then we'll prepare the **SED**. Of course, you're already familiar with this procedure.

George: Well, to tell you the truth, I've never…

Larry: Next, we prepare our invoice. We always specify shipping terms **FOB** our warehouse, not **FIO** or **FAS**. Payment terms are **CIA** for new customers or **CIF&E** by **L/C** for established customers – no exceptions. Welcome to the company!

Lesson Five

Translation of dialogue in standard English

Initials Used in International Trade

Larry: Since this is your first day at Apex Computer Company, there are a few simple things you need to know. We concentrate our export effort on those countries with **most favored nation** status. While there are always some **non-trade barriers** to deal with, a **counter-vailing duty** or **value added tax** is unlikely. Don't worry about routing through **free trade zones**; we leave that to the importer. I'm sure you understand exactly what I'm talking about.

George: Well, actually I…

Larry: Now, before you contact our **export management company**, pick up a copy of the **Standard International Trade Classification** and look up the **standard industrial classification** for all products in the shipment. Then we'll prepare the **shipper's export declaration**. Of course, you're already familiar with this procedure.

George: Well, to tell you the truth, I've never…

Larry: Next, we prepare our invoice. We always specify shipping terms as **free on board**, our warehouse, not **free in and out** or **free alongside ship**. Payment terms are **cash in advance** for new customers or **cost insurance freight & exchange** by **letter of credit** for established customers – no exceptions. Welcome to the company!

Lesson Five

Dialogue in slang as it would be heard

Initials Used in International Trade

Larry: Since this is y'r firs' day ad Apex C'mpuder Company, there'er a few simple things you need ta know. We conc'nchrade 'ar expord efford on those countries with **M-F-N** stadus. While there'er always s'm **N-T-B**s ta deal with, a **C-V-D** 'r **V-A-T** is unlikely. Don't worry about rouding through **F-T-Z**s; we leave that ta thee imporder. I'm sher you understand exactly whad I'm talking about.

George: Well, akshelly I...

Larry: Now, before you contact 'ar **E-M-C**, pick up a copy of thee **S-I-T-C** 'n look up thee **S-I-C** fer all produc's in the shipment. Then w'll prepare thee **S-E-D**. Of course, y'r already f'miliar with this procedure.

George: Well, ta tell you the truth, I've never...

Larry: Next, we prapare 'ar invoice. We always specify shipping terms **F-O-B** 'ar warehouse, nod **F-I-O** 'r **F-A-S**. Payment terms'er **C-I-A** fer new custamers 'r **C-I-F & E** by **L-C** fer established custamers – no exceptions. Welcome ta the company!

Vocabulary

CIA *exp.* (cash in advance) payment terms that specify that payment must be made in full before shipment of goods.

example: Our supplier will sell us replacement parts only on a **CIA** basis.

translation: Our supplier will sell us replacement parts only on a **cash in advance** basis.

as spoken: 'Ar supplier w'll sell us replacement parts only on a **CIA** basis.

CIF&E *exp.* (cost, insurance, freight, and [currency] exchange) a pricing term that specifies that cost, insurance, freight, and currency exchange are included in the quoted price.

example: Our Russian sales agent has specified terms of **CIF&E** on his order for educational materials.

translation: Our Russian sales agent has specified terms of **cost, insurance, freight, and (currency) exchange** on his order for educational materials.

as spoken: 'Ar Russian sales agent 'ez specified terms 'ev **C.I.F. 'n E** on 'is order fer edjacation'l materials.

CVD *n.* (countervailing duty) an extra duty imposed by the U.S. Secretary of Commerce on a particular product to counter the effects of a foreign government's subsidy.

example: The reason for the high cost of these components we have imported from France might be a **CVD**.

translation: The reason for the high cost of these components we have imported from France might be a **countervailing duty**.

as spoken: The reason fer the high cost 'a these c'mponents we've imporded fr'm France might be a **CVD**.

EMC *n.* (export management company) a company, usually compensated on a commission basis, which arranges foreign sales for domestic manufacturing companies.

example: We have retained an **EMC** to assist us with foreign sales for our products.

translation: We have retained an **export management company** to assist us with foreign sales for our products.

as spoken: We've retained 'n **EMC** ta assist us with forin sales fer 'ar produc's.

FAS *exp.* (free alongside ship) a term used on a quote indicating that the price includes delivery of the goods alongside a specified ship.

example: Since terms of our export shipment are **FAS**, we will have to arrange for delivery of goods to the vessel.

translation: Since terms of our export shipment are **free alongside ship**, we will have to arrange for delivery of goods to the vessel.

as spoken: Since terms of 'ar export shipment'er **FAS**, w'll hafta arrange fer delivery 'ev goods ta the vessel.

FIO *exp.* (free in and out) a term of sale indicating that the shipper is responsible for the cost of loading and unloading cargo.

example: **FIO** terms mean that we will have to pay for the cost of loading and unloading cargo.

translation: **Free in and out** terms mean that we will have to pay for the cost of loading and unloading cargo.

as spoken: **FIO** terms mean th't w'll hafta pay fer the cost of loading 'n unloading cargo.

FOB *exp.* (free on board) an international commercial term (INCOTERM). The seller pays for delivery and loading of cargo at a specified location.

example: **FOB** our warehouse, is a common term of sale in the United States.

translation: **Free on board** our warehouse, is a common term of sale in the United States.

as spoken: **FOB** our warehouse, is a common term 'ev sale in thee U.S.

FTZ *n.* (free trade zone) a special port outside a nation's custom's territory. No duties are paid if the merchandise is re-exported, otherwise duties are collected when goods pass out of the zone into an area subject to Customs Authority.

example: We can ship manufacturers' samples for exhibition without paying customs duties if the port of entry is in an **FTZ**.

translation: We can ship manufacturers' samples for exhibition without paying customs duties if the port of entry is in a **free trade zone**.

as spoken: We c'n ship manufacturers' samples fer exhibition without paying customs dudies if the pord of entry's 'n **FTZ**.

L/C *n.* (letter of credit) a bank's letter instructing payment to a named payee. Payment is made when terms specified in the letter are met.

example: Due to previous difficulties in receiving payment, we will ship to foreign distributors only when payment is guaranteed by **L/C**.

translation: Due to previous difficulties in receiving payment, we will ship to foreign distributors only when payment is guaranteed by **letter of credit**.

as spoken: Due da previous difficulties in receiving payment, we'll ship ta forin distribuders only when payment's guaranteed by **L/C**.

MFN *n.* (most-favored nation) a foreign country granted the most favorable terms in its international trade with the United States.

example: A country that loses its **MFN** status may experience a significant increase in import tariffs.

translation: A country that loses its **most-favored nation** status may experience a significant increase in import tariffs.

as spoken: A country that loses its **MFN** stadus may experience a significant increase in import tariffs.

NTB *n.* (nontariff barriers) any obstacle to trade other than a tariff barrier such as quotas and *VRAs*.

example: "Buy American" purchase policies are an example of an **NTB**.

translation: "Buy American" purchase policies are an example of a **nontariff barrier**.

as spoken: "Buy Americ'n" purchase policies are 'n example of 'n **NTB**.

SEE: **VRA**, *p. 130.*

SED *n.* (shipper's export declaration) a form prepared by a shipper that indicates the value, weight, destination, and other basic information about the export shipment.

example: An **SED** is required for many commercial shipments to a foreign destination.

translation: A **shipper's export declaration** is required for many commercial shipments to a foreign destination.

as spoken: An **SED**'s required fer many c'mmercial shipments ta a forin destination.

SIC *n.* (Standard Industrial Code) a uniform classification system published by the U.S. Department of Commerce for identifying products and services.

example: The **SIC** assigns numeric codes to products and services and is used to gather international trade statistics.

translation: The **Standard Industrial Code** assigns numeric codes to products and services and is used to gather international trade statistics.

as spoken: The **SIC** assigns numeric codes ta produc's 'n services and is used ta gather international trade statistics.

SITC *n.* (Standard International Trade Classification) a uniform system of codes developed by the United Nations and used for collecting international trade data.

example: The United Nations Statistical Office publishes the **SITC**.

translation: The United Nations Statistical Office publishes the **Standard International Trade Classification**.

as spoken: The Unided Nations Statisticle Office publishes thee **SITC**.

VAT *n.* (value-added tax) a sales tax on the increase in the monetary value of a product or service that has been improved by the addition of materials and/or processes.

example: The **VAT** is known as the GST (goods and services tax) in Canada.

translation: The **value-added tax** is known as the GST (goods services tax) in Canada.

as spoken: The **VAT**'s known as the GST (goods 'n services tax) in Canada.

Practice the Vocabulary

(Answers to Lesson 5, p. 273)

A. CROSSWORD PUZZLE
Fill in the crossword puzzle on the opposite page by choosing the correct initials from the list below.

CIA	**EMC**	**FOB**	**SIC**
CIF	**FAS**	**FTZ**	**SITC**
CVD	**FIO**	**SED**	**VAT**

ACROSS

7. ________ *n.* a uniform system of codes developed by the United Nations and used for collecting international trade data.

14. ________ *exp.* a term used on a quote indicating that the price includes delivery of the goods alongside a specified ship.

18. ________ *n.* a company, usually compensated on a commission basis, which arranges foreign sales for manufacturing companies.

20. ________ *n.* an extra duty imposed by the United States Secretary of Commerce on a particular product to counter the effects of a foreign government's subsidy.

26. ________ *n.* a special port outside a nation's custom's territory. No duties are paid if the merchandise is re-exported, otherwise duties are collected when the goods pass out of the zone into an area subject to Customs Authority.

32. ________ *exp.* an international commercial term (INCOTERM). The seller pays for delivery and loading of cargo at a specified location.

DOWN

2. ________ *exp.* payment terms which specify that payment must be made in full before shipment of goods.

8. ________**&E** *exp.* a pricing term which specifies that cost, insurance, freight, and exchange are included in the quoted price.

13. ________ *n.* a uniform classification system published by the U.S. Department of Commerce for identifying products and services.

15. ________ *n.* a form prepared by a shipper that indicates the value, weight, destination, and other basic information about the export shipment.

21. ________ *n.* a sales tax on the increase in the monetary value of a product or service that has been improved by the addition of materials and/or processes.

26 ________ *exp.* a term of sale indicating that the shipper is responsible for the cost of loading and unloading cargo.

CROSSWORD PUZZLE

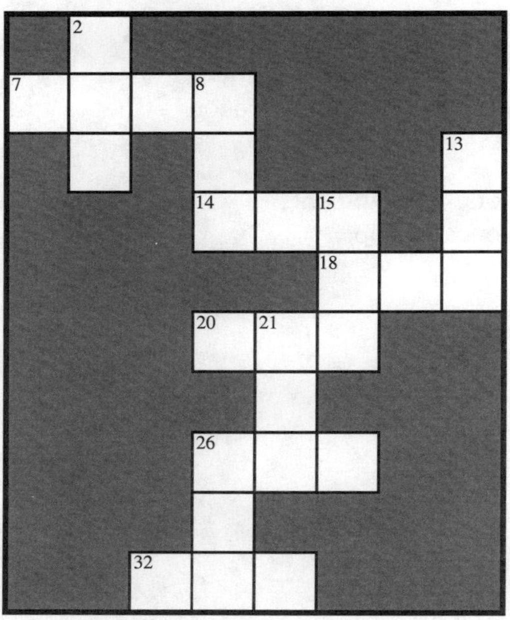

B. Circle the letter corresponding to the meaning of the initials in boldface.

1. **CVD:**
   a. customs values duty
   b. countervailing duty

2. **SIC:**
   a. standard industrial code
   b. standard international code

3. **MFN:**
   a. many foreign nations
   b. most-favored nation

4. **SED:**
   a. shipper's export duty
   b. shipper's export declaration

5. **CIA:**
   a. customs insurance act
   b. cash in advance

6. **EMC:**
   a. export management company
   b. export management corporation

7. **FAS:**
   a. free alongside shipment
   b. free alongside ship

8. **FIO:**
   a. free in and out
   b. free in only

9. **L/C:**
   a. letter certificate
   b. letter of credit

10. **FOB:**
    a. freight on boad
    b. free on board

C. Choose the correct definition of the initials in boldface.

1. **SITC (Standard International Trade Classification)**:

☐ a. a uniform system of codes developed by the United Nations and used for collecting domestic trade data.

☐ b. a uniform system of codes developed by the United Nations and used for collecting international trade data.

2. **SED (shipper's export declaration)**:

☐ a. a form prepared by customs that indicates the value, weight, destination, and other basic information about the export shipment.

☐ b. a form prepared by a shipper that indicates the value, weight, destination, and other basic information about the export shipment.

3. **EMC (export management company)**:

☐ a. a company, usually compensated on a commission basis, which arranges foreign sales for domestic manufacturing companies.

☐ b. a company, usually compensated on a commission basis, which arranges domestic sales for domestic manufacturing companies.

4. **MFN (most-favored nation)**:

☐ a. a country that is granted special tax privileges.

☐ b. a country that enjoys the most favorable trading terms.

5. **L/C (letter of credit)**:

☐ a. a bank's letter instructing payment to a named payee. Payment is made when terms specified in the latter are met.

☐ b. a financial institution's letter notifying the recipient that credit will not be given.

6. **FAS (free alongside ship)**:

☐ a. a term used on a quote indicating that the price does not include delivery of the goods alongside a specified ship.

☐ b. a term used on a quote indicating that the price includes delivery of the goods alongside a specified ship.

7. **FIO (free in and out)**:

☐ a. a term of sale indicating that the shipper is not responsible for the cost of loading and unloading cargo.

☐ b. a term of sale indicating that the shipper is responsible for the cost of loading and unloading cargo.

8. **CIA (cash in advance)**:

☐ a. payment terms that specify that payment must be made in full before shipment of goods.

☐ b. payment terms that specify that half of the payment must be made before shipment of goods and the other half when goods are received.

9. **SIC (standard industrial code)**:

☐ a. a uniform classification system published by the U.S. Department of Commerce for identifying products and services.

☐ b. a uniform classification system for identifying the crew in a large shipping company.

10. **FOB (free on board)**:

☐ a. an international commercial term meaning that the seller pays for delivery and loading of cargo at a specified location.

☐ b. an international commercial term meaning that the seller pays for delivery, but not for loading of cargo at a specified location.

A CLOSER LOOK:
Initials Used in International Trade

C & F *exp.* (cost and freight) a pricing term specifying that cost and freight are included in the quoted price.

example: Our distributor has specified terms of **C & F** on his book order.

translation: Our distributor has specified terms of **cost and freight** on his book order.

as spoken: 'Ar distribuder's specified terms of **C 'n F** on 'is book order.

C & I *exp.* (cost and insurance) a pricing term specifying that cost and insurance are included in the quoted price.

example: Our wholesaler always has us send shipments to him on a **C & I** basis.

translation: Our wholesaler always has us send shipments to him on a **cost and insurance** basis.

as spoken: 'Ar wholesaler always has us sen' shipments to 'im on a **C 'n I** basis.

CAD *exp.* (cash against documents) payment for goods in which an intermediary transfers title documents to the buyer upon payment in cash.

example: To take delivery of our merchandise from the importer, we have to bring payment. Terms are **CAD**

translation: To take delivery of our merchandise from the importer, we have to bring payment. Terms are **cash against documents**.

as spoken: Ta take delivery of 'ar merchandise fr'm the imporder, we hafta bring payment. Terms'er **CAD**.

CCC *n.* (Commodity Credit Corporation) a government corporation that is controlled by the Department of Agriculture. Its purpose is to control the marketing and exporting of a particular agricultural commodity.

example: The **CCC** guarantees commercial bank loans to farmers, and pays cash bonuses to food processors and farmers.

translation: The **Commodity Credit Corporation** guarantees commercial bank loans to farmers, and pays cash bonuses to food processors and farmers.

as spoken: The **CCC** guarantees commercial bank loans ta farmers, an' pays cash bonuses ta food processers 'n farmers.

CCCN *n.* (Customs Cooperation Council Nomenclature) a tariff structure used by most European countries as well as others worldwide. It is also known as the Brussels Tariff Nomenclature.

example: Before we ship our products to the European market, we need to determine if they're covered by the terms of the **CCCN**.

translation: Before we ship our products to the European market, we need to determine if they're covered by the terms of the **Customs Cooperation Council Nomenclature**.

as spoken: Before we ship 'ar produc's ta the European market, we need ta determine if they're covered by the terms of the **CCCN**.

CIF *exp.* (cost, insurance, freight) a pricing term specifying that cost, insurance, and freight are included in the quoted price.

example: Our importer always specifies terms of **CIF** on his tool orders.

translation: Our importer always specifies terms of cost, insurance, freight on his tool orders.

as spoken: 'Ar imporder always specifies terms 'ev **CIF** on 'is tool orders.

CIF & C *exp.* (cost, insurance, freight, and commission) a pricing term specifying that cost, insurance, freight, and commission are included in the quoted price.

example: Our foreign representative wants us to ship him medical supplies on a **CIF & C** basis.

translation: Our foreign representative wants us to ship him medical supplies on a **cost, insurance, freight, and commission** basis.

as spoken: 'Ar forin rep wants us ta ship 'im medic'l supplies on a **CIF 'n C** basis.

CWO *exp.* (cash with order) payment terms that requires a buyer to pay when placing an order.

example: The parts desk will sell you auto parts on a **CWO** basis.

translation: The parts desk will sell you auto parts on a **cash with order** basis.

as spoken: The parts desk will sell you audo parts on a **CWO** basis.

D/A *exp.* (Documents Against Acceptance) shipper's instructions to a bank specifying that title transfer documents will not be delivered to the buyer unless the buyer agrees to the terms of the attached draft.

example: Check the terms of the draft carefully. Delivery terms are **D/A**.

translation: Check the terms of the draft carefully. Delivery terms are **documents against acceptance**.

as spoken: Check the terms of the draft carefully. Delivery terms'er **D/A**.

D/P *exp.* (documents against payment) shipper's instructions to a bank specifying that title transfer documents will not be delivered to the buyer unless the buyer pays the attached draft.

example: If we want to take possession of that shipment today, we will need sufficient money to cover the amount of the draft. Delivery terms are **D/P**.

translation: If we want to take possession of that shipment today, we will need sufficient money to cover the amount of the draft. Delivery terms are **documents against payment**.

as spoken: If we wanna take possession of that shipment today, w'll need sufficient money ta cover the amount of the draft. Delivery terms'er **D/P**.

ECU *n.* (European currency unit) the currency unit of the European Community *(EC)* that is based on a basket of Common Market currencies.

example: The **ECU** is less volatile than each of the individual currencies upon which it is based.

translation: The **European currency unit** is less volatile than each of the individual currencies upon which it is based.

as spoken: The **ECU**'s less voladle than each 'ev thee individual currencies it's based on.

EEC *n.* (European Economic Community").

SEE: **Common Market**, *p. 69.*

EFTA *n.* (European Free Trade Association) composed of Austria, Faeroe Islands, Finland, Iceland, Norway, Portugal, Sweden, and Switzerland.

example: Trade between Austria and Finland may be subject to the regulations of the **EFTA**.

translation: Trade between Austria and Finland may be subject to the regulations of the **European Free Trade Association**.

as spoken: Trade b'tween Austria 'n Finland may be subject ta the regulations of the **EFTA**.

EMS *n.* (European Monetary System)

SEE: **Bloc**, *p. 68.*

ETC *n.* (export trading company) a company doing business in the United States chiefly to export domestic goods or services, or to facilitate exports.

example: An **ETC** can be foreign owned and can also import, barter, and arrange sales between third countries.

translation: An **export trading company** can be foreign owned and can also import, barter, and arrange sales between third countries.

as spoken: An **ETC** can be foreign owned and can also import, barter, and arrange sales between third countries.

ETCA *n.* (Export Trading Company Act) a law passed on October 8, 1982 to promote export of U.S. goods and services.

example: The **ETCA** establishes an Office of Export Trading Company Affairs in the United States Department of Commerce, reduces the restrictions on export financing by financial institutions, permits U.S. commercial banks to invest in *ETCs,* and limits the impact of antitrust legislation to certain export trade.

translation: The **Export Trading Company Act** establishes an Office of Export Trading Company Affairs in the United States Department of Commerce, reduces the restrictions on export financing by financial institutions, permits United States commercial banks to invest in *ETCs,* and limits the impact of antitrust legislation to certain export trade.

as spoken: The **ETCA** establishes 'n Office of Export Trading Company Affairs 'n thee U.S. Department of Commerce, r'duces the restrictions on export financing by financial institutions, permits U.S. commercial banks to invest 'n *ETCs,* 'n limits thee impact of an'itrust legislation ta certain export trade.

SEE: **ETC**, *(previous entry).*

Eximbank *n.* (Export-Import Bank of the United States) a bank that promotes export trade by providing financial assistance to exporters and credits to their customers overseas.

example: Let's see if we can improve our export trade by seeking assistance from the **Eximbank**.

translation: Let's see if we can improve our export trade by seeking assistance from the **Export-Import Bank of the United States**.

as spoken: Let's see if we c'n improve 'ar export trade by seeking assistance fr'm the **Eximbank**.

FAA *exp.* (free of all average) an insurance policy that excludes partial loss claims and covers only total loss claims.

example: With **FAA** terms, partial damage to our shipment will not be covered.

translation: With **free of all average** terms, partial damage to our shipment will not be covered.

as spoken: With **FAA** terms, partial damage ta 'ar shipment will not be covered.

FCIA *n.* (Foreign Credit Insurance Association) an association of commercial insurers who act as the insurance agent for the **Export/Import Bank of the United States** (also known as *Eximbank).*

example: An **FCIA** policy will insure an exporter against default on loans of short- to medium-term.

translation: A **Foreign Credit Insurance Association** policy will insure an exporter against default on loans of short- to medium-term.

as spoken: An **FCIA** policy'll insure 'n exporder against default on loans of short- ta medium-term.

FDI *n.* (foreign direct investment) a partial or total controlling investment in a foreign enterprise.

example: The construction of an overseas manufacturing subsidiary can be considered an **FDI**.

translation: The construction of an overseas manufacturing subsidiary can be considered an **foreign direct investment**.

as spoken: The c'nstruction of 'n overseas manufacturing subsidiary c'n be c'nsidered an **FDI**.

FI *exp.* (free in) a term of sale indicating that the shipper is responsible for the cost of loading cargo at the port of origin.

example: **FI** means that as the shipper, we will have to pay for the cost of loading cargo.

translation: **Free in** means that as the shipper, we will have to pay for the cost of loading cargo.

as spoken: **FI** means thad as the shipper, we'll hafta pay fer the cost of loading cargo.

FO *exp.* (free out) a term of sale indicating that the shipper is responsible for the cost of unloading cargo at its destination.

example: We will be responsible for the cost of unloading our shipment because the terms of the quote are **FO**.

translation: We will be responsible for the cost of unloading our shipment because the terms of the quote are **free out**.

as spoken: We'll be r'sponsible fer the cost of unloading 'ar shipment 'cuz the terms of the quode'er **FO**.

FPA *exp.* (free of particular average) the title of a marine insurance clause specifying that partial losses are covered if the salvage operation benefits all parties to a shipping transaction.

example: An **FPA** policy means that a partial loss will not be covered unless it is caused by stranding, burning, collision, or sinking.

translation: A **free of particular average** policy means that a partial loss will not be covered unless it is caused by stranding, burning, collision, or sinking.

as spoken: An **FPA** policy means thad a partial loss will not be covered unless it's caused by stranding, burning, collision, 'r sinking.

FSC *n.* (foreign sales corporation) an offshore company eligble for a preferential tax rate of 15-32%. To qualify for special tax treatment, the FSC must have a main office in a U.S. possession and at least one director resident outside of the U.S.

example: The Reagan Administration introduced the proposal for the **FSC** in the Tax Reform Act of 1984.

translation: The Reagan Administration introduced the proposal for the **foreign sales corporation** in the Tax Reform Act of 1984.

as spoken: The Reagan Administration intraduced the praposal fer thee **FSC** in the Tax Reform Act of 1984.

GATT *n.* (General Agreement on Tariffs and Trade) an agreement whose purpose is to lessen tariffs and reduce trade barriers among the participants.

example: The Trade Negotiations Committee is the principle **GATT** committee.

translation: The Trade Negotiations Committee is the principle **General Agreement on Tariffs and Trade** committee.

as spoken: The Trade Negotiations Commidee is the principle **GATT** commidee.

IMF *n.* (International Monetary Fund) an organization which promotes international exchange of goods and capital and acts as a clearing agency for member nations to assist them in avoiding *currency devaluations*.

example: When the **IMF** was created, the U.S. set the value of the dollar at $35 per ounce of gold and member nations tied their currencies to the dollar.

translation: When the **International Monetary Fund** was created, the United States set the value of the dollar at $35 per ounce of gold and member nations tied their currencies to the dollar.

as spoken: When the **IMF** was creaded, the U.S. set the value of the doller 'it $35 per ounce of gold an' member nations tied their currencies ta the doller.

SEE: currency devaluation, *p. 72*.

ITA *n.* (International Trade Administration) a division of the Department of Commerce which administers international trade agreements and domestic trade legislation.

example: The **ITA** helps to promote world trade and enhance the investment stance of the United States.

translation: The **International Trade Administration** helps to promote world trade and enhance the investment stance of the United States.

as spoken: The **ITA** helps ta pramote world trade and enhance the investment stance of the U.S.

LDC *n.* (less-developed country or least-developed country) an undeveloped country with limited natural resources and a poor supply of skilled labor. It is dependent on primary commodity exports for income.

example: Most **LDC**s are located in the Southern Hemisphere.

translation: Most **less-developed countries** are located in the Southern Hemisphere.

as spoken: Most **LDC**s'er locaded in the Southern Hemisphere.

MNC *n.* (multinational corporation) a firm which derives at least 25% of its annual sales income from its subsidiaries or branches located in other countries.

example: An **MNC** may benefit from lower labor costs and have access to reliable sources of inexpensive raw materials.

translation: A **multinational corporation** may benefit from lower labor costs and have access to reliable sources of inexpensive raw materials.

as spoken: An **MNC** may benefit fr'm lower labor costs an' have access ta reliable sources of inexpensive raw materials.

OECD *n.* (Organization for Economic Cooperation and Development) a group of twenty-four industrialized nations who meet to coordinate international, economic, and social policies.

example: The affairs of the **OECD** are administered by the secretariat based in Paris.

translation: The affairs of the **Organization for Economic Cooperation** are administered by the secretariat based in Paris.

as spoken: Thee affairs of thee **OECD**'er adminisdered by the secretariat based in Paris.

OPEC *n.* (Organization of Petroleum- Exporting Countries) a group of petroleum-producing countries, headquartered in Vienna, that attempts to influence the supply and price of oil.

example: **OPEC** was officially organized in 1961 in Caracas, Venezuela.

translation: **The Organization of Petroleum-Exporting Countries** was officially organized in 1961 in Caracas, Venezuela.

as spoken: **OPEC** was officially organized in 1961 in Caracas, Venezuela.

OPIC *n.* (Overseas Private Investment Corporation) a corporation (created by the Foreign Assistance Act of 1969) to finance and insure U.S. investment overseas.

example: The **OPIC** grants flexible-term direct loans for overseas investments in approximately 120 developing countries.

translation: The **Overseas Private Investment Corporation** grants flexible-term direct loans for overseas investments in approximately 120 developing countries.

as spoken: The **OPIC** grants flexible-term direct loans fer overseas investments in approximately a hundred 'n twen'y developing countries.

SDR *n.* (special drawing right) a universal reserve currency created by the *International Monetary Fund* (also referred to as the *IMF*).

example: **SDR**s are artificial currency units whose value is based on the British pound, the German mark, the Japanese yen, and the U.S. dollar.

translation: **Special Drawing Rights** are artificial currency units whose value is based on the British pound, the German mark, the Japanese yen, and the United States dollar.

as spoken: **SDR**s'er ardificial currency units whose value's based on the Bridish pound, the German mark, the Japanese yen, an' the U.S. doller.

SEE: **IMF**, *p. 127.*

VER *n.* (voluntary export restraint) a voluntary reciprocal trade restraint agreement.

example: To avoid an import quota, Japan agreed to a **VER**, and reduced export of automobiles to the U.S.

translation: To avoid an import quota, Japan agreed to a **voluntary export restraint**, and reduced export of automobiles to the United States.

as spoken: To avoid 'n import quoda, Japan agreed to a **VER**, an' r'duced expord 'ev audomobiles ta thee U.S.

Vertical ETC *n.* (Vertical Export Trading Company) an *ETC* that sells a wide range of products not organized around a particular product line or specific industry.

example: Since this *ETC* sells products ranging from agricultural commodities to high technology merchandise, it is considered a **Vertical ETC**.

translation: Since this *ETC* sells products ranging from agricultural commodities to high technology merchandise, it is considered a **Vertical Export Trading Company**.

as spoken: Since this *ETC* sells produc's ranging fr'm agricultural commodities ta high technology merchandise, it's c'nsidered a **V'rdicle ETC**.

SEE: **ETC**, *p.* 124.

VRA *n.* (voluntary restraint agreement) a reciprocal restraint agreement between a foreign government and a private company or group.

example: The successful negotiation of a **VRA** generally brings about a *VER* agreement.

translation: The successful negotiation of a **voluntary restraint agreement** generally brings about a voluntary export restraint agreement.

as spoken: The successful negotiation of a **VRA** generally brings aboud a *VER* agreement.

SEE: **VER**, *p. 130.*

WA *exp.* (with average) a term from marine insurance meaning that a shipment is covered for partial damage that exceeds a stipulated percentage of the value of the shipment.

example: The **WA** clause in our Marine Insurance policy states that damage which exceeds three percent of the total value of the cargo will be covered.

translation: The **with average** clause in our Marine Insurance policy states that damage which exceeds three percent of the total value of the cargo will be covered.

as spoken: The **WA** clause in 'ar Marine Insurance policy states th't damage which exceeds three percen' of the todle value 'ev the cargo w'll be covered.

WPA *exp.* (with particular average) a marine insurance policy that does not cover partial loss claims when the salvage operation aids only one party in the shipping arrangement.

example: Since the salvage operation will benefit only the ship's owner, our partial loss claims will not be covered under **WPA** terms.

translation: Since the salvage operation will benefit only the ship's owner, our partial loss claims will not be covered under **with particular average** terms.

as spoken: Since the salvage operation'll benefid only the ship's owner, 'ar partial loss claims won't be covered under **WPA** terms.

WTDR *n.* (world traders' data report) a report issued by the U.S. Department of Commerce that contains information on foreign firms such as product line and business reputation.

example: Before we contract with this foreign manufacturer, let's see if they are profiled by a **WTDR**.

translation: Before we contract with this foreign manufacturer, let's see if they are profiled by a **world traders' data report**.

as spoken: Before we contract with this foreign manufacturer, let's see if they are profiled by a **WTDR**.

Practice Using Initials in International Trade

(Answers, p. 274)

A. Draw a line to the correct definition of the initials in boldface.

1. **CAD:** cash against documents
   customs agency documents

2. **C&I:** cost and import
   cost and insurance

3. **CIF:** cost, insurance, financing
   cost, insurance, freight

4. **ECU:** European currency unit
   European customs unit

5. **EFTA:** European Foreign Trade Association
   European Free Trade Association

6. **ETCA:** Export Trading Company Act
   European Trading Company Act

7. **FCIA:** Free Company Insurance Act
   Foreign Credit Insurance Association

8. **FDI:** free distribution internationally
   foreign direct investment

9. **FO:** free out

for overseas

10. **GATT:** General Agreement on Tariffs and Trade

Government Agency on Tariffs and Trade

11. **IMF:** International Monetary Fund

International Marketing Team

12. **MNC:** multinational corporation

multinational clause

LESSON SIX

MORE Computer Slang

*Earl found a few **bugs** in his new computer program.*

Lesson Six

Dialogue in slang

Jan: I just bought a new **CD-ROM** drive for half-price from the local **computer superstore**. It came with a **soundboard** and all sorts of new **apps**, including **multimedia**.

Beth: Wasn't it hard to get it **up-and-running**?

Jan: Not a bit. It's **plug-and-play**. After you hook it up, you just turn on the **system** and you're off!

Beth: That sounds great! When I tried to install some **hardware** on my computer, I had a lot of problems with **interrupts** and then I discovered I couldn't **access** my **hard drive**!

Jan: Did you call **tech support**? They're supposed to be very helpful whenever you run into any **bugs**.

Beth: I called them, but after **camping on the line** for two hours, I gave up. I decided to get some information on the problem from an **on-line** service instead.

Jan: Be careful. In **cyberspace** you never know who is giving you the information!

Lesson Six

Translation of dialogue in standard English

MORE Computer Slang

Jan: I just bought a new **compact disk read-only memory** drive for half-price from the local **store that sells computers and accessories**. It came with a **circuit board that generates sound** and all sort of new **applications**, including the **combination of graphics, text, and sound on the computer**.

Beth: Wasn't it hard to get it **installed and operational**?

Jan: Not a bit. It **doesn't require configuration**. After you hook it up, you just turn on the **computer** and you're off!

Beth: That sounds great! When I tried to install some **equipment** on my computer, I had a lot of problems with **stop signals** and then I discovered that I couldn't **use** my **non-removable mass storage device**.

Jan: Did you call **the computer technicians who provide telephone assistance**? They're supposed to be very helpful whenever you run into any **problems**.

Beth: I called them, but after **being on hold** for two hours, I gave up. I decided to get some information on the problem from a **digital service available using a modem and telephone line** instead.

Jan: Be careful. In the **the electronic universe**, you never know who's giving you information!

Lesson Six

Dialogue in slang as it would be heard

MORE Computer Slang

Jan: I jus' bod a new **CD-ROM** drive fer half-price fr'm the local **c'mpuder superstore**. It came with a **soun'board** 'n all sorts 'ev new **apps**, including **multimedia**.

Beth: Wasn' it hard ta ged it **up-'n-running**?

Jan: Nod a bit. It's **plug-'n-play**. After ya hook id up, ya jus' turn on the **system** an' y'r off!

Beth: That soun's great! When I tried ta install s'm **hardware** on my c'mpuder, I had a lodda problems with **in(t)errup's** an' then I discovered I couldn't **access** my **hard drive**!

Jan: Didja call **tech support**? They're suppos'ta be very helpful whenever ya run inta any **bugs**.

Beth: I called 'em, bud after **camping on the line** fer two hours, I gave up. I decided ta get s'm infermation on the problem fr'm 'n **on-line** service instead.

Jan: Be careful. In **cyberspace** ya never know who's giving you thee infermation!

Vocabulary

access (to) *v.* to use some part of a computer system such as the *hard drive*, RAM, tape drive, *CD-ROM*, printer, etc.

example: I'm having trouble retrieving my file. For some reason, I can't **access** the hard disk!

translation: I'm having trouble retrieving my file. For some reason, I can't **use** the hard disk!

as spoken: I'm having trouble retrieving my file. Fer some reason, I can't **access** the hard disk!

SEE -1: **hard drive**, *p. 141.*

SEE -2: **CD-ROM**, *p. 140.*

app *exp.* (application) another term for "computer program."

example: Why are you using such an old word processing **app**? The newer ones have a lot more functions.

translation: Why are you using such an old word processing **program**? The newer ones have a lot more functions.

as spoken: Why'er ya using such 'n old word processing **app**? The newer ones have a lot more functions.

bug *n.* an error in a computer program that causes it to work incorrectly.

example: Stop using the accounting program right away! I discovered a **bug** in it that erases the entire document as soon as you try to store anything!

translation: Stop using the accounting program right away! I discovered a **problem** in it that erases the entire document as soon as you try to store anything!

as spoken: Stop using thee accoun'ing program ride away! I discovered a **bug** in it which erases thee entire docyam'nt 'ez soon 'ez ya try da store anything!

camp on the line (to) *exp.* to hold for a long time on the telephone.

example: Every time I call your company to get some information, I have to **camp on the line** for hours!

translation: Every time I call your company to get some information, I have to **stay on hold** for hours!

as spoken: Ev'ry time I call yer company ta get s'm infermation, I hafta **camp on the line** fer hours!

CD or CD-ROM *n.* (compact disc read-only memory) a removable plastic disc that can hold over 600 megabytes of digital information and is accessed through a special drive. Because this type of disc is read only memory, the user cannot change any information on the disc.

example: This **CD-ROM** of clip art contains over 5,000 images.

translation: This **compact disc read-only memory** of clip art contains over 5,000 images.

as spoken: This **CD-ROM** 'ev clip art c'ntains over 5,000 images.

computer superstore *n.* a store that sells computers, programs, games, accessories, printers, computer maintenance products, etc.

example: I used to have to go to one store to buy a computer, then to another store to purchase programs, then to a third store to buy accessories. Now I can go to the local **computer superstore** and buy everything at once!

translation: I used to have to go to one store to buy a computer, then to another store to purchase programs, then to a third store to buy accessories. Now I can go to the local **store that sells computers and accessories** and buy everything at once!

as spoken: I usta hafta go da one store da buy a c'mpuder, then to another store da purchase programs, then to a third store da buy accessories. Now I c'n go da the local **c'mpuder superstore** 'n buy ev'rything at once!

cyberspace *n.* a term given to the "place" where computer users meet on-line • *cyber* = electronic / *space* = universe.

example: There are millions of people who go into **cyberspace** every day.

translation: There are millions of people who connect to **on-line services** every day.

as spoken: There'er millions 'a people who go inta **cyberspace** ev'ry day.

hardware *n.* the computer itself and any other equipment such as the *hard drive, CD-ROM*, RAM, printer, etc.

example: I don't know why your computer isn't working. I checked all of the software and that seems to be fine. There must be a problem with your **hardware**. Maybe it's time to buy a new computer!

translation: I don't know why your computer isn't working. I checked all of the software and that seems to be fine. There must be a problem with your **physical computer system**. Maybe it's time to buy a new computer!

as spoken: I duuno why yer c'mpuder isn't working. I checked all 'a the software 'n that seems ta be fine. There must be a problem with yer **hardware**. Maybe it's time da buy a new c'mpuder!

SEE -1: **hard drive**, *(next entry)*.

SEE -2: **CD-ROM**, *p. 140*.

hard drive *n.* a mass storage device made of a non-removable metal disc that spins at a high rate and is capable of storing large amounts of programs and data for execution and retrieval.

example: When I dropped the computer, I hope I didn't damage the **hard drive**. If I did, I may have lost a lot of important information!

translation: When I dropped the computer, I hope I didn't damage the **mass storage device**. If I did, I may have lost a lot of important information!

as spoken: When I dropped the c'mpuder, I hope I didn' damage the **hard drive**. If I did, I may'ev lost a lod of important infermation!

SYNONYM: **hard disk** *n.*

interrupt *n.* a signal sent to the computer to stop a program currently running so that another function may be executed.

example: When the user makes a change to a drawing, it takes time for the screen to redraw the image. However, by simply moving the mouse, an **interrupt** is sent to the computer and the redraw will stop allowing the user to perform another function.

translation: When the user makes a change to a drawing, it takes time for the screen to redraw the image. However, by simply moving the mouse, a **stop signal** is sent to the computer and the redraw will stop allowing the user to perform another function.

as spoken: When the user makes a change to a drawing, it takes time fer the screen ta redraw the image. However, by simply moving the mouse, an **interrupt** is sent ta the c'mpuder an' the redraw will stop allowing thee user ta perform another function.

multimedia *n.* the combination of graphics, text, and sound on the computer to create programs (such as computer games, music programs, television interfacing, etc.).

example: Thanks to **multimedia**, computers have become more impressive, entertaining, and fun to use, attracting more and more new users.

translation: Thanks to **the joining of graphics, text, and sound on the computer to create programs**, computers have become more impressive, entertaining, and fun to use, attracting more and more new users.

as spoken: Thanks ta **multimedia**, c'mpuders'ev b'come more impressive, entertaining, an' fun ta use, attracting more 'n more new users.

on-line service *n.* a digital service available using a modem and telephone line. It gives users access to reference information over a wide range of subjects, as well as enabling users to communicate with one another.

example: I got some great new programs through the local **on-line service**.

translation: I got some great new programs through the local **telephone computer service**.

as spoken: I got s'm great new programs through the local **on-line** service.

plug-and-play *adj.* said of a device (such as a printer, scanner, etc.) which can be plugged into the computer and does not require configuration.

example: This CD-ROM drive I bought is supposed to be **plug-and-play**, but just look at the complicated instruction manual!

translation: This CD-ROM drive I bought is supposed to **configure itself automatically**, but just look at the complicated instruction manual!

as spoken: This CD-ROM drive I bod is supposs'ta be **plug-'n-play**, b't jus' look 'it the complicaded instruction manual!

sound board *n.* a special circuit board in the computer that generates audio.

example: Now that I bought a **sound board** for the computer, I can run this French language program and actually hear how to pronounce each word!

translation: Now that I bought a **special circuit board which generates audio** for the computer, I can run this French language program and actually hear how to pronounce each word!

as spoken: Now thad I bod a **soun' board** fer the c'mpuder, I c'n run this French language program 'n akshully hear how da pranounce each word!

system *n.* a computer (an abbreviation for *computer system*).

example: The boss just bought new **systems** for all the secretaries. He's hoping that work will get done a lot faster now.

translation: The boss just bought new **computers** for all the secretaries. He's hoping that work will get done a lot faster now.

as spoken: The boss jus' bod new **systems** for all the secretaries. He's hoping that work'll get done a lot faster now.

tech support *n.* (technical support) a department composed of computer technicians who provide telephone assistance to customers experiencing trouble with their computers or programs.

example: I don't understand how to install my photography program. I'm going to call **tech support** and get some help.

translation: I don't understand how to install my photography program. I'm going to call **the computer technicians who provide telephone assistance** and get some help.

as spoken: I don' understand how da install my fetogrufy program. I'm gonna call **tech suppord** 'n get s'm help.

up-and-running *exp.* said of a computer or program which has been installed and operational.

example: I just got my new computer **up and running**. You wouldn't believe how fast I can process documents now!

translation: I just got my new computer **installed and operational**. You wouldn't believe how fast I can process documents now!

as spoken: I jus' got my new c'mpuder **up 'n running**. You wouldn't believe how fast I c'n process docyam'nts now!

Practice the Vocabulary

(Answers to Lesson 6, p. 275)

A. Choose the correct answer from the list below.

app
bug
interrupt
multimedia
plug and play
sound board
system
tech support
to access
up and running

1. Another name for a computer is a:

Answer: ______________________________

2. If you're having trouble with your computer or software, you may want to call:

Answer: ______________________________

3. If your program starts to malfunction, you may have a:

Answer: ______________________________

4. If you want to hear audio with your computer game, you'll need to buy a:

Answer: ______________________________

5. Equipment that can be easily installed in your computer and does not require configuration is called:

   Answer: ______________________________

6. To use some part of a computer system such as the hard drive, RAM, tape drive, CD ROM, printer, etc.:

   Answer: ______________________________

7. If your computer is turned on and ready to use, it's:

   Answer: ______________________________

8. Another term for a computer program is an application or:

   Answer: ______________________________

9. The combination of graphics, text, and sound on the computer to create programs such as computer games, music programs, television interfacing, etc. is referred to as:

   Answer: ______________________________

10. A signal sent to the computer to stop a program currently running in order that another function may be executed, is known as an:

    Answer: ______________________________

B. True or false?

1. A **computer superstore** only sells computers.

   ☐ True ☐ False

2. Something that is **plug-and-play** can be used as soon as it is installed.

   ☐ True ☐ False

3. **Cyberspace** refers to the time it takes for the computer to turn on.

   ☐ True ☐ False

4. The term **hardware** is another name for a "program."

   ☐ True ☐ False

5. A **bug** is a special program which allows the user to make quick backups.

   ☐ True ☐ False

6. A **CD ROM** can only hold a megabyte of information.

   ☐ True ☐ False

7. The **hard drive** is one place where the computer stores and retrieves information.

   ☐ True ☐ False

8. If your computer is **up-and-running**, it's ready to use.

   ☐ True ☐ False

9. An **on-line service** is a special drawing program that uses lines and curves.

   ☐ True ☐ False

10. **Multimedia** refers to the combination of graphics, text, and sound on the computer to create elaborate programs such as computer games, music programs, television interfacing, etc.

    ☐ True ☐ False

C. Underline the word(s) that best complete(s) the phrase.

1. I just bought a new CD (**RAM**, **ROM**, **PC**) which has over a thousand photographs!

2. If you're having trouble with your computer, why don't you just call (**RAM**, **tech**, **hard drive**) support?

3. I'm going shopping for a new computer and some software at the computer (**grocery**, **department**, **super**) store.

4. Every time I call this telephone number for computer help, I have to camp on the (**hard drive**, **line**, **ROM**) for hours!

5. I just subscribed to a new (**on**, **off**, **up**)-line service. Now if I ever need information about anything, I can just call!

6. Something's wrong with this program. I think it has a (**hard drive**, **ROM**, **bug**).

7. The technician has been working on my computer for the past two hours. He said he should have it (**down**, **up**, **over**) and running in about ten minutes.

8. I can't store any more information in my computer because the (**CD-ROM**, **soft**, **hard**) drive is full.

9. In order to use this French language program, I need to purchase a (**sound board**, **hard drive**, **monitor**). That way, I'll be able to hear how each word is pronounced.

10. My brother spends hours sitting in front of his computer talking to other users in cyber(**universe**, **space**, **galaxy**).

A CLOSER LOOK: *MORE Computer Slang*

America Online *n.* (also referred to as *AOL*) a popular computer on-line service which paid subscribers can use to transfer files and various information to their own computers through the telephone wire.

example: I just got some great new programs from **America Online**. My subscription really paid off.

translation: I just got some great new programs from a popular **computer on-line service**. My subscription really paid off.

as spoken: I jus' got s'm great new programs fr'm **AOL**. My subscription really paid off.

append (to) *v.* to attach one document (or part of a document) to the end of another.

example: There is already a list of all of our clients in the computer. Instead of retyping all the names, you can save time if you simply **append** the list to your document.

translation: There is already a list of all of our clients in the computer. Instead of retyping all the names, you can save time if you simply **attach** the list to your document.

as spoken: There's already a list of all of 'ar clients in the c'mpuder. Instead of retyping all the names, you c'n save time if you simply **append** the list ta yer docyam'nt.

archive (to) *v.* to store computer files on a diskette, tape, CD, etc. where they can be retrieved at a future date.

example: Since you're not going to be using these documents in the near future, why don't you **archive** them. That way you'll free up some room in your computer for your current work.

translation: Since you're not going to be using these documents in the near future, why don't you **store** them? That way you'll free up some room in your computer for your current work.

as spoken: Since y'r not gonna be using these docyam'nts 'n the near future, why donchu **archive** 'em? That way you'll free up s'm room in yer c'mpuder fer yer current work.

ASCII *n.* (an acronym for *"American Standard Code for Information Interchange"*) a standard code for representing printable characters in binary format. It is understood by most computer systems and programs and includes certain control characters to indicate bell, carriage return, etc.

example: Since we have different word processing programs, make sure to give me your document in **ASCII**. That way I'll be able to use it in my word processing program.

translation: Since we have different word processing programs, make sure to give me your document in an **American Standard code for information Interchange** format. That way I'll be able to use it in my word processing program.

as spoken: Since we have different word processing programs, make sher da gimme yer docyam'nt in 'n **ASCII** format. That way a'll be able da use id in my word processing.

boilerplate *n.* general structure of a contract's language that does not change from contract to contract.

example: Instead of retyping the same contract for all of our clients, I'm using a **boilerplate**. Now all I have to do is to change the name and address on each one!

translation: Instead of retyping the same contract for all of our clients, I'm using a **standard version**. Now all I have to do is to copy the same document for each client and just change the name and address on each one!

as spoken: Instead of retyping the same contract fer all 'ev 'ar clients, I'm using a **boilerplate**. Now all I hafta is ta change the name 'n address on each one!

SYNONYM: **template** *n.*

boot-up (to) *v.* to start up a computer.

example: I have a lot of work to do this morning. I'm going to go **boot-up** my computer and get to work.

translation: I have a lot of work to do this morning. I'm going to go **start up** my computer and get to work.

as spoken: I have a lod 'a work ta do this morning. I'm gonna go **bood-up** my c'mpuder 'n get ta work.

btw *exp.* (by the way) used when chatting with someone on-line.

example: Thank you for the information you sent to me. It was very helpful. **Btw**, where did you do your research?

translation: Thank you for the information you sent to me. It was very helpful. **By the way**, where did you do your research?

as spoken: Thank you fer the infermation you sent ta me. It was very helpful. **Btw**, whered'ja do yer research?

buffer *n.* a storage area used to hold information temporarily.

example: When I send this document to the printer, its **buffer** stores the document until it's completely printed. That way, my computer is freed up for me to do other work while the document prints.

translation: When I send this document to the printer, its **storage area** stores the document until it's completely printed. That way, my computer is freed up for me to do other work while the document prints.

as spoken: When I sen' this docyam'nt ta the prin(t)er, its **buffer** stores the docyam'nt until it's completely prin(t)ed. That way, my c'mpuder's freed up fer me da do other work while the docyam'nt prints.

burn in (to) *v.* to run a computer (usually for a 48-72 hour period to test it for problems) before it is actually used for work. Most major failures occur during this time.

example: Don't forget to **burn in the computer**. Be sure the system doesn't have any hidden problems!

translation: Don't forget to **test the computer by running it for 48-72 hours**. Be sure the system doesn't have any hidden problems!

as spoken: Don't ferget ta **burn in the c'mpuder**. Be sure the system doesn' have any hidden problems!

bus *n.* an electronic highway for carrying information from the microprocessor to other parts of the computer such as video display, hard drive, RAM, etc.

example: My new computer has a 32-*bit* **bus** which can

carry information a lot faster than my old computer which only had an 8-*bit* bus.

translation: My new computer has a 32-*bit* "**electronic highway**" which can carry information a lot faster than my old computer which only had an 8-*bit* bus.

as spoken: My new c'mpuder has a 32-*bit* **bus** which c'n carry infermation a lot faster th'n my old c'mpuder which only had 'n 8-*bit* bus.

NOTE -1-: **bit** *n.* (an abbreviation for **bi**nary digi**t**) the fundamental unit of information stored in a computer.

NOTE -2: 8 bits = a byte; Half a byte = a nibble; One thousand bytes = a kilobyte; One million bytes = a megabyte; One billion bytes = a gigabyte.

coprocessor *n.* an additional processor optimized to perform specialized tasks more efficiently than the main processor.

example: I just bought a math **coprocessor** for my computer. You should see how fast it does calculations now!

translation: I just bought a **processor optimized to perform math operations** for my computer. You should see how fast it does calculations now!

as spoken: I jus' bod a math **coprocesser** fer my c'mpuder. You should see how fast it does calculations now!

crash • **1.** *n.* a sudden computer failure where the entire system freezes or shuts down • **2.** *v.* to fail suddenly (said of a computer).

example (1): My computer experienced a serious **crash** this morning. I'm waiting for a computer technician to arrive this afternoon.

translation: My computer experienced a serious **failure** this morning. I'm waiting for a computer technician to arrive this afternoon.

as spoken: My c'mpuder experienced a serious **crash** this morning. I'm waiding fer a c'mpuder technician ta arrive this afternoon.

example (2): My computer **crashed** just as I was finishing an important report. Now I'll never get it done in time for my meeting.

translation: My computer **failed** just as I was finishing

an important report. Now I'll never get it done in time for my meeting.

as spoken: My c'mpuder **crashed** just 'ez I was finishing 'n important r'port. Now a'll never ged it done in time fer my meeding.

NOTE: One of the most serious types of computer failures occurs when the hard disk drive heads (that read and write data to the drive) fall or "crash" onto the platter. This may cause a loss of information at the point of impact.

default • **1.** *n.* the initial settings a computer uses unless given instructions to the contrary • **2.** *v.* to reset back to an initial setting.

example (1): In most word processing programs, the **default** for line spacing is single space. If you want something different, you'll have to change the settings.

translation: In most word processing programs, the **pre-programmed initial setting** for line spacing is single space. If you want something different, you'll have to change the settings.

as spoken: In most word processing programs, the **default** fer line spacing is single space. If ya want something diff'r'nt, you'll hafta change the seddings.

example (2): Although you changed the settings to double space, the computer **defaults** to single space every time you recreate a new document.

translation: Although you changed the settings to double space, the computer **resets** to single space every time you recreate a new document.

as spoken: Although you changed the seddings ta double space, the c'mpuder **defaults** ta single space ev'ry time you recreade a new document.

desktop publishing *n.* a type of word processing program where text, graphics, and photographs can be manipulated on the computer to create a professional looking product.

example: Eight years ago, my partner and I began a **desktop publishing** business designing flyers for people. Now we design books for large publishers.

translation: Eight years ago, my partner and I began a **word processing and graphics** business designing flyers for people. Now we design books for large publishers.

as spoken: Eight years ago, my partner 'n I b'gan a **desktop publishing** business designing flyers fer people. Now we design books fer large publishers.

dialog box *n.* a rectangular box that appears on the computer screen to: **1.** request additional information from the user about a command just requested, or **2.** to give the user additional details.

example: Every time I hit a wrong key, a **dialog box** pops up asking me if I'm sure I hit the correct key. It's practically impossible to make a mistake on this computer!

translation: Every time I hit a wrong key, a **box with information** pops up asking me if I'm sure I hit the correct key. It's practically impossible to make a mistake on this computer!

as spoken: Ev'ry time I hid a wrong key, a **dialog box** pops up asking me if I'm sher I hit the correct key. It's practic'lly impossible da make a mistake on this c'mpuder!

dither (to) *v.* to combine two or more colors to simulate another color.

example: On some monitors, when you see the color pink, it's not really pink at all. The computer **dithers** red and white dots on the screen so that it appears pink from viewing distance.

translation: On some monitors, when you see the color pink, it's not really pink at all. The computer **combines the colors** of red and white dots on the screen so that it appears pink from viewing distance.

as spoken: On some moniders, when ya see the color pink, it's not really pink ad all. The c'mpuder **dithers** red 'n white dots on the screen so th'd id appears pink fr'm viewing dist'nce.

download (to) *v.* to receive files from another computer or *BBS* ("bulletin board system") through the telephone line.

example: I just **downloaded** some new graphics from the local *BBS*.

translation: I just **received** some new graphics from the local *BBS*.

as spoken: I jus' **down-loaded** s'm new graphics fr'm the local *BBS*.

ANTONYM: SEE — **upload (to)**, *p. 162.*

NOTE: **BBS** *n.* (an abbreviation for "*bulletin board system*") a digital service available using a modem and telephone line. It gives the user access to reference information over a wide range of subjects, as well as enabling users to communicate with one another.

fixed disk *n.*

SEE: **hard drive**, *p. 141*.

floppy disk *n.* a thin circular piece of plastic which has been magnetically-coated in order to store data.

example: After you enter your document in the computer, make sure to back it up on a **floppy disk**. If something ever happens to the computer, you'll still have a copy of your work.

translation: After you enter your document in the computer, make sure to back it up on a **thin circular piece of plastic which has been magnetically coated in order to store data**. If something ever happens to the computer, you'll still have a copy of your work.

as spoken: After you enter yer docyam'nt in the c'mpuder, make sher da back id up on a **floppy disk**. If something ever happens ta the c'mpuder, you'll still have a copy of your work.

NOTE: Floppy disks (also spelled: *discs*) typically come in two sizes: 3 1/2" (which can hold from 720 kilobytes to 2.88 megabytes of information) and 5 1/4" (which can hold from 360 kilobytes to 1.2 megabytes of information). The 3 1/2" disk is enclosed in a hard plastic case for protection.

greek text (to) *v.* to display text on the computer screen randomly for purposes of position only.

example: I hope you like the newsletter I created. Let me **greek the text** so that you can get a sense of the page composition without being distracted by the actual text.

translation: I hope you like the newsletter I created. Let me **display the text randomly for purposes of position only** so that you can get a sense of the page composition without being distracted by the actual text.

as spoken: I hope you like the newsledder I creaded. Lemme **greek the text** so that chu c'n ged a sense of the page compasition without being distracted by thee actual text.

hard copy *n.* a printed version of a document created on a computer.

example: Be sure to make a **hard copy** of everything you enter into the computer. If something happens to the computer, we don't want to be in a panic.

translation: Be sure to make a **printed version** of everything you enter in the computer. If something happens to the computer, we don't want to be in a panic.

as spoken: Be sher da make a **hard copy** of ev'rything you en(t)er in the c'mpuder. If something happens ta the c'mpuder, we don't wanna be ina panic.

house-keeping *n.* the process of deleting, moving, and/or backing up files in order to keep the hard disk organized.

example: There are so many old files on my hard disk that are just taking up room. I need to do some **house-keeping** right away.

translation: There are so many old files on my hard disk that are just taking up room. I need to do some **deleting, moving, and/or backing up of my files** right away.

icon *n.* a small picture on the computer screen which represents a particular computer function.

example: If you want to start the word processing program, put your cursor on the computer **icon** and double click your mouse.

translation: If you want to start the word processing program, put your cursor on the computer **picture** and double click your mouse.

as spoken: If ya wanna start the word processing program, put cher curser on the c'mpuder **icon** 'n double click yer mouse.

keyboard buffer *n.* an area of memory in the computer which holds a certain number of keystrokes.

example: My mother types so fast that she can finish typing an entire sentence before it's had a chance to appear on the screen. Fortunately, the **keyboard buffer** stores her keystrokes and puts the letters on the screen at a speed that the computer can handle.

translation: My mother types so fast that she can finish typing an entire sentence before it's had a chance to appear on the screen. Fortunately, the **area of memory dedicated to temporarily storing keystrokes** stores her keystrokes and puts the letters on the screen at a speed that the computer can handle.

as spoken: My mother types so fast th't she c'n finish typing 'n entire sen(t)ence before it's had a chance ta appear on the screen. Fortunately, the **keyboard buffer** stores 'er keystrokes 'n puts the ledders on the screen ad a speed th't the c'mpuder c'n handle.

landscape [orientation] *adj.* said of a page which is printed horizontally or lengthwise (as opposed to *portrait* [orientation] which is vertically).

example: This chart is rather large. I think you'd better print it in **landscape [orientation]**.

translation: This chart is rather large. I think you'd better print it **lengthwise**.

as spoken: This chard is rather large. I think ya bedder prin' id in **lan'scape [orientation]**.

SEE: portrait [orientation], *p. 159.*

log on (to) *v.* to enter a name and password in a computer in order to gain access.

example: I can't **log on** to my computer. It looks like someone changed my password!

translation: I can't **gain access** to my computer. It looks like someone changed my password!

as spoken: I can't **log on** ta my c'mpuder. It looks like someone changed my password!

logical drive *n.* a partition of a single physical *hard drive* that has been created by the user for program and data storage.

example: I've divided my *hard drive* into three **logical drives**; C, D, and E. I keep all of my programs stored on C, our client documents on D, and my personal work on E.

translation: I've divided my *hard drive* into three **program and data storage**; C, D, and E. I keep all of my programs stored on C, our client documents on D, and my personal work on E.

as spoken: I divided my *hard drive* inta three **logical drives**; C, D, 'n E. I keep all 'a my programs stored on C, 'ar client docyam'nts on D, an' my personal work on E.

SEE: **hard drive**, *p.*141.

monochrome *adj.* referring to a computer screen, or *monitor,* which displays information in shades of one color (amber, green, or white) as opposed to a color monitor.

example: If you want to use your paint program, you'll have to replace your **monochrome** monitor with a color one.

translation: If you want to use your paint program, you'll have to replace your **one-color display** monitor with a color one.

as spoken: If ya wanna use yer paint program, you'll hafta r'place yer **monachrome** monider with a color one.

morph (to) *v.* to smoothly transform one image into another.

example: Watch this great graphics effect on my monitor. I'm going to **morph** this image of our biology teacher into an ape.

translation: Watch this great graphics effect on my monitor. I'm going to **tranform** this image of our biology teacher into an ape.

as spoken: Watch this great graphics affect on my monider. I'm gonna **morph** this image of 'ar biology teacher into 'n ape.

motherboard *n.* the main circuit board of the computer.

example: In many cases, the performance of a computer system can be greatly improved by upgrading only the **motherboard**.

translation: In many cases, the performance of a computer system can be greatly improved by upgrading only the **main circuit board**.

as spoken: In many cases, the performance of a c'mpuder system c'n be greatly improved by upgrading only the **motherboard**.

multitasking *n.* the computer's ability to run more than one program ("tasks") at the same time.

example: Since my computer allows **multitasking**, I can use my word processing program while I download files from a *BBS* in the background.

translation: Since my computer allows **more than one program to be run at the same time**, I can use my word processing program while I download files from a *BBS* in the background.

as spoken: Since my c'mpuder allows **multitasking**, I c'n use my word processing program while I download files fr'm a *BBS* in the background.

SEE: **BBS**, under the heading **download, to**, *p. 155.*

portrait [orientation] *adj.* said of a page which is printed vertically (as opposed to *landscape* [orientation] which is horizontally).

example: Business letters should always be printed in **portrait [orientation]**!

translation: Business letters should always be printed **vertically**!

as spoken: Business ledders should always be prin(t)ed in **portred [orientation]**!

SEE: **landscape [orientation]**, *p. 157.*

power down (to) *v.* to turn off an electrical applicance.

example: We've all worked hard today. Let's **power down** our computers and go home early today!

translation: We've all worked hard today. Let's **turn off** our computers and go home early today!

as spoken: We've all worked hard today. Let's **power down** 'ar c'mpuders 'n go home early today!

ANTONYM: SEE — **power up (to)**, *p. 159.*

power up (to) *v.* to turn on an electrical appliance.

example: It's time to **power up** the computers and start working.

translation: It's time to **turn on** the computers and start working.

as spoken: It's time ta **power up** the c'mpuders 'n start working.

SYNONOYM: SEE — **boot up (to)**, *p. 150.*

ANTONYM: SEE — **power down (to)**, *p. 159.*

pull-down menu *n.* a list of options displayed on a computer moitor and usually accessed with a mouse. This action resembles closing a "pull-down" window shade.

example: To print this document, use the **pull-down menu** and choose the correct printer.

translation: To print this document, use the **pull-down list of options** and choose the correct printer.

as spoken: Ta print this docyam'nt, use the **pull-down menu** 'n choose the correct prin(t)er.

pull up (to) *v.* to retrieve a computer file.

example: Please **pull up** the budget report on your computer. I need to verify some numbers.

translation: Please **retrieve** the budget report on your computer. I need to verify some numbers.

as spoken: Please **pull up** the budget r'pord on yer c'mpuder. I need ta verify s'm numbers.

queue *n.* (from the British term for a waiting line of persons or vehicles) documents that have been sent to a printer and are "waiting in line" to be printed.

example: I need to print this document right away, but there are five print jobs ahead of me in the print **queue.**

translation: I need to print this document right away, but there are five print jobs ahead of me in the **print line.**

as spoken: I need ta print this docyam'nt ride away, b't there'er five print jobs ahead 'ev me in the print **queue.**

root directory *n.* the main directory, created when the *hard drive* is formatted.

example: Command programs and configuration files are usually stored in the **root directory** of the *hard drive.*

translation: Command programs and configuration files are usually stored in the **main directory** of the *hard drive.*

as spoken: Command programs an' c'nfiguration files'er ujally stored in the **root directery** 'ev the *hard drive.*

SEE: **subdirectory**, *(next entry).*

SEE: **hard drive**, *p.*141.

subdirectory *n.* a partition of a directory or subdirectory.

example: On my root directory, I have created a **subdirectory** called "clients." Under that directory are separate **subdirectories** for each customer. That way, each customer file can be stored in its proper location.

<u>translation:</u> On my root directory, I have created a **partition** called "clients." Under that directory are separate **partitions** for each customer. That way, each customer file can be stored in its proper location.

<u>as spoken:</u> On my root directery, I've creaded a **subdirectery** called "clients." Under that directery'er sep'rit **subdirecteries** fer each custamer. That way, each custamer file c'n be stored in its proper location.

surf (to) *v.* to explore *cyberspace* using an on-line service.

<u>example:</u> George spends too much time on his computer **surfing** when he should be working.

<u>translation:</u> George spends too much time on his computer **exploring cyberspace** when he should be working.

<u>as spoken:</u> George spen's too much time on 'is c'mpuder **surfing** when 'e should be working.

SEE: **cyberspace**, *p. 141.*

sysop *n.* (an acronym for "system operator") a term given to the person in charge of managing a *BBS* ("bulletin board service") or website.

<u>example:</u> The **sysop** gave me a one month free trial period on the *BBS*.

<u>translation:</u> The **system operator** gave me a one month free trial period on the *BBS*.

<u>as spoken:</u> The **sysop** gave me a one month free trial period on the *BBS*.

SEE: **BBS**, under the heading **download, to** – *p. 155.*

tractor-feed *n.* a mechanism used for feeding continuous form paper into a dot-matrix printer.

<u>example:</u> Something is wrong with the **tractor-feed**. The paper isn't being fed into the printer evenly.

<u>translation:</u> Something is wrong with the **paper feeding mechanism**. The paper isn't being fed into the printer evenly.

<u>as spoken:</u> Something's wrong with the **tracter-feed**. The paper isn't being fed inta the prin(t)er evenly.

Trojan horse *n.* a highly destructive program created by irresponsible programmers. It is hidden inside a genuine program and intended to cause data damage or loss.

example: If someone gave that program to you, I'd be careful. You never know, it may contain a **Trojan horse**.

translation: If someone gave that program to you, I'd be careful. You never know, it may contain a **hidden destructive program intended to cause data damage or loss**.

as spoken: If someone gave that progr'm ta you, I'd be careful. Ya never know, it may c'ntain a **Troj'n horse**.

typeface *n.* a group of characters sharing a common design (whereas a "font" refers to the combination of "typeface" and "point size").

example: Times Roman and Helvetica are the most common **typefaces** used in newspapers.

translation: Times Roman and Helvetica are the most common **character designs** used in newspapers.

as spoken: Times Roman an' Helvedica'er the most common used **typefaces** used in newspapers.

upload (to) *v.* to send files from one computer to another computer or to a *BBS* through the telephone line.

example: I'm going to **upload** my desktop publishing files to our service bureau's *BBS*.

translation: I'm going to **send** my desktop publishing files to our service bureau's *BBS*.

as spoken: I'm gonna **upload** my desktop publishing files ta 'ar service bureau's *BBS*.

ANTONYM: SEE — **download (to)**, *p. 154*.

SEE: **BBS**, under the heading **download, to** – *p. 155*.

write-protect (to) *v.* to modify a disk or file so that the user cannot change or delete information.

example: Don't worry about accidentally deleting the program on the disk. It's been **write-protected**.

translation: Don't worry about accidentally deleting the program on the disk. It's been **modified so that the user cannot change or delete information**.

as spoken: Don't worry about accident'lly deleding the program on the disk. It's been **write-pratected**.

Practice Using MORE Computer Slang

(Answers, p. 275)

A. Circle the letter which corresponds to the correct definition of the words in boldface.

1. **default**:
   a. a computer document that is used repeatedly, but can be customized by changing certain words.
   b. the initial setting of a computer function.

2. **to append**:
   a. to backup computer files onto a diskette, tape, CD, etc. where they can be retrieved at a future date.
   b. to attach one document (or part of a document) to the end of another.

3. **to dither**:
   a. to combine two or more colors to simulate another color.
   b. to reset back to an inital setting.

4. **to download**:
   a. to send files from one computer to another (or bulletin board system) through the telephone lines.
   b. to receive files from another computer (or bulletin board system) through the telephone lines.

5. **to write protect**:
   a. to copyright a file.
   b. to modify a disk or file so that the user cannot change or delete information.

6. **Trojan horse**:
   a. a group of characters sharing a common design.
   b. a highly destructive program that is created by irresponsible programmers. It is hidden inside a genuine program and intended to cause data damage or loss.

7. **typeface**:
   a. a group of characters sharing a common design.
   b. a mechanism used for pulling continuous form paper into a dot-matrix printer.

8. **to surf**:
   a. to attach an existing document (or part of a document) to a document currently on the computer screen.
   b. to explore cyberspace using an on-line service.

9. **to morph**:
   a. to turn off an electrical appliance.
   b. to smoothly transform one image into another.

10. **multitasking**:
   a. the computer's ability to run more than one program at the same time.
   b. the process of deleting, moving, and/or backing up files in order to keep a hard drive organized.

LESSON SEVEN

Bureaucratese

Timmy had all the signs of
a ***whistle-blower*** *at an early age.*

Lesson Seven

Dialogue in slang

The Mayor: Jenkins, I'd like your **feedback** on the progress of our **task force** assigned to clean up the city.

Jenkins: I don't want to be a **whistle-blower**, but it is my **role** to bring you **up-to-speed**.

The Mayor: Is the group **dysfunctional**? It was understanding that these people are hard workers.

Jenkins: That's **counterfactual**, sir. The littering problem is getting worse. There are many **causal factors** for this but the main problem is that the people in the group are **motivationally deficient**.

The Mayor: Jenkins, I'm assigning you to **spearhead** the task force. I am aware of your **past history** and know you can do it.

Jenkins: I've already come up with some ideas that I'm sure you'll find **doable** and not **cost-prohibitive**. I know the **private sector** will appreciate that, although I'll need some **seed money** to **implement** them.

The Mayor: Well, we have experienced a **revenue shortfall** this year, but we'll see what we can do. Let's talk about this again tomorrow. I'll **pencil you in** for a 2:00 meeting.

Lesson Seven

Translation of dialogue in standard English

Bureaucratese

The Mayor:	Jenkins, I'd like your **reaction** on the progress of our **small committee** assigned to clean up the city.
Jenkins:	I don't want to be an **informant**, but it is my **responsibility** to bring you **current information**.
The Mayor:	Is the group **ineffective**? It was my understanding that these people are hard workers.
Jenkins:	That's **not true**, sir. The littering problem is getting worse. There are many **reasons** for this but the main problem is that the people in the group are **lazy**.
The Mayor:	Jenkins, I'm assigning you to **take charge of** the task force. I am aware of your **history** and know you can do it.
Jenkins:	I've already come up with some ideas that I'm sure you'll find **achievable** and not **expensive**. I know the **business community** will appreciate that, although I'll need some **money upfront** to **start** them.
The Mayor:	Well, we have experienced a **shortage of money** this year, but we'll see what we can do. Let's talk about this again tomorrow. I'll **tentatively schedule** you for a 2:00 meeting.

Lesson Seven

Dialogue in slang as it would be heard

Bureaucratese

The Mayor: Jenkins, I'd like yer **feedback** on the progress of 'ar **task force** assign' ta clean up the cidy.

Jenkins: I don' wanna be a **whistle blower**, bud it's my **role** ta bring you **up-ta-speed**.

The Mayor: Is the group **dysfunctional**? It was my understanding th't these people'er hard workers.

Jenkins: That's **coun(t)erfactual**, sir. The liddering problem's gedding worse. There'er many **causal facters** fer this but the main problem is th't the people in the group 'ar **modivationally deficient**.

The Mayor: Jenkins, I'm assigning you ta **spearhead** the task force. I'm aware 'ev yer **past histery** n' know you c'n do it.

Jenkins: I've already come up with s'm ideas th'd I'm sher you'll fin' **do-able** 'n not **cost prohibidive**. I know the **private secter** will appreciate that, although A'll need s'm **seed money** ta **implement** th'm.

The Mayor: Well, we have experienced a **revenue shortfall** this year, but we'll see what we c'n do. Let's talk about this again tomorrow. A'll **pencil you in** fer a 2:00 meeding.

Vocabulary

causal factors *n.* reasons.

example: There are many **causal factors** for our poor sales, but I think that the primary one is our packaging.

translation: There are many **reasons** for our poor sales, but I think that the primary one is our packaging.

as spoken: There'er many **causal facters** fer 'ar poor sales, bud I think th't the primary one is 'ar packaging.

cost-prohibitive *adj.* too expensive.

example: Repairing the streets in the city would be **cost-prohibitive** at this time.

translation: Repairing the streets in the city would be **too expensive** at this time.

as spoken: R'pairing the streets in the cidy would be **cost-prohibidive** 'it this time.

counterfactual *adj.* false.

example: Your statement is **counterfactual**.

translation: Your statement is **false**.

as spoken: Yer statement's **coun(t)erfactual**.

ALSO (1): **categorical inaccuracy** *n.* a lie.

ALSO (2): **counterfactual propostion** *n.* a lie.

doable (to be) *adj.* to be achievable.

example: I propose that we shorten the work day in order to reduce traffic problems. I think you'll find this to be a **doable** solution.

translation: I propose that we shorten the work day in order to reduce traffic problems. I think you'll find this to be an **achievable** solution.

as spoken: I prapose th't we shorten the work day in order ta r'duce traffic problems. I think you'll fin' this ta be a **doable** solution.

dysfunctional *adj.* ineffective.

example: Our new committee has turned out to be completely **dysfunctional**.

translation: Our new committee has turned out to be completely **ineffective**.

as spoken: 'Ar new commidee's turned out ta be completely **dysfunction'l**.

feedback *n.* reaction.

example: I'd like to hear your **feedback** regarding yesterday's meeting.

translation: I'd like to hear your **reaction** regarding yesterday's meeting.

as spoken: I'd like ta hear yer **feedback** r'garding yesderday's meeding.

implement (to) *v.* to start.

example: We're ready **to implement** our plan.

translation: We're ready **to start** our plan.

as spoken: W'r ready **da implemen'** 'ar plan.

motivationally deficient *adj.* lazy.

example: The employees seem to be getting more and more **motivationally deficient** every day!

translation: The employees seem to be getting more and more **lazy** every day!

as spoken: The employees seem ta be gedding more 'n more **modivationally deficient** ev'ry day!

past history *exp.* history.

example: Before I hire him, I want to know his **past history**.

translation: Before I hire him, I want to know his **history**.

as spoken: Before I hire 'im, I wanna know 'is **past histery**.

NOTE: If you have noticed that the phrase "past history" is redundant, you're right! This phrase is certainly not correct, although it *is* popular.

pencil in (to) *exp.* to tentatively schedule (written in pencil so that it can be easily changed if necessary).

example: Let's have a meeting next week. Let me **pencil** you **in** for next Thursday.

translation: Let's have a meeting next week. Let me **tentatively schedule** for next Thursday.

as spoken: Let's have a meeding next week. Lemme **pencil** you **in** fer nex' Thursday.

private sector *n.* business.

example: The new president will give tax breaks to the **private sector**.

translation: The new president will give tax breaks to **businesses**.

as spoken: The new president'll give tax breaks ta the **private sector**.

SEE: **public sector**, *p. 179*.

revenue shortfall *n.* a smaller gross income than forecast or budgeted.

example: Mr. President, I must report that our company is experiencing a **revenue shortfall** this year.

translation: Mr. President, I must report that our company is experiencing a **reduced gross income** this year.

as spoken: Mr. President, I must r'port th'd 'ar company is experiencing a **revenue shortfall** this year.

role *n.* function, responsibility.

example: It's not my **role** to supervise you.

translation: It's not my **function** to supervise you.

as spoken: It's not my **role** ta supervise you.

seed money *n.* funds used to start a project.

example: Where are we going to get the **seed money** for this project?

translation: Where are we going to get the **funds to start** this project?

as spoken: Where 'er we gonna get the **seed money** fer this project?

spearhead (to) *v.* to lead.

example: I was just assigned **to spearhead** our committee.

translation: I was just assigned **to lead** our committee.

as spoken: I w's just assigned **ta spearhead** 'ar commidee.

task force *n.* a small temporary committee.

example: We need to set up a **task force** to help clean the park.

translation: We need to set up a **temporary committee** to help clean the park.

as spoken: We need ta sed up a **task force** ta help clean the park.

up to speed *exp.* to be up-to-date, current.

example: Let me bring you **up to speed** on what's been going on in the trial.

translation: Let me bring you **up-to-date** on what's been going on in the trial.

as spoken: Lemme bring you **up ta speed** on what's b'n going on in the trial.

whistle blower *n.* an informant.

NOTE: **to blow the whistle** on someone. *v.* to inform on someone.

example: I just found out who our **whistle blower** is!

translation: I just found out who our **informant** is!

as spoken: I jus' found out who 'ar **whistle blower** is!

Practice the Vocabulary

(Answers to Lesson Seven, p. 276)

A. Complete the sentences by choosing the appropriate word(s) from the list below.

feedback
doable
cost prohibitive
counterfactual
history
implement
pencil
revenue shortfall
seed
spearhead
up-to-speed
whistle blower

1. I'd like your ________________. What do you think about our new product?

2. Let me bring you ____________________ on what happened at yesterday's conference.

3. If you think you'll be free tomorrow afternoon, I'll ______________ you in for a 2 o'clock meeting.

4. Your ideas are all certainly __________________, I'm just afraid that they may be ________________________________ given our current budget.

5. We've experienced a ______________________________ this year but next year, I'm hopeful we'll make a lot more money.

6. If you don't want this to get back to the boss, don't say anything to Greg. He's known for being a ______________________________ .

7. Your statement is ______________________________ . If you knew the facts, you wouldn't make that accusation.

8. Before hiring him, we need to know about his past ______________ .

9. I'm going to need some ______________ money in order to ______________________ this project.

10. Roger, I'm assigning you to ____________________ our committee.

B. Underline the word(s) in parentheses that best complete(s) the sentence.

1. I'd like your (**past history**, **feedback**, **role**) on the progress of our committee. How do you think it's going?

2. I'm sorry to have to contradict you, but that's completely (**past history**, **dysfunctional**, **counterfactual**).

3. Let's tentatively plan on having lunch together tomorrow. I'll (**pencil**, **draw**, **sketch**) you in for noon.

4. It may be rather costly to begin this project. Let's see how much (**seed**, **doable**, **feedback**) money we'll need.

5. That's going to cost a million dollars?! I'm afraid that's (**dysfunctional**, **cost-prohibitive**, **doable**)!

6. I'd like to get more information on her. What's her past (**future**, **present**, **history**)?

7. You won't believe what happened yesterday. Let me bring you up to (**seed**, **speed**, **quick**).
8. Your ideas sound very (**doable**, **counterfactual**, **motivationally deficient**). I think we'll use them!
9. There are many (**deficient**, **dysfunctional**, **causal**) factors for this problem.
10. We need to create a (**task**, **feedback**, **spearhead**) force to clean up our city.

C. CONTEXT EXERCISE
Match the columns.

☐	1. Advertising is going to cost us a million dollars?!	A. That's **cost-prohibitive**!
☐	2. Let's tentatively plan on meeting tomorrow.	B. I'll **pencil you in** for 3:00.
☐	3. So you're interested in working for our company?	C. They all seem very **doable**.
☐	4. Our products don't seem to be selling as well as they used to.	D. In fact, I'm assigning you to **spearhead** our new committee.
☐	5. Welcome back from your vacation.	E. Tell me something about your **past history**.
☐	6. Our employees don't seem happy here.	F. Let me bring you **up-to-speed** on everything that happened while you were gone.
☐	7. I like your suggestions.	G. I'm not surprised. Everyone knows he's a **whistle-blower**.
☐	8. I have to disagree with you.	H. It's obvious that they're **motivationally deficient**.
☐	9. You seem like a leader to me.	I. That statement is simply **counterfactual**.
☐	10. Mark got me in trouble with the boss yesterday.	J. Do we need to rethink our advertising strategy? I'd like your **feedback**.

A CLOSER LOOK:
Popular Bureaucratese

brainstorm (to) *v.* to gather in a group in order to contribute ideas for solving problems.

example: We need to find an immediate solution to this problem. Why don't you come into my office so we can **brainstorm**.

translation: We need to find an immediate solution to this problem. Why don't you come into my office so we can **contribute ideas for solving problems together**.

as spoken: We need ta find 'n immediate s'lution ta this problem. Why don'chu come inta my office so we c'n **brainstorm**.

coequal *adj.* to be equal.

example: We're all **coequal** in this room.

translation: We're all **equal** in this room.

as spoken: W'r all **coequal** in this room.

CYA *exp.* an abbreviation for "cover your ass" meaning document everything so you can't be blamed later.

example: Before you fire him, make sure to document everything. Remember, **CYA**!

translation: Before you fire him, make sure to document everything. Remember, **cover your ass**!

as spoken: Before you fire 'im, make sure da docyam'nt ev'rything. R'member, **CYA**!

NOTE: The term ass, meaning "buttocks," is considered crude and should be used with caution.

ALSO: **CYA memo** *n.* a memorandum used to document one's actions and avoid blame if something does not get done correctly.

detention center *n.* jail.

example: The criminals were ordered to spend five years in the **detention center**.

translation: The criminals were ordered to spend five years in **jail**.

as spoken: The criminals were ordered ta spen' five years in the **detention cen(t)er**.

domicile *n.* home.

example: His **domicile** is in Europe.

translation: His **home** is in Europe.

as spoken: His **domicile**'s in Europe.

dysfunctional *adj.* ineffective.

example: We tried to implement his plan, but I'm afraid that it turned out to be **dysfunctional**.

translation: We tried to implement his plan, but I'm afraid that it turned out to be **ineffective**.

as spoken: We tried da implemen'is plan, bud I'm afraid th'd it turned out ta be **dysfunction'l**.

etched in stone (not) *exp.* to be changeable.

example: These rules **are not etched in stone**.

translation: These rules **are changeable**.

as spoken: These rules **aren't etched in stone**.

ALSO: **written in sand** *exp.* flexible.

example: Don't worry about all the requirements for this job. They're really **written in sand**.

translation: Don't worry about all the requirements for this job. They're really **flexible**.

as spoken: Don't worry aboud all the r'quirements fer this job. They're really **written in sand**.

fund (to) *v.* to pay for.

example: There isn't enough money in the budget **to fund** the housing project.

translation: There isn't enough money in the budget **to pay for** the housing project.

as spoken: There isn' enough money in the budget **ta fun'** the housing project.

funding *n.* money.

example: The **funding** for this project was made possible by the telephone company.

translation: The **money** for this project was made possible by the telephone company.

as spoken: The **funding** fer this project was made possible by the phone company.

hands-off *adj.* uninvolved.

example: The president of our company has a **hands-off** style.

translation: The president of our company has a **don't-get-involved** style.

as spoken: The president of 'ar company has a **han's-off** style.

interpersonal skills *n.* ability to get along with other people.

example: It's important that the person we hire have good **interpersonal skills** since he'll be dealing directly with our customers.

translation: It's important that the person we hire have the **ability to get along with people** since he'll be dealing directly with our customers.

as spoken: It's important th't the person we hire have good **in(t)erpersonal skills** since 'e'll be dealing directly with 'ar custamers.

irrespective *prep.* regardless.

example: **Irrespective** of the cost, we need to repair the sidewalks in the neighborhood.

translation: **Regardless** of the cost, we need to repair the sidewalks in the neighborhood.

as spoken: **Irrespective** of the cost, we need ta r'pair the sidewalks in the neighberhood.

live with *exp.* to accept circumstances or consequences.

example: I can **live with** his decision.

translation: I can **accept** his decision.

as spoken: I c'n **live with** 'is decision.

phase out (to) *v.* to gradually discontinue .

example: We're going **to phase out** our health insurance plan.

translation: We're going **gradually discontinue** our health insurance plan.

as spoken: We're gonna **phase oud** 'ar health insurance plan.

ANTONYM: **phase in (to)** *v.*

phase zero *exp.* the planning stage of a project, usually before significant resources have been committed.

example: Since our worker retraining project has reached **phase zero**, we need to submit a starting budget.

translation: Since our worker retraining project has reached the **planning stage**, we need to submit a starting budget.

as spoken: Since our worker retraining project has reached phase zero, we need to submit a starting budget.

public sector *n.* the government, the people.

example: The **public sector** will not tolerate any more tax increases.

translation: The **people** will not tolerate any more tax increases.

as spoken: The **public sector** won't tolerade any more tax increases.

SEE: **private sector**, *p. 171.*

qualitative *adj.* relating to quality or certain other characteristics that have not been measured or specified.

example: While we don't know the actual cost of these items, **qualitatively** they appear to be valuable.

translation: While we don't know the actual cost of these items, **judging by their characteristics** they appear to be valuable.

as spoken: While we don't know the actual cost 'a these idems, **qualitadively** they appear da be valu'ble.

reskill (to) *v.* to retrain.

example: Since most of our employees don't know about computers, we're going to have **to reskill** everyone.

translation: Since most of our employees don't know about computers, we're going to have **to retrain** everyone.

as spoken: Since most 'ev 'ar employees don't know about c'mpuders, w'r gonna haf**ta reskill** ev'ryone.

root cause *n.* cause.

example: The **root cause** for this country's unemployment problem is the lack of job skills.

translation: The **cause** for this country's unemployment problem is the lack of job skills.

as spoken: The **root cause** fer this country's unemployment problem's the last of job skills.

surviving spouse *n.* widow/widower.

example: That woman is the **surviving spouse** of Mr. Green, our former CEO.

translation: That woman is the **widow** of Mr. Green, our former CEO.

as spoken: That woman's the **surviving spouse** 'ev Mr. Green, 'ar former CEO.

unsubstantiated rumor *exp*. rumor.

example: It's an **unsubstantiated rumor** that the company is going out of business.

translation: It's a **rumor** that the company is going out of business.

as spoken: It's 'n **unsubstanchiaded rumer** that the company's going oudda business.

NOTE: This expression is redundant since a **rumor** is an unsubstantiated remark. Although this expression is grammatically incorrect, it *is* common.

utilize (to) *v*. to use, expend.

example: How do you plan to **utilize** this money?

translation: How do you plan to **use** this money?

as spoken: Howdy'a plan ta **udilize** this money?

viable *adj*. possible, workable, practical.

example: Your plan to increase the company's productivity is **viable**.

translation: Your plan to increase the company's productivity is **workable**.

as spoken: Yer plan ta increase the company's productividy's **viable**.

whole ball of wax (the) *exp*. everything.

example: This morning I heard that only the computer division would be sold. Now it turns out that the **whole ball of wax** is up for sale.

translation: This morning I heard that only the computer division would be sold. Now it turns out that **everything** is up for sale.

as spoken: Th's morning I heard th'd only the c'mpuder division would be sold. Now it turns out th't the **whole ball 'a wax** is up fer sale.

SYNONYM -1: **whole megillah (the)** *exp*.

SYNONYM -2: **whole nine yards (the)** *exp*.

SYNONYM -3: **whole shebang (the)** *exp*.

wiggle room *exp*. flexibility, room to maneuver.

example: Don't specify a completion date for our software update project. We'll need some **wiggle room** if anything goes wrong.

translation: Don't specify a completion date for our

software update project. We'll need some **flexibility** if anything goes wrong.

as spoken: Don't specify a c'mpletion date fer 'ar software update project. W'll need s'm **wiggle room** if anything goes wrong.

SYNONYM: **latitude** *n.*

zero fund *exp.* a process whereby a program receives no money for its operations.

example: Rather than be criticized for cancelling our research program, the director decided **to zero fund** it.

translation: Rather than be criticized for cancelling our research program, the director decided **not to make any money available for** it.

as spoken: Rather th'n be cridisized fer canc'lling 'ar research program, the directer d'cided **ta zero fund** it.

Practice Bureaucratese

(Answers, p. 276)

A. Circle the letter which corresponds to the correct definition of the term in boldface.

1. **coequal**:
   a. almost equal
   b. exactly equal

2. **to fund**:
   a. to pay for
   b. to use

3. **viable**:
   a. impossible
   b. possible

4. **detention center**:
   a. location
   b. jail

5. **to reskill**:
   a. to train
   b. to schedule

6. **wiggle room**:
   a. flexibility
   b. said of a program which receives no money for its operations

7. **surviving spouse**:
   a. parent
   b. widow/widower

8. **phase zero**:
   a. the beginning of something
   b. the end of something

9. **the private sector**:
   a. the business community
   b. the government

10. **ball of wax**:
    a. the entire situation
    b. excessive bureaucracy

11. **to phase out**:
    a. to discontinue
    b. to implement

12. **CYA**:
    a. a common acronym for "check your addition"
    b. an abbreviation for "cover your ass" meaning document everything so you can't be blamed later

LESSON EIGHT

Political Slang & Jargon

*Wally loves **to press the flesh** with his supporters.*

Lesson Eight

Dialogue in slang

Carl: I think you'd better go on a **junket** to the midwest and start **stumping** before your opponent does.

Wally: You're right. I guess it's time **to press the flesh**. I still can't believe that Bob decided **to run for office** against me. His **platform** is weak and he keeps **waffling** on the issues. In his **gubernatorial race**, his critics accused him of **sitting on the fence**.

Carl: That's all changed. He's **solidified his position** on the issues and he's no longer **running on a third party ticket**. Not only is he a member of the **GOP**, but the guy's a **right winger** and a **hawk**.

Wally: Well, I do have to admit one thing. He does know how **to ramrod** a bill through **Capitol Hill** and that's what the **private sector** is going to be looking for.

Carl: But you are better at **mud slinging** than he is! And no one is better at **demagoguery** than you are! Besides, the **polls** are showing that Bob's popularity is **slipping** among the elderly **bloc** while yours is improving with the **middle of the road** vote.

Wally: That's what I want to hear! As long as we get a good voter **turnout**, I'll have this election **all wrapped up**! I can't wait to see those **returns**!

Lesson Eight

Translation of dialogue in standard English

Political Slang & Jargon

Carl: I think you'd better go on an **information-gathering trip** to the midwest and start **doing speaking tours** before your opponent does.

Wally: You're right. I guess it's time **to meet the people**. I still can't believe that Bob decided **to campaign for an elected position in government** against me. His **political plan** is weak and he keeps **evading** the issues. In his race for **election as governor**, his critics accused him of **being indecisive**.

Carl: That's all changed. He's **formed a definite opinion** on the issues and in fact, he's **no longer representing an independent party**. Not only is he a member of the **Republican Party**, but the guy's a **conservative** and a **supporter of agressive military policy**.

Wally: Well, I do have to admit one thing. He does know how **to push** a bill through **the House of Representatives and Congress** and that's what the **the business community** is going to be looking for.

Carl: But you are better at **making disparaging remarks** than he is! And no one is better at **getting people roused** than you are! Besides, the **surveys** are showing that Bob's popularity is **diminishing** among the elderly **group of voters** while yours is improving with the **voters who are neutral**.

Wally: That's what I want to hear! As long as we get a good voter **attendance**, I think I'll **win** this election! I can't wait to see those **results**!

Lesson Eight

Dialogue in slang as it would be heard

Political Slang & Jargon

Carl: I think ya bedder go on a **junket** ta the midwest 'n start **stumping** before yer apponent does.

Wally: Y'r right. I guess it's time **ta press the flesh**. I still can't believe th't Bob d'cided **ta run fer office** against me. His **platform**'s weak 'n 'e keeps **waffling** on the issues. In his **gubernatorial race**, his cridics accused 'im of **sidding on the fence**.

Carl: That's all changed. He's **solidified 'is position** on the issues and e's no longer **running on a third pardy ticket**. Nod only is 'e a member of the **GOP**, but the guy's a **right winger** and a **hawk**.

Wally: Well, I do hafta admit one thing. He does know how **da ramrod** a bill through **Capid'l Hill** 'n that's wh't the **private sector**'s gonna be looking for.

Carl: But y'r bedder at **mud slinging** th'n he is! An' no one's bedder at **demagoguery** th'n you are! Besides, the **polls** are showing th't Bob's popularidy's **slipping** among the elderly **bloc** while yers is improving with the **middle 'a the road** vote.

Wally: That's whad I want ta hear! As long as we ged a good voter **turnout**, a'll have this election **all wrapped up**! I can't wait ta see those **r'turns**!

Vocabulary

bloc *n.* a group of people united by a commonality such as age, race, religion, etc.

example: The elderly **bloc** is opposed to cutbacks in social security.

translation: The elderly **group** is opposed to cutbacks in social security.

as spoken: The elderly **bloc**'s opposed ta cutbacks in social securidy.

Capitol Hill *n.* site of the United States Senate and House of Representatives (it is located on a hill in the nation's capital).

example: We just heard some interesting news today from **Capitol Hill**.

translation: We just heard some interesting news today from **the Senate and House of Representatives**.

as spoken: We jus' heard s'm int'resting news today fr'm **Capid'l Hill**.

VARIATION: **The Hill** *n.*

demagoguery *n.* the use of popular prejudices and misleading claims to gain political power.

example: I'm so tired of the **demagoguery** that goes on during campaigns. The goal of so many politicians is to say what the people want to hear.

translation: I'm so tired of the **use of popular prejudice and false claims to gain political power** that goes on during campaigns. The goal of so many politicians is to say what the people want to hear.

as spoken: I'm so tired 'ev the **demamgoguery** th't goes on during campaigns. The goal of so many politicians is ta say what the people wanna hear.

GOP *n.* an abbreviation for the "Grand Old Party," also known as the Republican Party.

example: My parents always argue on political issues because my mother is a Democrat and my father is a member of the **GOP**

translation: My parents always argue on political issues because my mother is a democrat and my father is a member of the **Republican Party**

as spoken: My parents always argue on polidical issues 'cuz my mother's a Democrat an' my father's a member 'a the **GOP**

gubernatorial race *n.* a contest for the election of governor.

example: I lost the **gubernatorial race** this year, but next time I'm determined to win!

translation: I lost the **contest for the election of governor** this year, but next time I'm determined to win!

as spoken: I lost the **gubernatorial race** this year, b't nex' time I'm d'termin' ta win!

NOTE: **gubernatorial** *adj.* having to do with a governor.

hawk *n.* one who supports aggressive military policy.

example: My uncle is a real **hawk**. He believes that we should use our military forces without hesitation.

translation: My uncle is a real **supporter of aggressive military policy**. He believes that we should use our military forces without hesitation.

as spoken: My uncle's a real **hawk**. He believes th't we should use 'ar military forces without hesitation.

ANTONYM: **dove** *n.* one who believes in keeping peace at all costs.

junket *n.* a trip made at public expense by a politician to conduct official business or gather information.

example: The governor is going on a **junket** to Los Angeles to inspect damage caused by the earthquake.

translation: The governor is going on a **political business trip** to Los Angeles to inspect damage caused by the earthquake.

as spoken: The govern'r's goin' ona **junket** ta L.A. ta inspect damage caused by the quake.

middle-of-the-road *adj.* politically neutral.

example: I'm definitely **middle-of-the-road** when it comes to politics.

translation: I'm definitely **neutral** when it comes to politics.

as spoken: I'm def'nitely **middle-'a-the-road** when it comes ta politics.

NOTE -1: **right winger** *n.* one who has conservsative views.

NOTE -2: **left winger** *n.* one who has liberal views.

mudslinging *n.* criticism and condemnation of an opponent.

example: The growing voter discontent with the political process has a lot to do with the **mudslinging** that goes on. The important issues are rarely discussed.

translation: The growing voter discontent with the political process has a lot to do with the **personal criticizing and condemnation** that goes on. The important issues are rarely discussed.

as spoken: The growing voder disc'ntent with the polidic'l process has a lot ta do with the **mudslinging** th't goes on. The important issues'er rarely discussed.

platform *n.* the plan presented by a person running for office.

example: I like that candidate's **platform**. He is a big advocate of better education for our youth.

translation: I like that candidate's **plan**. He is a big advocate of better education for our youth.

as spoken: I like that can'idut's **platform**. He's a big advocade of bedder edjacation fer 'ar youth.

poll • **1.** *n. & v.* survey; to survey • **2.** *n.* the place where voting takes place (usually in the plural: *polls*).

example (1): According to the latest **poll**, Meyers is leading the race for presidency.

translation: According to the latest **survey**, Meyers is leading the race for presidency.

as spoken: According ta the lates' **poll**, Meyers 'ez leading the race fer presidency.

example (2): Remember, tomorrow is election day. See you at the **polls**!

translation: Remember, tomorrow is election day. See you at the **voting location**!

as spoken: Remember, tomorrow's election day. See ya at the **polls**!

ALSO -1: **pollster** *n.* one who conducts a poll or survey.

ALSO -2: **straw poll** *v.* a random sampling of opinion.

press the flesh (to) *v.* to mingle with the public and shake hands.

example: If a candidate wants to be popular with the people, he has to spend a lot of time **pressing the flesh**.

translation: If a candidate wants to be popular with the people, he has to spend a lot of time **shaking hands**.

as spoken: If a can'idut wants ta be popul'r with the people, he hasta spend a lod 'a time **pressing the flesh**.

SYNONYM: SEE — **glad hand**, *p. 203*.

private sector *n.* the business community.

example: The **private sector** is angry with the president because he didn't keep his promise to cut taxes.

translation: The **business community** is angry with the president because he didn't keep his promise to cut taxes.

as spoken: The **private sect'r**'s angry with the president 'cuz 'e didn't keep 'is promise ta cut taxes.

ALSO: **public sector** *n.* the government.

ramrod (to) *v.* to push something through forcefully and quickly.

example: She was able to **ramrod** the bill through Congress without a problem.

translation: She was able to **push** the bill through Congress without a problem.

as spoken: She was able da **ramrod** the bill through Congress withoud a problem.

NOTE: The verb *to ramrod* refers to the action of taking a metal rod and using it to force the charge into the barrel of a cannon.

returns *n.* election results.

example: The **returns** are just starting to come in from the polls.

translation: The **election results** are just starting to come in from the polls.

as spoken: The **r'turns**'er jus' starding ta come in fr'm the polls.

right-winger *n.* a person with conservative views.

example: My grandfather is a **right-winger**. He strongly supports states' rights.

translation: My grandfather is a **person of conversative views**. He strongly supports states' rights.

as spoken: My gran'father's a **right-winger**. He strongly supports states' rights.

ANTONYM: **left-winger** *n*. a person with liberal views.

run for office (to) *exp*. to compete in an election for a position in government.

example: This is the second time Ed has **run for office**. I think he has a good chance this time.

translation: This is the second time Ed has **competed in an election**. I think he has a good chance this time.

as spoken: This is the secon' time Ed's **run fer office**. I think 'e has a good chance this time.

sit on the fence (to) *exp*. to be indecisive.

example: I wish he would stop **sitting on the fence**. He needs to take a strong position on this issue!

translation: I wish he would stop **being indecisive**. He needs to take a strong position on this issue!

as spoken: I wish 'e'd stop **sidding on the fence**. He needs ta take a strong position on this issue!

SYNONYM: **wishy-washy (to be)** *adj*.

ANTONYM: **take a stand (to)** *exp*. to be decisive.

slip (to) *v*. to decline.

example: Tim's popularity is starting to **slip**.

translation: Tim's popularity is starting to **decline**.

as spoken: Tim's popyalaridy's starding ta **slip**.

solidify one's position (to) *exp*. to form a definite opinion, take a stand.

example: The candidate has **solidified her position** on school busing.

translation: The candidate has **formed a definite opinion** regarding school busing.

as spoken: The can'idut's **solidified 'er position** on school busing.

stump (to) *v.* to travel from town to town making political speeches.

example: Mr. President, since elections are coming up soon, I think it would be a good idea for you to start **stumping**.

translation: Mr. President, since elections are coming up soon, I think it would be a good idea for you to start **touring and making political speeches**.

as spoken: Mr. President, since elections'er coming up soon, I think it'd be a good idea fer you da start **stumping**.

NOTE: At one time, it was common to see a politician making speeches while standing on a tree stump.

third party ticket (run on a) *exp.* to enter an election campaign representing an independent party (other than the Democratic or Republican party).

example: She's **running on a third party ticket**, probably as a Libertarian.

translation: She's **entering the election campaign representing an independent party**, probably as a Libertarian.

as spoken: She's **running on a third pardy ticket**, prob'ly as a Libertarian.

turnout *n.* attendance.

example: We had a terrific **turnout** at the rally on campus!

translation: We had a terrific **attendance** at the political demonstration on campus!

as spoken: We had a terrific **turnoud** at the rally on campus!

waffle (to) *v.* to be vague and misleading, to evade an issue.

example: I just don't trust him. He keeps **waffling** on the issues. First he takes one position on an issue, then suddenly states a different position.

translation: I just don't trust him. He keeps **evading** the issues. First he takes one position on an issue, then suddenly states a different position.

as spoken: I jus' don't trust 'im. He keeps **waffling** on the issues. First 'e takes one position on 'n issue, th'n suddenly states a diff'rent p'sition.

wrapped up *adj.* to be won.

example: Even before the final results come in, I think we can safely assume that you have this election all **wrapped up**!

translation: Even before the final results come in, I think we can safely assume that you have this election **won**!

as spoken: Even before the final r'sults come in, I think we c'n safely assume th't chu have this election all **wrapped up**!

SYNONYM: **all sewn up** *adj.*

Practice the Vocabulary

(Answers to Lesson 8, p. 277)

A. Underline the appropriate word that best completes the phrase.

1. Last week the senator went on a (**junket**, **gubernatorial race**, **GOP**) to California.

2. The governor is not being decisive. Instead, he's (**standing**, **lying**, **sitting**) on the fence.

3. In every political race, there is always a lot of mud-(**throwing**, **slinging**, **tossing**).

4. The laws of the United States are passed on Capitol (**Hill**, **GOP**, **Mountain**).

5. We have to go to the (**platform**, **polls**, **private sector**) today and vote.

6. There was a good voter turn(**up**, **down**, **out**) today!

7. In another hour, this election should be all wrapped (**up**, **down**, **out**).

8. The president meets hundreds of people every day. I don't think I'd like pressing the (**hands**, **flesh**, **people**) all day long.

9. Some day, I'm going to (**run**, **press the flesh**, **turnout**) for office.

10. I wish the senator would stop (**waffling**, **mud-slinging**, **ramrodding**) on the issues and take a firm position!

B. CROSSWORD
Fill in the crossword puzzle on page 198 by choosing the correct word(s) from the list below.

waffle	**stump**	**office**
clip	**ticket**	**gubernatorial**
turnout	**platform**	**wrapped**
hawk	**sector**	**returns**
demagoguery	**bloc**	**fence**
ramrod	**junket**	**mud**
road	**winger**	**press**
position	**hill**	**poll**

ACROSS

13. ____ **(to)** *v.* to be vague and misleading, to evade an issue.

26. ____ *n.* attendance.

37. ____ *n.* one who supports agressive military policy.

42. ____ *n.* the use of popular prejudices and misleading claims to gain political power.

50. ____ **(to)** *v.* to push something through forcefully and quickly.

54. **middle of the** ____ *exp.* neutral.

55. **solidify one's** ____ **(to)** *exp.* to form a definite opinion.

59. ____ **(to)** *v.* to travel from town to town making political speeches.

61. **run on a third party** ____ **(to)** *exp.* to enter an election campaign representing an independent party.

69. ____ *n.* the plan represented by a person running for office.

78. **private** ____ *exp.* the business community.

DOWN

8. ____ *n.* a group of people united by a commonality such as age, race, religion, etc.

12. ____ *n.* a trip made at public expense by a politician to conduct official business.

13. **right-** ____ *exp.* a person with conservative views.

27. **run for** ____ **(to)** *exp.* to compete in an election for a position in government.

33. ____ **race** *exp.* a contest for the election of governor.

38. ____ **up (to be all)** *exp.* to be won.

43. ____ *n.* election results.

51. **sit on the** ____ **(to)** *exp.* to be indecisive.

60. ____**-slinging** *exp.* criticizing and condemnation of an opponent.

66. ____ **the flesh (to)** *exp.* to go around meeting people and shaking hands.

69. ____ *n.* survey.

CROSSWORD PUZZLE

C. True or false?

1. A **hawk** does not support military intervention.
   ☐ True ☐ False

2. A **junket** is a trip made by a politician to conduct official business.
   ☐ True ☐ False

3. A politician who goes around **pressing the flesh** is in the process of meeting people and shaking hands.
   ☐ True ☐ False

4. A **right-winger** is a person with conservative views and opinions.
   ☐ True ☐ False

5. The **private sector** refers to the group of people living in private residences.
   ☐ True ☐ False

6. A **bloc** is a group of people united by a commonality such as age, race, religion, etc.
   ☐ True ☐ False

7. A politician who is said to **sit on the fence** is very decisive.
   ☐ True ☐ False

8. If a politician's popularity starts to **slip**, he or she is gaining support.
   ☐ True ☐ False

9. A politician who **waffles on the issues** is being vague and misleading.
   ☐ True ☐ False

10. To **stump** means to lose an election.
    ☐ True ☐ False

A CLOSER LOOK:
Common Political Slang & Jargon

absentee ballot *n.* a ballot completed prior to an election by a voter who will not able to be present at the polling place.

example: Since we're not going to be in town on election day, let's be sure to request an **absentee ballot.**

translation: Since we're not going to be in town on election day, let's be sure to request a **ballot completed prior to an election by a voter who will not be present at the polling place**.

as spoken: Since w'r not gonna be in town on election day, let's be sher da request 'n **absentee ballot**.

affair *n.* a fund-raising event.

example: Tomorrow's Congressional **affair** is going to cost $1,000 a plate.

translation: Tomorrow's Congressional **fund-raising event** is going to cost $1,000 a plate.

as spoken: Tamorrow's Congressional **affair**'s gonna cost a thousan' dollers a plate.

bill *n.* a draft of a proposed law presented to a legislative body for enactment.

example: Our **bill** will probably require many changes before we can expect it to be passed.

translation: Our **draft of proposed law** will probably require many changes before we can expect it to be passed.

as spoken: 'Ar **bill** will prob'ly r'quire many changes before we c'n expect it ta be passed.

carpetbagger *n.* an arrogant politician who anticipates success in a new locality.

example: The recent election brought a lot of **carpet baggers** to the House of Representatives.

translation: The recent election brought a lot of **arrogant politicians who anticipate success in their new locality** to the House of Representatives.

as spoken: The recen' election brod a lod 'a **carpet baggers** ta the House of Represen'adives.

caucus *n.* • **1.** a group of people with similar political beliefs and goals • **2.** a meeting.

example (1): The new legislation isn't popular with the Congressional Black **Caucus**.

translation: The new legislation isn't popular with the Congressional Black **group**.

as spoken: The new legislation isn't popul'r with the Congression'l Black **Caucus**.

example (2): There will be a **caucus** at noon regarding the new tax law.

translation: There will be a **meeting** at noon regarding the new tax law.

as spoken: They'll be a **caucus** 'ut noon r'garding the new tax law.

censure (to) *v.* to reprimand, criticize.

example: The Senator was **censured** because of his unacceptable comments regarding women.

translation: The Senator was **reprimanded** because of his unacceptable comments regarding women.

as spoken: The Senader was **censured** 'cuz of 'is unacceptable comments r'garding women.

convene (to) *v.* to assemble (as in a meeting), to come together.

example: We are going to **convene** at noon to discuss the new law.

translation: We are going to **meet** at noon to discuss the new law.

as spoken: W'r gonna **convene** 'ut noon ta discuss the new law.

deliberate (to) *v.* to discuss, ponder, consider, or reflect.

example: The group **deliberated** the new environmental laws for several weeks.

translation: The group **discussed** the new environmental laws for several weeks.

as spoken: The group **deliberaded** the new envi'ermen'al laws fer sev'ral weeks.

filibuster • **1.** *v.* to speak for a lengthy period of time, preventing legislative activity •

2. *n.* a tactic used to delay or prevent legislative activity.

example (1): Senator Foghorn usually **filibusters** by reading from the Bible.

translation: Senator Foghorn usually **speaks for a lengthy period of time** by reading from the Bible.

as spoken: Senader Foghorn ujally **filibusders** by reading fr'm the Bible.

example (2): Senator Foghorn began his **filibuster** by reading from the Bible.

translation: Senator Foghorn began his **delay tactic** by reading from the Bible.

as spoken: Senader Foghorn began 'is **filibusder** by reading fr'm the Bible.

floor *n.* the main area of the Senate or the House of Representatives where debating and voting occurs.

example: The discussion on the **floor** of the Senate was very heated.

translation: The discussion on the **main area** of the Senate was very heated.

as spoken: The discussion on the **floor** of the Senate was very heeded.

ALSO: **have the floor (to)** *exp.* to have permission to speak (permission granted by the chairperson).

example: Mr. Jones, you **have the floor**.

translation: Mr. Jones, you **have permission to speak**.

as spoken: [no change]

freshman *n.* an elected official serving his/her first term.

example: It's unlikely that Steve will be appointed to a committee because he's a **freshman**.

translation: It's unlikely that Steve will be appointed to a committee because he's an **elected official serving his first term**.

as spoken: It's unlikely that Steve'll be appoin(t)ed to a commidee 'cuz 'e's a **freshm'n**.

gag rule *n.* a ruling that forbids anyone from revealing information presented during an official meeting or hearing.

example: The chairman of the Senate imposed a **gag rule** on the recent hearing.

translation: The chairman of the Senate imposed a **ruling that forbids anyone from revealing information presented during the official meeting**.

as spoken: The chairm'n 'a the Senate imposed a **gag rule** on the recent hearing.

gavel-to-gavel *adj.* a period from the opening session to the closing session of the Senate or the House of Representatives (also used in reference to a court trial).

example: The media coverage of the recent Senate hearing was **gavel-to-gavel**.

translation: The media coverage of the recent Senate hearing was **from the opening session to the closing session**.

as spoken: The media coverage 'a the recent Senate hearing was **gavel-da-gavel**.

NOTE: This is commonly referred to as *gavel-to-gavel coverage*.

glad-hand (to) *v.* said of a politician who goes around meeting people and shaking hands to stay in good favor with the public.

example: You can always tell it's election time. All of the politicians are busy **glad-handing**.

translation: You can always tell it's election time. All of the politicians are busy **meeting people and shaking hands to stay in good favor with the public**.

as spoken: You c'n always tell it's alection time. All 'a the politicians'er busy **glad-handing**.

SYNONYM: SEE — **press the flesh (to)**, *p. 190*.

GOP *n.* (an abbreviation for the "*Grand Old Party*") another name for the Republican Party.

example: In 1860, four years after the formation of the **GOP**, Abraham Lincoln became the first Republican president.

translation: In 1860, four years after the formation of the **Grand Old Party**, Abraham Lincoln became the first Republican president.

as spoken: In 1860, four years after the f'rmation of the **GOP**, Abraham Lincoln b'came the first Republican president.

grandstand (to) *v.* to try to impress an audience through speech or action.

example: I'm sick and tired of watching these politicians **grandstand**.

translation: I'm sick and tired of watching these politicians **trying to impress an audience**.

as spoken: I'm sick 'n tired of watching these politicians **gran'stand**.

grass roots *n.* having to do with the general public or the average person.

example: John will be helped in his bid for election because his popularity comes right from the **grass roots**.

translation: John will be helped in his bid for election because his popularity comes right from the **average person**.

as spoken: John'll be helped in 'is bid fer alection 'cuz 'is popyalaridy comes right fr'm the **grass roots**.

hearing *n.* a meeting held to investigate actions or behavior.

example: The **hearing** has been delayed because one of the members is busy on another committee.

translation: The **meeting held to investigate actions or behavior** has been delayed because one of the members is busy on another committee.

as spoken: The **hearing**'s been delayed 'cuz one 'a the members is busy on another commidee.

hit list *n.* a list of regulations or laws that a political group wishes to modify or eliminate.

example: The Republican Party has put environmental regulations on their **hit list**.

translation: The Republican Party has put environmental regulations on their **list of regulations or laws that they wish to eliminate**.

as spoken: The Republic'n Pardy'z pud envi'ermen(t)al regulations on their **hit list**.

incumbent *n.* someone currently holding office.

example: I always vote for **incumbents** because they have the most experience.

translation: I always vote for **those currently holding office** because they have the most experience.

as spoken: I always vote fer **incumbents** 'cuz they have the most experience.

in the running *exp.* to be under consideration for (a job, a government position, an appointment, etc.).

example: I've just heard that Jane is **in the running** for the new Cabinet post.

translation: I've just heard that Jane is **under consideration** for the new Cabinet post.

as spoken: I've just heard that Jane is **in the running** for the new Cabinet post.

lame duck *n.* an elected official who is not eligible to run for another term.

example: The President of the United States is a **lame duck** in his second term.

translation: The President of the United States is **not eligible to run again for president** in his second term.

as spoken: The President of the United States is a **lame duck** in 'is secon' term.

legislation *n.* • **1.** proposed law • **2.** a law which has already been passed.

example (1): There was a heated discussion in the House of Representatives concerning **legislation** to increase taxes.

translation: There was a heated discussion in the House of Representatives concerning a **proposed law** to increase taxes.

as spoken: There was a heeded discussion in the House of Represen'adives c'ncerning **legislation** ta increase taxes.

example (2): The President has just signed the new environmental **legislation**.

translation: The President has just signed the new environmental **law already passed in Congress**.

as spoken: The President jus' signed the new envi'ermen'al **legislation**.

PAC *n.* (Political Action Committee) a group of politically active people who try to influence legislation.

example: The Forest Products **PAC** has been trying to weaken United States Forest Service regulations for years.

translation: The Forest Products **Political Action Committee** has been trying to weaken United States Forest Service regulations for years.

as spoken: The Forest Produc's **PAC** 'ez been trying ta weaken U.S. Forest Service regulations for years.

panel *n.* a group of individuals assembled for a hearing.

example: The Senate **panel** will be appointed later this year.

translation: The Senate **group assembled for a hearing** will be appointed later this year.

as spoken: The Senate **panel** will be appoin(t)ed lader this year.

pigeonhole (to) *v.* to postpone voting on a bill by delaying its presentation to a voting body.

example: After reviewing the Crime Bill, some members of the Committee have threatened to **pigeonhole** it.

translation: After reviewing the Crime Bill, some members of the Committee have threatened to **delay its presentation to the voting body**.

as spoken: After r'viewing the Crime Bill, some members 'a the Commidee 'ev threatened ta **pigeonhole** it.

pork barrel *n.* government funding that results in significant patronage benefits.

example: Senator Claghorn complains about unnecessary government spending but when it comes to his own state, he's very generous with the **pork barrel**.

translation: Senator Claghorn complains about unnecessary government spending but when it comes to his own state, he's very generous with **government funding that results in significant patronage benefits**.

as spoken: Senader Claghorn c'mplains aboud unnecessary gover'ment spending b't when it comes to 'is own state, he's very generous with the **pork barrel**.

precinct *n.* an election district of a city or town.

example: We won't know if our representative has been re-elected until the results from the last **precinct** come in.

translation: We won't know if our representative has been re-elected until the results from the last **election district** come in.

as spoken: We won't know if 'ar represen'adive 'es been re-elected until the r'sults fr'm the las' **precinct** come in.

prop *n.* (proposition) a proposed law presented directly to the voting public for enactement.

example: **Prop** 13 passed overwhelmingly!

translation: **Proposition** 13 passed overwhelmingly!

as spoken: [no change]

ride one's coattails (to) *exp.* said of a successful candidate who identifies with a popular elected official.

example: The only reason Mark won the election is because the voters identify him with a popular governor. He certainly **rode on his coattails** in this election.

translation: The only reason Mark won the election is because the voters identify him with a popular governor. He certainly **identified himself with a popular elected official** in this election.

as spoken: The only reason Mark won the election is 'cuz the voders iden'ify 'im with a popul'r gove'ner. He certainly **rode on 'is coattails** in this alection.

running mate *n.* political companion in an election, especially president and vice president.

example: The governors' **running mate** has been very popular in her district.

translation: The governors' **political companion** has been very popular in her district.

as spoken: The governers' **running mate** has b'n very popul'r in 'er distric.

sweep *n.* an overwhelming election victory.

example: The mayor is so popular that his campaign staff expects him to win by a **sweep**.

translation: The mayor is so popular that his campaign staff expects him to win by an **overwhelming victory**.

as spoken: The mayor's so popular thad 'is campaign staff expects 'im ta win by a **sweep**.

SYNONYM: **landslide** *n.*

table an issue (to) *v.* to postpone discussion on, or consideration of, a piece of legislation.

example: The subcommittee has decided to **table** the new legislation because of questions regarding its constitutionality.

translation: The subcommittee has decided to **postpone discussion on** the new legislation because of questions regarding its constitutionality.

as spoken: The subcommidee's decided ta **table** the new legislation 'cuz of questions regarding its constitutionalidy.

term *n.* a period of time during which an elected official holds office.

example: A United States senator has a **term** of six years, whereas the president's term is four years.

translation: A United States senator **holds office** for six years, whereas the president's term is four years.

as spoken: A U.S. senader has a **term** of six years, whereas the president's term is four years.

veto (to) *v.* to reject, cancel.

example: The President has stated that he will **veto** this new bill.

translation: The President has stated that he will **reject** this new bill.

as spoken: The President stated that he'll **vedo** this new bill.

Practice Political Slang & Jargon

(Answers, p. 278)

A. Choose the correct definition of the words in boldface.

1. **bill**:
   a. a ballot completed prior to an election by a voter who will not be present at the polling place
   b. a draft of proposed law presented to a legislative body

2. **caucus**:
   a. a group of people or a meeting
   b. the main area of the Senate or the House of Representatives

3. **grassroots**:
   a. having to do with the general public or the average person
   b. a meeting to investigate actions or behavior.

4. **carpet bagger**:
   a. a tactic used to delay or prevent legislative activity
   b. an arrogant politician who anticipates success in a new locality

5. **to deliberate**:
   a. to reprimand
   b. to discuss

6. **lame duck**:
   a. someone currently holding office
   b. an elected official who is not eligible to run for another term

7. **to filibuster**:
   a. to assemble
   b. to speak for a lengthy period of time to prevent legislative activity

8. **to grandstand**:
   a. said of a politician who goes around meeting people and shaking hands to stay in good favor with the public
   b. to speak or act so as to impress an audience

9. **to pigeonhole**:
   a. said of a successful candidate who identifies with a popular elected official
   b. to postpone voting on a bill by delaying its presentation to a voting body

10. **gag rule**:
   a. a ruling that forbids anyone from revealing information which was presented during an official meeting or hearing
   b. a ruling that allows anyone to reveal information which was presented during an official meeting or hearing

LESSON NINE

Management Slang & Jargon
(Part A)

*Laura always believes in applying the **KISS** principle.*

Lesson Nine

Dialogue in slang

Kim: So, how did your **power lunch** go with the new **consultants**?

Laura: Really well. They're scheduled to **interface** with our **CEO**s and suggest changes to our **business plan** that will help us **restructure**. In fact, they've even offered to help us rewrite the plan.

Kim: H'mm, I see a **glitch**. Our **bean counters** aren't going to let us spend a lot of money on consultants. The **honchos** are always telling them to watch the **bottom line**. In fact, if we don't get some **rainmakers** in here soon, they're talking about **downsizing** and you know what that means...**the ax**!

Laura: Don't worry. The consultants are doing this **on spec**. It'll be **quick-and-dirty**, but it'll give the **corporation** a good idea of how we can effectively **license** our products. They really seem to understand the **nuts and bolts** of our company. They're convinced that we're the **sunrise industry** of the next decade!

Kim: Sounds exciting. Keep me **in the loop** on this. And don't forget to apply the **KISS** principle along the way!

Lesson Nine

Translation of dialogue in standard English

Management Slang & Jargon (Part A)

Kim: So, how did your **important business lunch** go with the new **independent specialist**?

Laura: Really well. They're scheduled to **communicate** with our **chief executive officers** and suggest changes to our **company blueprint** that will help us **make big changes in operation**. In fact, they've even offered to help us rewrite the plan.

Kim: H'mm, I see a **problem**. Our **accountants** aren't going to let us spend a lot of money on consultants. The **executives** are always telling them to watch **how we spend money**. In fact, if we don't get some **successful salespeople** in here soon, they're talking about **reducing the staff** and you know what that means...**the end of our jobs**!

Laura: Don't worry. The consultants are doing this **speculatively**. It'll be **done quickly without a lot of attention to details**, but it'll give the **business, which is composed of investors** a good idea on how we can effectively **charge and authorize people to use** our products. They really seem to understand the **details** of our company. They're convinced that we're **the potential growth industry** of the next decade!

Kim: Sounds exciting. Keep me **informed** on this. And don't forget to apply the **Keep It Simple, Stupid** principle along the way!

Lesson Nine

Dialogue in slang as it would be heard

Management Slang & Jargon (Part A)

Kim: So, how'd your **power lunch** go with the new **consultants**?

Laura: Really well. They're scheduled ta **in(t)erface** with 'ar **CEO**s 'n suggest changes ta 'ar **bizness plan** that'll help us **restructure**. In fact, they even offered ta help us rewrite the plan.

Kim: H'mm, I see a **glitch**. Our **bean coun(t)ers** aren't gonna let us spend a lod 'ev money on consultants. The **honchos**'er always telling th'm ta watch the **boddom line**. In fact, if we don't get s'm **rainmakers** in here soon, they're talking about **downsizing** and 'ju know what that means...**thee ax**!

Laura: Don't worry. The consultants'er doing this **on spec**. Id'll be **quick-'n-dirdy**, bud id'll give the **corperation** a good idea 'ev how we c'n effectively **license** 'ar produc's. They really seem ta understand the **nuts 'n bolts** 'ev 'ar company. They're convinced that we're the **sunrise industry** of the next decade!

Kim: Soun's exciting. Keep me **in the loop** on this. And don't ferget ta apply the **KISS** principle along the way!

Vocabulary

ax (the) *exp.* to be dismissed from one's job, fired.

example: Did you hear the news? John got **the ax** this morning!

translation: Did you hear the news? John got **fired** this morning!

as spoken: Didja hear the news? John got **the ax** this morning!

ALSO: **get axed (to)** *v.* to get fired.

bean counter *n.* shortsighted accountant or bureaucrat.

example: We'll have to cancel our project. The **bean counters** don't want us to spend any more money on it.

translation: We'll have to cancel our project. The **accountants** don't want us to spend any more money on it.

as spoken: We'll hafta cancel 'ar project. The **bean coun(t)ers** don't wan' us ta spend any more money on it.

bottom line *n.* **1.** the last line of an income or financial statement • **2.** the basic issue in a discussion.

example (1): The value of our stock will continue to drop if we can't do something about our **bottom line**.

translation: The value of our stock will continue to drop if we can't do something about our **income**.

as spoken: The value of 'ar stock'll c'ntinue da drop if we can't do something aboud 'ar **boddom line**.

example (2): I've listened to all of your concerns. But let's get to the **bottom line**. If we don't cut our expenses, we'll be out of business within the year.

translation: I've listened to all of your concerns. But let's get to the **the basic issue**. If we don't cut our expenses, we'll be out of business within the year.

as spoken: I've listened to all of yer c'ncerns. But let's get ta the **boddom line**. If we don't cud "R" expenses, w'll be oudda business within thee year.

business plan *n.* a blueprint by which a new business lists its executive, financial, and product goals for the purpose of obtaining financing.

example: We need to have a well-written **business plan** before the bank will consider giving us a loan.

translation: We need to have a well-written **blueprint of our company which lists our executive, financial and product goals** before the bank will consider giving us a loan.

as spoken: We need ta have a well-written **business plan** before the bank'll c'nsider giving us a loan.

CEO *n.* (chief executive officer) the person ultimately responsible for a company's success or failure.

example: After Acme Corporation lost money for the fourth quarter in a row, the **CEO** was fired.

translation: After Acme Corporation lost money for the fourth quarter in a row, the **chief executive officer** was fired.

as spoken: After Acme Corperation lost money fer the fourth quarder in a row, the **C-E-O** was fired.

consultant *n.* an independent contractor (hired on a time or project basis) who gives professional or expert advice.

example: We're going to need a software **consultant** to develop our new product.

translation: We're going to need a software **specialist** to develop our new product.

as spoken: W'r gonna need a software **c'nsultant** ta develop 'ar new product.

corporation *n.* a business entity composed of investors (or stockholders), each of whose liability is limited to the amount invested.

example: Remember that as a stockholder in our **corporation**, your liability is limited to the amount you choose to invest.

translation: Remember that as a stockholder in our **business, which is composed of investors**, your liability is limited to the amount you choose to invest.

as spoken: R'member th'd 'ez a stockholder in 'ar **corperation**, yer liabilidy's limided ta thee amount you choose ta invest.

downsizing *v.* reducing staff or personnel to minimize operating costs and improve efficiency.

example: Joe is pretty worried because his company is in the process of **downsizing** and he doesn't know if his job is secure.

translation: Joe is pretty worried because his company is in the process of **reducing personnel** and he doesn't know if his job is secure.

as spoken: Joe's preddy worried 'cuz 'is company's in the process of **downsizing** an'e doesn' know if 'is job's secure.

glitch *n.* a problem, "bug," obstacle which prevents the completion of a project.

example: We can't perform our final accounting procedure until we resolve this **glitch**.

translation: We can't perform our final accounting procedure until we resolve this **problem**.

as spoken: We can't perform 'ar fin'l accoun(t)ing pracedure until we r'solve this **glitch**.

honcho *n.* (from the Japanese term *hancho*) squad or group leader; person in charge of a work detail.

example: With two consecutive quarters of poor profits, it's important that we get all of our **honchos** in here for a sales meeting.

translation: With two consecutive quarters of poor profits, it's important that we get all of our **group leaders** in here for a sales meeting.

as spoken: With two consecudive quarders 'ev poor profits, it's important th't we ged all of 'ar **honchos** in here fer a sales meeding.

VARIATION: **head honcho** *n.*

ALSO -1: **big banana** *n.* boss.

ALSO -2: **top dog** *n.* boss.

interface (to) *v.* to communicate or interact with (another person).

example: We'd better clear up the discrepancies on these sales brochures. I want the sales and graphics departments to **interface** as soon as possible.

translation: We'd better clear up the discrepancies on these sales brochures. I want the sales and graphics departments to **communicate** as soon as possible.

as spoken: We bedder clear up the discrep'ncies on these sales broch'res. I want the sales 'n graphics d'partm'nts ta **in(t)erface** 'ez soon 'ez possible.

KISS *exp.* (an acronym for Keep It Simple, Stupid) general advice to focus on reliability rather than unncessary features.

example: This morning I reviewed the plans for the addition to our office building and there are just too many unncessary features. We need to apply the **KISS** principle here.

translation: This morning I reviewed the plans for the addition to our office building and there are just too many unncessary features. We need to apply the **Keep It Simple, Stupid** principle here.

as spoken: Th's morning I r'viewed the plans fer the addition ta 'ar office building an' there'er jus' too many unncessary features. We need ta apply the **KISS** principle here.

license (to) *v.* to authorize, for a royalty or fee, the right to use a patent, trademark, process, or other item of value.

example: The illustrations that we used in our book are very clever. Let's see if we can **license** them for printing on T-shirts.

translation: The illustrations that we used in our book are very clever. Let's see if we can **authorize the use of** them for printing on T-shirts.

as spoken: The illustrations th't we used in 'ar book'er very clever. Let's see if we c'n **license** th'm fer prin(t)ing on T-shirts.

loop *n.* a process by which information travels inter- or intra-office.

example: That's the third time this month I haven't received the sales figures. It's frustrating being out of the **loop**.

translation: That's the third time this month I haven't received the sales figures. It's frustrating being out of the **inter-office information process**.

as spoken: That's the third time this month I haven't received the sales figures. It's frustrading being oudda the **loop**.

nuts and bolts • **1.** *n.* the working parts • **2.** *adj.* (as an adjective, hyphens are used: nuts-and-bolts) experienced or well-trained in the fundamentals.

example (1): This is a very complicated business. It's going to take us some time to learn the **nuts and bolts** of this operation.

translation: This is a very complicated business. It's going to take us some time to learn the **basics** of this operation.

as spoken: This is a very complicaded business. It's gonna take us s'm time ta learn the **nuts 'n bolts** of this operation.

example (2): With all the complicated equipment we're installing, we have to consider adding a **nuts-and-bolts** person to our management team.

translation: With all the complicated equipment we're installing, we have to consider adding a **person well-trained in the basics** to our management team.

as spoken: With all the complicaded equipment w'r installing, we hafta c'nsider adding a **nuts-'n-bolts** person ta 'ar management team.

on spec *exp.* work of a speculative nature; performing preliminary development for no fee hoping that the client will agree to a full contract.

example: We've been asked to submit a proposal for the software rewrite **on spec**. Let's make sure we do a good job so we will land the contract.

translation: We've been asked to submit a proposal for the software rewrite **on a speculative basis**. Let's make sure we do a good job so we will land the contract.

as spoken: We've b'n asked ta submid a prapos'l fer the software rewride **on spec**. Let's make sher we do a good job so w'll lan' the contract.

NOTE: **land a contract (to)** *exp.* to sign a contract with a client.

power lunch *n.* a midday meal where major business deals are discussed and confirmed.

example: Charlie's back from his **power lunch**. That's the fifth major contract he's landed this week.

translation: Charlie's back from his **business lunch**. That's the fifth major contract he's landed this week.

as spoken: Charlie's back fr'm 'is **power lunch**. That's the fifth major contract 'e's landed this week.

ALSO: **power breakfast** *n.*

quick-and-dirty *adj.* said of work performed rapidly and without careful planning, fast and simple.

example: Let's not worry about the details. We just need a **quick-and-dirty** financial report.

translation: Let's not worry about the details. We just need a **fast and simple** financial report.

as spoken: Let's not worry about the details. We jus' need a **quick-'n-dirdy** financial r'port.

rainmaker *n.* a successful salesperson, one who brings in a lot of business due to his/her influence.

example: Look at all the clients Susan has signed up this month. She's a real **rainmaker**.

translation: Look at all the clients Susan has signed up this month. She's a real **successful salesperson**.

as spoken: Look 'it all the clients Susan's signed up this month. She's a real **rainmaker**.

restructure (to) *v.* to make significant and fundamental changes in a company's financial structure or operations.

example: The new CEO has been brought in for one reason: to **restructure** the company.

translation: The new Chief Executive Officer has been brought in for one reason: to **make significant and fundamental changes** in the company.

as spoken: The new CEO's been brod in fer one reason: ta **restructure** the company.

sunrise industry *n.* a new potential growth industry (such as micro-computers in the 1970s.)

example: It's hard to predict what the **sunrise industry** will be in the year 2020.

translation: It's hard to predict what the **new potential growth industry** will be in the year 2020.

as spoken: It's hard ta predict wh't the **sunrise industry**'ll be in the year two thousan' twen'y.

Practice the Vocabulary

(Answers to Lesson Nine, p.278)

A. Complete the sentences by choosing the appropriate word from the list below.

bolts	**honchos**	**rainmaker**
dirty	**loop**	**spec**
downsizing	**power**	**sunrise**

1. I don't have time to make you a detailed report right now. For the moment, I'll just give you something quick-and-__________ .

2. Make sure to keep me in the ______________ on this project. It's important that I stay informed.

3. I'm having a ____________ lunch today with the sales department to try and figure out new ways to increase our sales.

4. I agreed to do this one project on ____________ . Hopefully, the client will like my work and give me a large profitable job.

5. The new manager really understands the nuts and __________ of our company.

6. I just heard that the ____________ are considering giving you a promotion!

7. If the company doesn't make more money this year, they may start _________________ .

8. It looks like we're a _________________ industry. Our business grows every year.

9. Our new salesperson is a real ____________________ . It's amazing how much money he brought in last month.

B. Underline the correct definition of the word(s) in boldface.

1. **the ax**:
   a. employment
   b. dismissal from one's job

2. **bean counter**:
   a. lawyer
   b. accountant

3. **to interface**:
   a. to communicate or interact with another person
   b. to fire an employee

4. **glitch**:
   a. a product that makes a company a lot of money
   b. an obstacle, problem

5. **KISS**:
   a. an acronym for "Keep International Shipments Safe"
   b. an acronym for "Keep It Simple, Stupid"

6. **bottom line**:
   a. the loading dock
   b. the last line of an income or financial statement

7. **business plan**:
   a. a company's list of employees
   b. a blueprint by which a new business lists its goals and objectives for the purpose of obtaining financing

8. **downsizing**:
   a. the process of hiring new employees
   b. the process of reducing personnel

9. **nuts and bolts**:
   a. useless and unproductive employees
   b. details, technicalities

10. **loop**:
    a. a process by which information travels inter- or intra-office
    b. the telephone

C. CONTEXT EXERCISE
Write the letter of the phrase from the right column that goes with the phrase to the left.

☐ 1. We need to hire an advertising **consultant** to help us promote our new products.

☐ 2. Karen is a real **rainmaker**.

☐ 3. This one time, I'll do all my work on **spec**.

☐ 4. This new computer program doesn't work correctly. It has a severe **glitch**.

☐ 5. After ABC Corporation lost money for the fifth time, the **CEO** was fired.

☐ 6. I hope the new **bean counter** will be able to help us budget our finances.

☐ 7. I just heard that the company is about to **restructure**!

☐ 8. Why don't we **license** our cartoon characters for some commercial products?

☐ 9. Did you meet the new **honcho**?

☐ 10. Steve got the **ax** this morning!

A. You'd better not use it in case it does some irreversible damage to a computer file.

B. He said he would fire anyone who is ever late!

C. We could contact shirt companies and see if they would be interested in printing them on T-shirts!

D. I sure wouldn't want to be responsible for the success or failure of a company!

E. Next time I'm going to have to charge you.

F. Last year she made more money for the company than anyone else.

G. I never even had a chance to say goodbye.

H. That means that none of our jobs is secure!

I. I'm not sure about him. He keeps complaining that his checkbook is never balanced!

J. Once the public knows that they exist, I'm convinced that they will sell extremely well.

A CLOSER LOOK:
Management Slang & Jargon (Part A)

analysis-paralysis *exp.* all talk and no action.

example: Nothing ever gets done at this company because of their **analysis-paralysis** style of management.

translation: Nothing ever gets done at this company because of their **all-talk-and-no-action** style of management.

as spoken: Nothing ever gets done 'it this company 'cuz 'a their **analysis-paralysis** style of management.

audit trail *n.* the method of recording each step of a transaction.

example: We need an **audit trail** to check the accuracy of our financial report.

translation: We need a **method of recording each step of our transactions** to check the accuracy of our financial report.

as spoken: We need 'n **audit trail** ta check the accuracy 'ev 'ar financial report.

black magic *n.* used to refer to the skills of a technical specialist who is able to accomplish results no one else can.

example: Get George down here right away. We need his **black magic** to fix our computer.

translation: Get George down here right away. We need some of his **special skills** to fix our computer.

as spoken: Get George down here ride away. We need some of 'is **black magic** ta fix 'ar c'mpuder.

boilerplate *n.* general structure of a contract's language that does not change from contract to contract.

example: We have the **boilerplate** of the contract on the computer. However, some specific points will need to be negotiated.

translation: We have the **general structure** of the contract on the computer. However, some specific points will need to be negotiated.

as spoken: We have the **boilerplade** of the contract on the c'mpuder. However, s'm specific points'll need ta be negotiated.

bootstrapping *n.* using a company's own resources to start up a new product line.

example: We're not going to be able to raise money at the bank for this new product line. We'll have to look at **bootstrapping**.

translation: We're not going to be able to raise money at the bank for this new product line. We'll have to look at **using our own resources**.

as spoken: W'r not gonna be able da raise money 'it the bank fer this new product line. W'll hafta look 'it **bootstrapping**.

bottom-up *exp.* a management style in which low-level personnel are encouraged to make suggestions for business operations.

example: Our **bottom-up** management style has greatly improved morale among the assembly line workers.

translation: Our **style of management where low-level personnel are encouraged to make suggestions for business operations** has greatly improved morale among the assembly line workers.

as spoken: 'Ar **boddom-up** management style 'ez greatly improved morale among the assembly line workers.

bulletize (to) *v.* to draw attention to important points in a document by the use of "bullets" (bold marks).

example: This memo is poorly organized. Why don't you **bulletize** it so readers can focus on the important points.

translation: This memo is poorly organized. Why don't you **draw attention to important points by using bullets (or bold marks)** so readers can focus on the important points.

as spoken: This memo's poorly org'nized. Why donchu **bulletize** it so readers c'n focus on thee important points.

bypass *v.* use of a company's internal resources to accomplish tasks not normally performed by that company.

example: Let's **bypass** the telephone company and simply install the new telephone lines ourselves.

translation: Let's **use our company's own internal resources to accomplish tasks usually performed by** the telephone company and simply install the new telephone lines ourselves.

as spoken: Let's **bypass** the phone company an' simply install the new phones lines 'ar-selves.

call report *n.* a report detailing a salesperson's calls/visits and customer responses to those calls/visits.

example: Let's evaluate our salespeople's performance by reviewing the **call reports**.

translation: Let's evaluate our salespeople's performance by reviewing their **reports detailing their customer reponses**.

as spoken: Let's evaluade 'ar salespeople's performance by r'viewing their **call r'ports**.

camel *exp.* ("a horse designed by committee") a project in which the elements are assembled by separate individuals without a clear picture of the final product. They intend to create a horse, but instead end up with a camel.

example: The new accounting software we developed turned out to be a **camel**. All of the modules work well individually, but are not compatible with each other.

translation: The new accounting software we developed turned out to be **poorly designed**. All of the modules work well individually, but are not compatible with each other.

as spoken: The new accoun(t)ing software we developed turned out ta be a **camel**. All 'a the modules work well individually, bud aren't c'mpadible w'th each other.

class action *n.* a legal action started by a small group of people on behalf of a larger group.

example: Your car broke down again?! Why don't you call Bill. He's organizing a **class action** against the manufacturer.

translation: Your car broke down again?! Why don't you call Bill. He's organizing **group legal action** against the manufacturer.

as spoken: Yer car broke down again?! Why donchu call Bill. He's org'nizing a **class action** against the manufacturer.

competition analysis *exp*. a euphemism for "corporate spying."

example: Joe conducted his **competition analysis** by reviewing phone records taken from our competitors' trash.

translation: Joe conducted his **corporate spying** by reviewing phone records taken from our competitors' trash.

as spoken: Joe c'nducted 'is **competition analysis** by r'viewing phone records taken from 'ar c'mpediders' trash.

conglomerate *n*. a big corporation made up of smaller companies, generally in unrelated businesses.

example: In today's market, a small company has great difficulty competing with **conglomerates**.

translation: In today's market, a small company has great difficulty competing with **big corporations made up of smaller companies**.

as spoken: In today's marked, a small company has great difficulty c'mpeding with **c'nglomerates**.

contract services *n*. work performed by outside contractors with a formal agreement.

example: These **contract services** are too expensive. In the future, in-house personnel will have to install software upgrades.

translation: These **outside contractors** are too expensive. In the future, in-house personnel will have to install software upgrades.

as spoken: These **contract services**'er too expensive. In the future, in-house personnel will hafta install software upgrades.

corpocracy *exp*. duplicate or excessive corporate management caused by multiple companies having merged.

example: With the **corpocracy** around here, it seems decisions are never finalized.

translation: With the **excessive corporate management** around here, it seems decisions are never finalized.

as spoken: With the **corpocracy** around here, it seems decisions'er never finalized.

corporate veil *n*. a shield under which stockholders are immune from legal action resulting from business failure.

example: Don't worry about the pending bankruptcy action. The **corporate veil** can't be pierced.

translation: Don't worry about the pending bankruptcy action. The **shield of immunity** can't be pierced.

as spoken: Don't worry about the pending bankrup'cy action. The **corp'rit veil** can't be pierced.

DBA *exp.* (doing business as; also referred to as a "fictitious name") used when a person or business known by one name choses to do business under a different name.

example: If we're going to start this new business, we're going to need to file a **DBA** statement.

translation: If we're going to start this new business, we're going to need to file a **doing-business-as** statement.

as spoken: If w'r gonna start this new business, w'r gonna need ta file a **D-B-A** statement.

de-diversify *v.* to sell off individual companies or divisions of a corporation not compatible with its main line of business.

example: I hope you're not going to lose your job when your company **de-diversifies**.

translation: I hope you're not going to lose your job when your company **sells off individual companies or divisions within your corporation**.

as spoken: I hope y'r not gonna lose yer job when yer company **de-diversifies**.

delphi technique *n.* a method of using outside experts in an interactive fashion to make company forecasts.

example: The company's forecasts have been very accurate since we applied the **delphi technique**.

translation: The company's forecasts have been very accurate since we applied **a method of using outside experts to make company forecasts**.

as spoken: The company's forecas'ev been very accurate since we applied the **delphi technique**.

delta *n.* Greek character depicted by a triangular symbol (Δ); used in mathematics to indicate "change in" – often used in business to represent a change.

example: What's the **delta** in our sales figures for this month compared to last month?

translation: What's the **change** in our sales figures for this month compared to last month?

as spoken: What's the **delta** in 'ar sales figures fer this month c'mpared ta las' month?

diagonal slice *n.* a randomly chosen employee cross-section (ranging from assembly line to middle management workers); the group is intended to meet with management as a way of improving communication.

example: We need to select a new **diagonal slice** for our upper level management meeting next month.

translation: We need to select a new **employee cross-section** for our upper level management meeting next month.

as spoken: We need ta select a new **diagn'l slice** fer 'ar upper level management meeding nex' month.

divest (to) *v.* said of a large company selling off certain lines of its business.

example: Management has decided **to divest** the accounting software division of the company we recently accquired. It just doesn't fit in with our current merchandise.

translation: Management has decided **to sell off** the accounting software division of the company we recently accquired. It just doesn't fit in with our current merchandise.

as spoken: Management's d'cided **ta divest** the accoun(t)ing software division of the company we recently accquired. It jus' doesn' fid in with 'ar current merchandise.

NOTE: **divestiture** *n.* the process of a large company selling off certain lines of its business.

downstream *v.* a movement of goods or funds from a parent company to a subsidiary company.

example: Rather than finding an outside vendor for starting materials, let's **downstream** our own product directly to our subsidiary.

translation: Rather than finding an outside vendor for starting materials, let's **move** our own product directly to our subsidiary.

as spoken: Rather th'n finding 'n outside vender fer starding materials, let's **downstream** 'ar own product directly ta 'ar s'bsidiary.

downtime *n.* an interval when no work can be performed due to equipment breakdown, power failure, employee breaks, etc.

example: We have to purchase more reliable machinery. With all the equipment failures, our **downtime** has been excessive this month.

translation: We have to purchase more reliable machinery. With all the equipment failures, **the interval when no work can be performed** has been excessive this month.

as spoken: We hafta perchase more reliable machinery. With all the equipment failures, 'ar **downtime** 'ez been excessive this month.

entrepreneur *n.* one who starts a business; founder.

example: George is quite the **entrepreneur**. He has started another flower shop!

translation: George is quite the **businessman**. He has started another flower shop!

as spoken: George is quite thee **entraprener**. He's starded another flower shop!

Filthy Five *n.* a list of companies compiled annually by *Mother Jones* magazine based on their poor environmental record.

example: I see that our company is not on the **Filthy Five** this year. The cleanup effort on our toxic waste pit has paid off.

translation: I see that our company is not on the **list of companies compiled annually by *Mother Jones* magazine.** The cleanup effort on our toxic waste pit has paid off.

as spoken: I see th'd 'ar company's nod on the **Filthy Five** this year. The cleanup efford on 'ar toxic waste pit 'ez paid off.

finder's fee *n.* a commission paid to a third party who locates a buyer, property, personnel, etc. that leads to a business deal between two other parties.

example: Our agent has a buyer for the business but his **finder's fee** might be more than we can afford.

translation: Our agent has a buyer for the business but his **commission** might be more than we can afford.

as spoken: 'Ar agent has a buyer fer the business bud 'is **finder's fee** might be more th'n we c'n afford.

functional management *n.* a management system based on a function, such as marketing or advertising, in contrast to being arranged around an end product.

example: Now that we are no longer a manufacturer, we need to take a serious look at **functional management**.

translation: Now that we are no longer a manufacturer, we need to take a serious look at **a management system based on a function, rather than arranged around an end product**.

as spoken: Now that w'r no longer a manufacturer, we need ta take a serious look 'it **functional management**.

general partner *n.* a partner who is generally responsible for the business and has unlimited liability.

example: Think carefully about this opportunity to become a **general partner**. If something goes wrong, your financial loss could be substantial.

translation: Think carefully about this opportunity to become a **partner who is generally responsible for the business and has unlimited liability**. If something goes wrong, your financial loss could be substantial.

as spoken: Think carefully about this oppertunidy da b'come a **general partner**. If something goes wrong, yer financial loss could be substantial.

SEE: **limited partner**, *p. 254*.

gold plating *n.* Useful but unnecessary features.

example: Since we bought new computers with these high performance options, we spent much more money than we needed to. We should have never let ourselves get talked into all of this **gold plating**.

translation: Since we bought new computers with these high performance options, we spent much more money than we needed to. We should have never let ourselves get talked into all of these **unnecessary features**.

as spoken: Since we bought new c'mpuders with these high performance options, we spent much more money th'n we needed to. We should've never led 'ar-selves get talked inta all 'a this **gold plading**.

governance *n.* a method or system of management that must be followed by the officers of a company.

example: This policy reflects our **governance**. We must adhere to it.

translation: This policy reflects our **system of management**. We must adhere to it.

as spoken: This policy r'flec's 'ar **governance**. We must adhere to it.

grandfather clause *n.* a provision in a new rule that exempts those already engaged in the activity affected by the rule.

example: I was worried that the new bank owners would raise the interest on my loan. Then I discovered that because of a **grandfather clause**, the interest rate cannot be increased.

translation: I was worried that the new bank owners would raise the interest on my loan. Then I discovered that because of a **provision that exempts those already engaged in the activity affected by the rule**, the interest rate cannot be increased.

as spoken: I was worried th't the new bank owners would raise the interest on my loan. Then I discovered that 'cuz of a **gran'father clause**, the interest rate can't be increased.

NOTE: The term originated during the Reconstruction following the U.S. Civil War when blacks were allowed to vote only if their grandfathers had voted before 1867.

hands-on *adj.* describes management style characterized by active personal involvement.

example: Joe's a very effective supervisor because of his **hands-on** management style.

translation: Joe's a very effective supervisor because of his **involved** management style.

as spoken: Joe's a very effecdive superviser 'cuz of 'is **han's-on** management style.

heuristics *n.* problem-solving by experimental or trial-and-error methods rather than formal mathematical techniques.

example: Since we have no formal mathematical model of the U.S. economy, we must rely on **heuristics** to assess the effects of a tax increase.

translation: Since we have no formal mathematical model of the United States economy, we must rely on **trail-and-error methods** to assess the effects of a tax increase.

as spoken: Since we have no form'l math'madic'l model of thee U.S. aconamy, we must rely on **heuristics** to assess thee effec's 'ev a tax increase.

housekeeping *n.* routine management of any system such as an office filing system.

example: If we can't get the **housekeeping** figured out in this office, we're not going to be able to keep anything organized.

translation: If we can't get the **routine management** figured out in this office, we're not going to be able to keep anything organized.

as spoken: If we can't get the **housekeeping** figured oud in this office, w'r not gonna be able to keep anything organized.

know-how license *n.* a contract for licensing a technology process to a vendor for commercial development.

example: We have a vendor interested in our new technology but we should finalize a **know-how license** before we provide any more details.

translation: We have a vendor interested in our new technology but we should finalize a **licensing contract** before we provide any more details.

as spoken: We have a vender int'rested in 'ar new technolagy but we should finalize a **know-how license** before we provide any more details.

Practice Management Slang & Jargon

(*Answers p. 279*)

A. Underline the word(s) that best complete(s) the phrase.

1. Since the bank won't give us a loan, we'll have to investigate (**corpocracy**, **bootstrapping**, **black magic**).

2. We have the (**boiler**, **audit**, **competition**)plate of the contract on the computer. However, some specific points will have to be negotiated.

3. Management has decided to (**bypass**, **divest**, **bulletize**) the accounting software division of the company that we recently acquired. It just doesn't fit in with our current merchandise.

4. Think carefully about this opportunity to become a general (**plating**, **venture**, **partner**). If something goes wrong, your financial loss could be substantial.

5. If we want a successful software business in China, we'll probably have to form a joint (**housekeeping**, **venture**, **heuristics**) with a Chinese software publisher.

6. If we can't get the (**housekeeping**, **know-how license**, **governance**) figured out in this office, we're not going to be able to keep anything organized.

7. Because these rules are (**hands-on**, **governance**, **gold plating**), we have no choice but to follow them.

8. Joe's a very effective supervisor because of his (**downstream**, **delta**, **hands-on**) management style.

9. George is quite the (**audit trail**, **conglomerate**, **entrepreneur**). He has started another flower shop!

10. We have to purchase more reliable machinery. With all the equipment failures, our (**finder's fee**, **downtime**, **downstream**) has been excessive this month.

B. Match the term with its definition.

analysis-paralysis	**delphi technique**
audit trail	**entrepreneur**
black magic	**filthy five**
camel	**finder's fee**
competition analysis	**functional management**
contract services	**general partner**
corporate veil	**heuristics**
DBA	**know-how license**

1. ____________________________ *exp.* all talk and no action.

2. ________________ *n.* problem-solving by experimental and trial-and-error methods rather than formal mathematical techniques.

3. ________________ *exp.* (doing business as; also referred to as a fictitious name) used when a person or business known by one name choses to do business under a different name.

4. ________________ *exp.* ("a horse designed by committee") a project in which the elements are assembled by separate individuals without a clear picture of the final product.

5. ________________ *n.* a list of companies compiled annually by *Mother Jones* magazine based on their poor environmental record.

6. ________________ *n.* a management system based on a function, such as marketing or advertising, in contrast to being arranged around an end product.

7. ________________ *exp.* a euphemism for "corporate spying."

8. ________________ *n.* the method of recording each step of a transaction.

9. ________________ *n.* a method of using outside experts in an interactive fashion to make company forecasts.

10. ________________ *n.* used to refer to the skills of a technical specialist who is able to accomplish results no one else can.

11. ________________ *n.* a partner who is generally responsible for the business and has unlimited liability.

12. ________________ *n.* a commission paid to a third party who locates a buyer, property, personnel, etc. that leads to a business deal.

13. ________________ *n.* work performed by outside contractors with a formal agreement.

14. ________________ *n.* one who starts a business; founder.

15. ________________ *n.* a shield under which stock holders are immune from legal action resulting from business failure.

16. ________________ *n.* a contract for licensing a technology process to a vendor for commercial development.

LESSON TEN

Management Slang & Jargon
(Part B)

*Acme Corporation is loaded with **heavy hitters**.*

Lesson Ten

Dialogue in slang

Earl: How do you like your new job?

Pete: Well, the **corporate culture** is pretty **buttoned-down**. The **COO**, who's a real **slave driver**, likes to run a **tight ship**. So at least there won't be the **Chinese fire drills** we had at my last company, R&O Corporation, **aka** Rip 'em Off Inc. That **Mickey Mouse** company was **dead in the water**. All the **execs** were just **figureheads** and believed in the **MBI** approach. Fortunately, this new company is loaded with **heavy-hitters**.

Earl: It sounds like your new employer has a pretty **deep bench**.

Pete: To tell you the truth, I wouldn't be surprised if we made the **Fortune 500** next year. The **front end** of the company is full of **go-getters**. It's hard to believe that the company was a **greenfield** just two years ago. In fact, **Inc. 100** did a big **spread** on us last month. They were really impressed by the managers' **MBWA** approach.

Earl: H'mm. With all those managers wandering around, I hope someone stays **behind the wheel**!

Lesson Ten

Translation of dialogue in standard English

Management Jargon (Part B)

Earl: How do you like your new job?

Pete: Well, the **company's values and standards** are pretty **strict.**. The **chief operating officer**, who's a real **demanding boss**, likes to run a **well-organized operation**. So at least there won't be the **mass confusion** we had at my last company, R&O Corporation, **also known as** Rip 'em Off Inc. That **poorly organized** company was **lacking direction**. All the **executives** were just **chosen for their reputation and not for their participation in the decision-making process** and believed in the **management by intimidation** approach. Fortunately, this new company is loaded with **powerful individuals**.

Earl: It sounds like your new employer has a pretty **powerful management team**.

Pete: To tell you the truth, I wouldn't be surprised if we made the **annual list of the 500 largest U.S. industrial corporations compiled by *Fortune Magazine*** next year. The **marketing end** of the company is full of **ambitious people**. It's hard to believe that the company was **brand new** just two years ago. In fact, **the magazine which publishes an annual list of the 100 fastest-growing small public companies in the U.S.** did a big **news story** on us last month. They were really impressed by the managers' **management by wandering around** approach.

Earl: H'mm. With all those managers wandering around, I hope someone stays **in charge**!

Lesson Ten

Dialogue in slang as it would be heard

Management Jargon (Part B)

Earl: Howdy'a like yer new job?

Pete: Well, the **corp'rate culture**'s preddy **button'-down**. The **C-O-O**, who's a real **slave driver**, likes ta run a **tight ship**. So 'it least there won't be the **Chinese fire drills** we had 'it my last company, R 'n O Corperation, **aka** Rip 'em Off Inc. That **Mickey Mouse** company was **dead in the wader**. All the **execs** were jus' **figureheads** 'n believed in thee **M-B-I** approach. Fortunately, this new company's loaded with **heavy-hidders**.

Earl: It sounds like yer new employer has a preddy **deep bench**.

Pete: Ta tell ya the truth, I wouldn't be sarprised if we made the **Fortune 500** next year. The **fron' end** 'a the company's full of **go-gedders**. It's hard da believe th't the company was a **greenfield** jus' two years ago. In fact, **Inc. 100** did a big **spread** on us last month. They were really impressed by the managers' **M-B-W-A** approach.

Earl: H'mm. With all those managers wandering around, I hope someone stays **b'hin' the wheel**!

Vocabulary

aka *exp.* (also known as)

example: I've been working for IBM, **aka** "Big Blue" for fifteen years.

translation: I've been working for IBM, **also known as** "Big Blue" for fifteen years.

as spoken: I've been working fer IBM, **aka** "Big Blue" fer fifteen years.

behind-the-wheel *exp.* to be in control or in charge.

example: With Kim **behind-the-wheel** of this project, we have nothing to worry about.

translation: With Kim **in charge** of this project, we have nothing to worry about.

as spoken: With Kim **b'hin'-the-wheel** of this project, we have nothing ta worry about.

buttoned-down *adj.* formal, bureaucratic, executive style.

example: If you go to work for that company, you're going to need to buy a suit. Their style is very **buttoned-down**.

translation: If you go to work for that company, you're going to need to buy a suit. Their style is very **formal**.

as spoken: If ya go da work fer that company, y'r gonna need ta buy a suit. Their style's very **button'-down**.

Chinese fire drill *exp.* mass confusion.

example: When our main computer crashed, there was a **Chinese fire drill** in the data processing department.

translation: When our main computer crashed, there was **mass confusion** in the data processing department.

as spoken: When 'ar main c'mpuder crashed, there was a **Chinese fire drill** in the dada processing department.

COO *n.* (chief operating officer) one who reports to the chief executive officer.

example: Why don't you talk to the **COO** since he's more involved in the operation of the company than the CEO.

translation: Why don't you talk to the **chief operating officer** since he's more involved in the operation of the company than the Chief Executive Officer.

as spoken: Why don't you talk to the **COO** since he's more involved in the operation of the company than the CEO.

SEE: **CEO** (chief executive officer), *p. 216.*

corporate culture *n.* a company's values and standards, represented through mission statement, dress code, style of management, and goals.

example: In this company, there's no problem wearing casual clothing. Our **corporate culture** is very relaxed.

translation: In this company, there's no problem wearing casual clothing. Our **company's style** is very relaxed.

as spoken: In this company, there's no problem wearing casual clothing. Our **corp'rit culture**'s very ralaxed.

dead-in-the-water *adj.* a company lacking direction or failing to succeed.

example: This company's been **dead-in-the-water** ever since the original owner sold out.

translation: This company's been **lacking direction** ever since the original owner sold out.

as spoken: This company's been **dead-in-the-wader** ever since thee origin'l owner sold out.

deep bench *exp.* (from sports) a company with a lot of management talent.

example: It's a shame that Karen decided to leave the company but with our **deep bench**, we'll adjust.

translation: It's a shame that Karen decided to leave the company but with so much **management talent**, we'll adjust.

as spoken: It's a shame th't Karen d'cided ta leave the company but w'th 'ar **deep bench**, w'll adjust.

exec *n.* (executive) director or controller of a company.

example: Congratulations! I hear you've been promoted to **exec**!

translation: Congratulations! I hear you've been promoted to **executive**!

as spoken: Congrajalations! I hear ya've been pramoded ta **exec**!

figurehead *n.* a person who is a chief or head in name only, and does not participate in the decision-making process.

example: After the merger, the company president lost most of his authority. Now he's just a **figurehead**.

translation: After the merger, the company president lost most of his authority. Now he's just **president in name only**.

as spoken: After the merger, the company president lost most of 'is athoridy. Now 'e's just a **figurehead**.

Fortune 500 *n.* annual list of the 500 largest U.S. industrial corporations compiled by *Fortune* magazine.

example: The new management team was worth the expense. This is the first year we've made the **Fortune 500**.

translation: The new management team was worth the expense. This is the first year we've been chosen for the **annual list of the 500 largest U.S. industrial corporations**.

as spoken: The new management team was worth the expense. This is the first year we've made the **Fortune 500**.

front end *n.* the marketing division of a business, as opposed to the manufacturing division.

example: This product can be so easily manufactured, that we can focus on the **front end**.

translation: This product can be so easily manufactured, that we can focus on the **marketing side of the business**.

as spoken: This product c'n be so easily manufactured, th't we c'n focus on the **fronnend**.

go-getter *n.* a highly ambitious person.

example: Maggie is going to be very successful some day. She's a real **go-getter**.

translation: Maggie is going to be very successful some day. She's a real **ambitious person**.

as spoken: Maggie's gonna be very successful some day. She's a real **go-gedder**.

greenfield *n.* a general business term referring to any business venture or project that is new.

example: We'll have to use our own money for this startup. The bank won't give us a loan because it's a **greenfield** project.

translation: We'll have to use our own money for this startup. The bank won't give us a loan because it's a **new** project.

as spoken: We'll hafta use 'ar own money fer this stardup. The bank won't give us a loan 'cuz it's a **greenfield** project.

heavy hitter *n.* a powerful individual; someone with money, influence, or experience.

example: If we want to have success with our new business venture, we're going to need a **heavy hitter** on our management team.

translation: If we want to have success with our new business venture, we're going to need a **person with a lot of money, influence, or experience** on our management team.

as spoken: If we wanna have success w'ith 'ar new business venture, w'r gonna need a **heavy hidder** on 'ar management team.

Inc. 100 *n.* annual list of the 100 fastest-growing small public companies in the U.S. compiled by *Inc. Magazine.*

example: Our sales growth has really taken off this quarter. At this rate, we'll definitely make the **Inc. 100** this year.

translation: Our sales growth has really taken off this quarter. At this rate, we'll definitely make the **annual list of the 100 fastest-growing small public companies in the U.S.** this year.

as spoken: 'Ar sales growth 'ez really taken off this quarder. At this rate, w'll def'nitely make thee **Inc. 100** this year.

MBI *exp.* (Management By Intimidation) a tactic by management to increase job performance through threats or coercion.

example: Watch out! The new manager they brought in believes in **MBI**.

translation: Watch out! The new manager they brought in believes in **management by intimidation**.

as spoken: Watch out! The new manager they brod in believes in **MBI**.

MBWA *exp.* (Management By Wandering Around) a system of visible management whereby executives "wander around" the work site in order to assess the work process and enable employee interaction.

example: This is the third time this week I've seen our new Chief Executive Officer down in production. He must be an advocate of **MBWA**.

translation: This is the third time this week I've seen our new Chief Executive Officer down in "Production". He must be an advocate of **management by wanding around**.

as spoken: This 'ez the third time this week I've seen 'ar new CEO down in praduction. He mus' be 'n advocad of**MBWA**.

Mickey Mouse *adj.* said of a business that is poorly organized, inadequately financed, and lacking management talent.

example: The company I bought this software from must be a real **Mickey Mouse** operation. They didn't include a manual with my software.

translation: The company I bought this software from must be a real **poorly organized** operation. They didn't include a manual with my software.

as spoken: The company I bought this software from must be a real **Mickey Mouse** operation. They didn' include a manual with my software.

run a tight ship *exp.* to operate a well-organized and structured company.

example: The last manager we had was so disorganized that work was never done. I have a feeling that the new manager is going to be very effective. He's known for **running a tight ship**.

translation: The last manager we had was so disorganized that work was never done. I have a feeling that the new manager is going to be very effective. He's known for **operating a well-organized and structured company**.

as spoken: The last manager we had was so disorg'nized th't work was never done. I have a feeling th't the new manager's gonna be very effective. He's known fer **running a tight ship**.

slave driver *n.* an overly demanding employer who makes employees work like slaves without regard to their well-being.

example: My boss is making us work through the fourth weekend in a row! He sure is a **slave driver**!

translation: My boss is making us work through the fourth weekend in a row! He sure is an **overly demanding employer**!

as spoken: My boss 'ez making us work through the fourth weekend in a row! He sher is a **slave driver**!

spread *n.* a large newpaper or magazine article ("spreading" across more than one page).

example: Did you see the **spread** on our company in the newspaper this morning? This is the best publicity we could have hoped for!

translation: Did you see the **large news story** on our company in the newspaper this morning? This is the best publicity we could have hoped for!

as spoken: Didja see the **spread** on 'ar company in the newspaper th's morning? This 'ez the best publicidy we could've hoped for!

Practice the Vocabulary

(Answers to Lesson Ten, p. 279)

A. Circle the letter corresponding to the correct definition of the word(s) in boldface.

1. **greenfield:**
   a. a general business term referring to any brand new business venture or project
   b. an annual list of the 100 fastest-growing small public companies in the U.S. compiled by *Inc. Magazine*

2. **heavy hitter:**
   a. a highly ambitious person
   b. a powerful individual

3. **front end:**
   a. the marketing part of a business as opposed to the manufacturing
   b. the manufacturing part of a business as opposed to the marketing

4. **buttoned-down:**
   a. formal, bureaucratic executive style
   b. a company lacking direction or failing to succeed

5. **to be behind the wheel:**
   a. to be close to the age of retirement
   b. to be in control or in charge

6. **Chinese fire drill:**
   a. a test performed on a factory's equipment to ensure its safety
   b. mass confusion

7. **corporate culture:**
   a. said of a company lacking direction or failing to succeed
   b. a company's values and standards as represented by mission statement, dress code, style of management, and goals.

8. **figurehead:**
   a. a popular abbreviation for "executive"
   b. a chief or head in name only

9. **Mickey Mouse:**
   a. said of a business that is poorly organized, inadequately financed, and lacking management talent
   b. said of a business whose employees are happy and energetic

10. **to run a tight ship:**
   a. to operate a poorly-organized and unstructured company
   b. to operate a well-organized and structured company

B. Underline the word(s) in boldface that best complete(s) the following.

Earl: How do you like your new job?

Pete: Well, the (**corporate culture**, **Fortune 500**) is pretty (**buttoned-down**, **Mickey Mouse**). The (**deep bench**, **COO**), who's a real (**aka**, **slave driver**), likes to run a (**tight ship**, **greenfield**). So at least there won't be the (**Chinese fire drills**, **heavy hitters**) that there were in my last company, R&O Corporation, (**aka**, **MBI**) Rip 'em Off Inc. That (**front end**, **Mickey Mouse**) company was (**Mickey Mouse**, **dead in the water**). All the (**execs**, **figureheads**) were just (**figureheads**, **execs**) and believed in the (**MBI**, **Inc. 100**) approach. Fortunately, this new company is loaded with (**heavy hitters**, **slave drivers**).

Earl: It sounds like your new employer has a pretty (**Fortune 500**, **deep bench**).

Pete: To tell you the truth, I wouldn't be surprised if we made the (**Fortune 500**, **greenfield**) next year. The (**deep bench**, **front end**) of the company is full of (**go-getters**, **figureheads**). It's hard to believe that the company was a (**heavy hitter**, **greenfield**) just two years ago. In fact, (**Mickey Mouse**, **Inc. 100**) did a big (**aka**, **spread**) on us just last month. They were really impressed by the managers' (**MBWA**, **aka**) approach.

Earl: H'mm. With all those managers wandering around, I hope someone stays (**front end**, **behind-the-wheel**)!

C. FIND-THE-WORD CUBE

Step 1: Fill in the blanks with the correct word from the list below.

Step 2: Find and circle the word in the grid on the opposite page.

buttoned	**hitter**
drill	**Mickey Mouse**
driver	**ship**
figurehead	**water**
getters	**wheel**

1. With Kim behind-the-__________________ of this project, we have nothing to worry about.

2. You're going to go work for a corporation? Are you sure you'll be able to tolerate the __________________-down style?

3. When the electricity went off, you should have seen the Chinese fire __________ . Everyone panicked!

4. Ever since they brought in a new manager, this company's been dead-in-the-________________ .

5. Before our company merged with a large corporation, I had a lot of authority. Now I'm just a ____________________ .

6. We need a lot more go-__________________ like you on our sales force. You've brought in more money for this company than any other salesperson!

7. David was hired because he knows influential people in this town. He's a real heavy __________________ .

8. This company is so ________________ . I'm surprised anything ever gets done!

9. Mr. Collins works us so hard. What a slave ________________ !

10. You've turned into a fine manager. I'm particularly impressed with the way you run a tight ________________ .

FIND-A-WORD CUBE

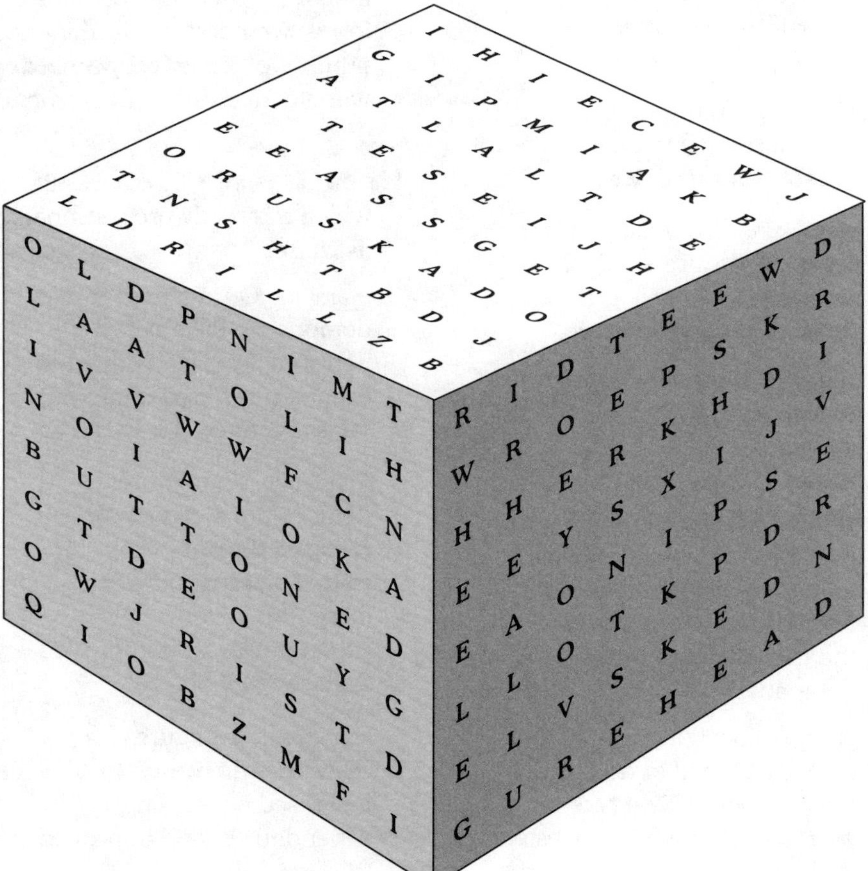

A CLOSER LOOK: *Management Slang & Jargon (Part B)*

learning experience *exp.* a euphemistic term for a business mistake.

example: We really *lost our shirts* on this business deal. We'll just have to look at it as a **learning experience**.

translation: We really *lost our shirts* on this business deal. We'll just have to look at it as a **business mistake**.

as spoken: We really *lost 'ar shirts* on this bizness deal. W'll just hafta look ad it as a **learning experience**.

NOTE: **lose one's shirt** *exp.* to lose everything in a business deal.

limited partner *n.* a partner in a business whose liability is limited to his/her investment and who has no involvement in the management of the company.

example: To complete our tax forms, we need to determine the number of **limited partners** who have invested in the business.

translation: To complete our tax forms, we need to determine the number of **partners with limited liability** who have invested in the business.

as spoken: Ta c'mplede 'ar tax forms, we need ta d'termine the number of **limided partners** who've invesded in the bizness.

linearity *adj.* said of a result which is directly proportional to its cause.

example: Our figures demonstate **linearity** between increased advertising expenditures, and improved sales revenues.

translation: Our figures demonstate **a directly proportional relationship** between increased advertising expenditures, and improved sales revenues.

as spoken: 'Ar figures demonstate **linearity** b'tween increased advertising expenditures, and improved sales revenues.

lowball (to) *v.* to quote low prices early in a sales negotiation, then raise them once the customer appears committed.

example: The figures on this quote are much higher than we received originally. It looks like the vendor **lowballed** his prices.

translation: The figures on this quote are much higher than we received originally. It looks like the vendor **quoted lower prices early and then raised** his prices.

as spoken: The figures on this quode'er much higher th'n we r'ceived originally. It looks like the vender **lowballed** 'is prices.

mature industries *n.* an industry producing a product no longer in demand.

example: Year after year of flat sales in the computer business demonstrates that it is becoming a **mature industry**.

translation: Year after year of flat sales in the computer business demonstrates that it is becoming an **industry producing a product no longer in demand.**

as spoken: Year after year 'ev flat sales in the c'mpuder bizness demonstrates thad it's b'coming a **mature industry**.

MBO *exp.* (Management By Objective) a set of mutually acceptable performance goals developed through collaboration between management and employees.

example: Management and employees are scheduled to assemble this afternoon to develop **MBO** standards.

translation: Management and employees are scheduled to assemble this afternoon to develop **management by objective** standards.

as spoken: Management 'n employees'er scheduled ta assemble th's afdernoon ta develop **M-B-O** standards.

mini-merger *n.* a merger between a small high-tech, cash-starved company and a large company with substantial cash reserves.

example: This **mini-merger** will give us the cash we need for further development but will take away much of our control.

translation: This **merger between our small cash-starved company and a larger company** will give us the cash we need for further development but will take away much of our control.

as spoken: This **mini-merger**'ll give us the cash we need fer ferther d'velopment bud'll take away much of 'ar c'ntrol.

mouse milking *n.* a project requiring substantial effort but producing minimal return.

example: Our rewrite of this accounting software amounted to nothing more than **mouse milking**. It still causes computer failures several times a day.

translation: Our rewrite of this accounting software amounted to nothing more than **a project requiring substantial effort but producing minimal return**. It still causes computer failures several times a day.

as spoken: "Ar rewrite of this accoun(t)ing software amounted ta nothing more th'n **mouse milking**. It still causes c'mpuder failures sev'ral times a day.

Murphy's Law *exp.* "Whatever can go wrong, will go wrong."

example: **Murphy's Law**: the computer crashed, the network went down, the power failed, and the deadline is tomorrow.

translation: **Whatever could go wrong did go wrong**: the computer crashed, the network went down, the power failed, and the deadline is tomorrow.

as spoken: **Murphy's Law**: the c'mpuder crashed, the network went down, the power failed, an' the deadline's tomorrow.

NIH *exp.* (Not Invented Here) a close-minded view that if an idea was not created locally, it is not worth consideration.

example: The new management ideas brought up in the meeting look very interesting. Unfortunately, we'll probably never adopt them because they're **NIH**.

translation: The new management ideas brought up in the meeting look very interesting. Unfortunately, we'll probably never adopt them because they're **not invented here**.

as spoken: The new management ideas brod up in the meeding look very int'resting. Unfortunately, we'll prob'ly never adopt th'm 'cuz they're **N-I-H**.

NIMBY *exp.* (Not In My Back Yard) said of people who are opposed to anything undesirable in their community such as a factory, new prison, etc.

example: It'll be difficult to get a new factory built in this community. The entire city council has a bad case of the **NIMBY** syndrome.

translation: It'll be difficult to get a new factory built in this community. The entire city council has a bad case of the **not-in-my-back-yard** syndrome.

as spoken: Id'll be difficult ta ged a new factery built in this c'mmunidy. Thee entire cidy council has a bad case 'a the **NIMBY** syndrome.

oil patch *n.* a descriptive term for the oil industry.

example: Jack knows more about oil refining than anybody else. He was born in the **oil patch**.

translation: Jack knows more about oil refining than anybody else. He was born in the **oil industry**.

as spoken: Jack knows more aboud oil r'fining th'n anybody else. He was born in thee **oil patch**.

open-collared *adj.* a corporate culture characterized by an informal and relaxed atmosphere.

example: Now that I took this job with XYZ Corporation, I can retire my suit and tie. This is an **open-collared** company.

translation: Now that I took this job with XYZ Corporation, I can retire my suit and tie. This is an **informal and relaxed** company.

as spoken: Now th'd I took this job with XYZ Corperation, I c'n r'tire my suit 'n tie. This is 'n **open-coller'd** company.

"opportunity" *exp.* a euphemistic expression for a problem encountered in business.

example: I heard all your top sales people quit at the same time. Good luck with this **"opportunity."**

translation: I heard all your top sales people quit at the same time. Good luck with this **business problem**.

as spoken: I heard all yer top sales people quid 'it the same time. Good luck with this **"oppertunidy."**

order taker *n.* a salesperson who doesn't aggressively pursue potential business.

example: It looks like you have two **order takers** on your sales staff. Both have written less than three percent of your total orders.

translation: It looks like you have two **non-aggressive salespeople** on your sales staff. Both have written less than three percent of your total orders.

as spoken: It looks like you have two **order takers** on yer sales staff. Both 've written less th'n three percen' of yer todal orders.

outside directors *n.* individuals elected by shareholders to boards of public companies to protect investor interests.

example: Look at the stockholder dividends this quarter! The new **outside directors** really forced this company to shape up!

translation: Look at the stockholder dividends this quarter! The new **board of individuals elected to protect investor interests** really forced this company to shape up!

as spoken: Look 'it the stockholder dividen's this quarder! The new **outside directers** really forced this company da shape up!

Parkinson's law *exp.* a proverb coined by C. Orthcote Parkinson: "Work expands so as to fill the time available for its completion."

example: I thought this job would only take a day to complete but it actually took right up until the deadline. This is a good example of **Parkinson's law**.

translation: I thought this job would only take a day to complete but it actually took right up until the deadline. This is a good example of **"work expands so as to fill the time available for its completion."**

as spoken: I thought th's job'ed only take a day da c'mplete bud it akshelly took ride up until the deadline. This is a good example of **Parkinson's law**.

partnership *n.* a business entity composed of two or more individuals, corporations, or other partnerships. Each partner is fully liable for the debts of the partnership and the partnership is responsible for the acts of each partner.

example: Consider the proposal for the formation of this **partnership** very carefully. You would be liable for all debts incurred by the partnership.

translation: Consider the proposal for the formation of this **business entity which is composed of two or more individuals, corporations, or other partnerships** very carefully. You would be liable for all debts incurred by the partnership.

as spoken: C'nsider the praposal fer the fermation of this **partnership** very carefully. You'd be li'ble fer all debts incurred by the partnership.

point man *n.* a person appointed to a highly prominent lobbying position.

example: You are the most photogenic member of our sales force. You should be the **point man** for our new product launch.

translation: You are the most photogenic member of our sales force. You should be the **prominent lobbyist** for our new product launch.

as spoken: Y'r the most phodagenic member 'ev 'ar sales force. You should be the **point man** fer 'ar new product launch.

NOTE: Originally, a military term for a lead soldier taking enemy fire.

proactive *adj.* taking action in anticipation of future problems or needs; taking the initiative.

example: We need a **proactive** approach to deal with declining sales of our product.

translation: We need a **vigorous** approach to deal with declining sales of our product.

as spoken: We need a **proactive** approach ta deal with d'clining sales of 'ar product.

product life-cycle *n.* refers to the seven stages in the lifetime of a product: research and development, introduction, market development, exploitation, maturation, saturation, and decline.

example: Now that we've completed the marketing development, we're in the middle of the **product life-cycle**.

translation: Now that we've completed the marketing development, we're in the middle of the **seven stages in the lifetime of our product**.

as spoken: Now th't we've c'mpleded the markeding d'velopment, w'r in the middle 'a the **product life-cycle**.

profit center *n.* part of a company that maximizes revenue and minimizes costs.

example: When we compare our hardware and software divisions, it's clear that software is the **profit center**.

translation: When we compare our hardware and software divisions, it's clear that software is the **part of our company that maximizes revenue and minimizes costs**.

as spoken: When we c'mpare 'ar hardware and software divisions, it's clear th't software is the **profit cen(t)er**.

proprietary *adj.* exploited, produced, and sold only by the owner having the exclusive rights to a particular product or technology.

example: We can't use this new technology in our computers because it's **proprietary**.

translation: We can't use this new technology in our computers because it's **owner has the exclusive rights**.

as spoken: We can't use this new technalogy in 'ar c'mpuders 'cuz it's **praprietary**.

QWL *exp.* (Quality of Work-Life) a term for actions taken to create a humane working environment.

example: Based on the positive results we received from our employee questionnaire, our **QWL** changes were popular.

translation: Based on the positive results we received from our employee questionnaire, our **quality of work-life** changes were popular.

as spoken: Based on the positive r'sults we r'ceived fr'm 'ar employee questionnaire, 'ar **QWL** changes were popyaler.

reinvent the wheel (to) *v.* to start from the beginning, to develop something that already exists.

example: Let's bring a consultant in on this project. We don't want to **reinvent the wheel**.

translation: Let's bring a consultant in on this project. We don't want to **start from the beginning only to develop something that already exists**.

as spoken: Let's bring a c'nsultant in on this project. We don't wanna **reinvent the wheel**.

runaway *n.* a business that relocates or shuts down to avoid organized labor or compliance with local regulations.

example: Be careful about investing in ABC corporation; they're probably going to be a **runaway**.

translation: Be careful about investing in ABC corporation; they're probably going to be a **business that relocates or shuts down to avoid organized labor or compliance with local regulations**.

as spoken: Be careful aboud investing in ABC corperation; they're prob'ly gonna be a **runaway**.

secrecy agreement *n.* an agreement authorizing a person or organization to evaluate or research a particular technology, but generally prohibiting its commercial development.

example: We'd better draw up a **secrecy agreement** before we reveal the details of our new technology to Apex Corporation.

translation: We'd better draw up an **agreement authorizing an organization to evaluate a particular technology** before we reveal the details of our new technology to Apex Corporation.

as spoken: We bedder draw up a **secrecy agreement** before we reveal the details 'ev 'ar new technalagy ta Apex Corperation.

service business *n.* a company whose primary product is a service i.e. temporary office workers, typesetting, printing, etc.

example: Now that we have sold our manufacturing facilities, we have become a **service business**.

translation: Now that we have sold our manufacturing facilities, we have become a **company whose primary product is a service**.

as spoken: Now th't we've sold 'ar manufacturing facilidies, we've b'come a **service business**.

smokestack America *n.* a descriptive term for automobiles, steel, and glass manufacturers (from a time when huge old-fashioned factories dominated American manufacturing).

example: Ever since high-quality foreign imports came on the scene, we've seen a decline of **smokestack America**.

translation: Ever since high-quality foreign imports came on the scene, we've seen a decline of **huge old-fashioned factories that once dominated American manufacturing**.

as spoken: Ever since high-qualidy forin imports came on the scene, we've seen a decline of **smokestack America**.

squeaky wheel *exp.* (from the expression "The squeaky wheel gets the grease") said of someone whose assertiveness gets results.

example: When you are dealing with insurance companies, you often have to be a **squeaky wheel**.

translation: When you are dealing with insurance companies, you often have to be **someone whose assertiveness gets results**.

as spoken: When y'r dealing with insurance companies, ya offen hafta be a **squeaky wheel**.

SRO *n.* (Self-Regulating Organization) an association of professionals who set industry standards to avoid government regulation.

example: To avoid government regulation in our industry, we should become an **SRO**.

translation: To avoid government regulation in our industry, we should become a **self-regulating organization**.

as spoken: Ta avoid government regulation in 'ar industry, we should b'come 'n **S-R-O**.

subsidiary *n.* a company completely controlled by another company through majority ownership.

example: Now that we have a controlling interest in ABC Corporation, they've become our **subsidiary**.

translation: Now that we have a controlling interest in ABC Corporation, they've become our **company completely controlled by another company through majority ownership**.

as spoken: Now that we have a c'ntrolling int'rest in ABC Corperation, they've b'come our **subsidiary**.

Sullivan principles *n.* a code of conduct formulated by the Reverend Leon Sullivan of Philadelphia. It directs U.S. corporations who have dealings with South Africa to treat black and white workers equally.

example: Before we authorize PMA Distributors to sell our product in South Africa, let's ensure that they adhere to the **Sullivan principles**.

translation: Before we authorize PMA Distributors to sell our product in South Africa, let's ensure that they adhere to the **code of conduct ensuring that blacks and whites are treated equally**.

as spoken: Before we autherize PMA Distribyaders ta sell 'ar product in South Africa, let's ensure th't they adhere da the **Sulliv'n principles**.

sunset industry *n.* a no-growth industry in decline.

example: Structural steel production in the United States has become a **sunset industry**.

translation: Structural steel production in the United States has become a **no-growth industry in decline**.

as spoken: Structural steel praduction in the U.S. 'ez b'come a **sunsed industry**.

sweat equity *n.* an investment of labor (rather than capital) in a business when cash is in short supply.

example: You don't need a lot of money to buy into this business. You could invest **sweat equity**.

translation: You don't need a lot of money to buy into this business. You could invest **labor instead of capital**.

as spoken: You don't need a lod 'a money ta buy inta this bizness. You could 'nvest **swead equidy**.

SWOT *exp.* (Strengths, Weaknesses, Opportunities, and Threats) information a company needs in order to perform strategic planning.

example: In this competitive industry, we really need to know our **SWOT**.

translation: In this competitive industry, we really need to know our **strengths, weaknesses, opportunities, and threats**.

as spoken: In this c'mpedidive industry, we really need ta know 'ar **SWOT**.

synergy *n.* combined action or operation, i.e. cooperation, leading to improved results.

example: The **synergy** of our two agencies has led to accomplishments that neither could have achieved individually.

translation: The **combined operation** of our two agencies has led to accomplishments that neither could have achieved individually.

as spoken: The **synergy** 'ev 'ar two agencies has led to accomplishments th't neither could'ev achieved individually.

threshold company *n.* a business that has passed the entrepreneurial stage and is attempting to establish a solid financial footing and a pattern of long-term growth and prosperity.

example: Now that you have become a **threshold company**, you need to find a bank that will arrange long-term financing.

translation: Now that you have become a **business that has passed the entrepreneurial stage**, you need to find a bank that will arrange long-term financing.

as spoken: Now th't chuv b'come a **threshold company**, you need ta find a bank thad'll arrange long-term financing.

tin-cupping *exp.* interdivisional soliciting for resources and support for a new product or idea within a corporation.

example: I hear that our overseas division is going to be **tin cupping** to get this new idea funded.

translation: I hear that our overseas division is going to be **soliciting other divisions for resources and support** to get this new idea funded.

as spoken: I hear th'd 'ar overseas division is gonna be **tin cupping** to get this new idea funded.

upstream (to) *v.* to steer goods or funds from a subsidiary to its parent company.

example: It will cost a great deal of money to set up manufacturing for these new products. Why not just **upstream** them?

translation: It will cost a great deal of money to set up manufacturing for these new products. Why not just **steer them from the subsidiary to the parent company**?

as spoken: It'll cost a great deal of money ta set up manufacturing fer these new produc's. Why not just **upstream** th'm?

value-driven *adj.* said of a well-organized corporate culture that uses the values of a founder or top executives to motivate employees and improve the company's productivity.

example: After all of the frustrating jobs I've had with shortsighted large corporations, it would be nice to work for a **value-driven** company.

translation: After all of the frustrating jobs I've had with shortsighted large corporations, it would be nice to work for a **well-organized company that uses the values of the top executives to motivate employees and improve productivity**.

as spoken: After all 'a the frustrading jobs I've had with shortsided large corperations, it'd be nice ta work fer a **value-driven** company.

vertical integration *exp.* corporate control of all major aspects of a business from collection of raw materials to distribution of finished products.

example: After the purchase of the new mining division, we now have **vertical integration** in this industry.

translation: After the purchase of the new mining division, we now have **corporate control of all major aspects of the business from collection of raw materials to distribution of finished products**.

as spoken: After the purchase of the new mining division, we now have **verdic'l integration** in this industry.

vertical supplier *n.* a company-owned supplier; or independent vendor of raw goods, components or services to a vertically integrated industry.

example: That airframe fabricator is a **vertical supplier**. As long as the aircraft industry does well, they will prosper.

translation: That airframe fabricator is a **company-owned supplier or independent vendor of components**. As long as the aircraft industry does well, they will prosper.

as spoken: Thad airframe fabricader's a **verdic'l supplier**. As long 'ez thee aircraft industry does well, they'll prosper.

visuals *n.* slides, illustrations, flip charts, graphs, videocassettes, etc. used in a presentation.

example: Put in a call to the graphic arts department! We need to make sure that those **visuals** are ready on time.

translation: Put in a call to the graphic arts department! We need to make sure that those **slides and charts** are ready on time.

as spoken: Pud in a call da the graphic arts department! We need ta make sher th't those **visuals** 'r ready on time.

Practice Management Slang & Jargon

(Answers p. 281)

A. Underline the correct word that best completes the phrase.

1. We lost a lot of money on this business deal. We'll have to look at it as a (**learning**, **lowball**, **linearity**) experience.

2. It will cost a lot of money to set up manufacturing for these new products. Why not just (**up**, **down**, **side**)stream them?

3. The final figures on this quote are much higher than we received originally. It looks like the vendor (**high**, **low**, **medium**)balled his prices.

4. Rewriting this new accounting software amounts to nothing more than (**mouse**, **mousse**, **squirrel**) milking. It still causes computer failures several times a day.

5. Murphy's (**Law**, **MBO**, **runaway**): the computer crashed, the network went down, the power failed, and the deadline is tomorrow.

6. Now that I took this job with XYZ Corporation, I can retire my suit and tie. This is an open-(**collared**, **sleeved**, **belted**) company.

7. When we compare our hardware with our software sales, it's clear that software is the profit (**center**, **runaway**, **mini-merger**).

8. Let's bring a consultant in on this project. We don't want to reinvent the (**tire**, **wheel**, **ball**).

9. When you are dealing with insurance companies, you have to learn to be a squeaky (**wheel**, **tire**, **NIH**).

10. You don't need a lot of money to buy into this business. You could invest (**mouse milking**, **Parkinson's Law**, **sweat**) equity.

ANSWERS TO LESSONS 1-10

LESSON ONE - *General Business Slang & Jargon (Part A)*

Practice the Vocabulary (*p. 11*)

A. 1. We'll be making more money soon.
2. I want you to be as concise as possible.
3. We talked in great detail.
4. We don't have any problems at all!
5. It started at 2 o'clock and ended around 3 o'clock.
6. We're all ready!
7. He feels much better now.
8. Each employee cooperates with the other.
9. I didn't realize you were so knowledgeable!
10. Let's celebrate our future together!
11. In fact, I'll give it to you in a few weeks.
12. We need to increase our advertising.

B. 1. G
2. F
3. A
4. B
5. D
6. H
7. C
8. E
9. J
10. I

C. CROSSWORD PUZZLE

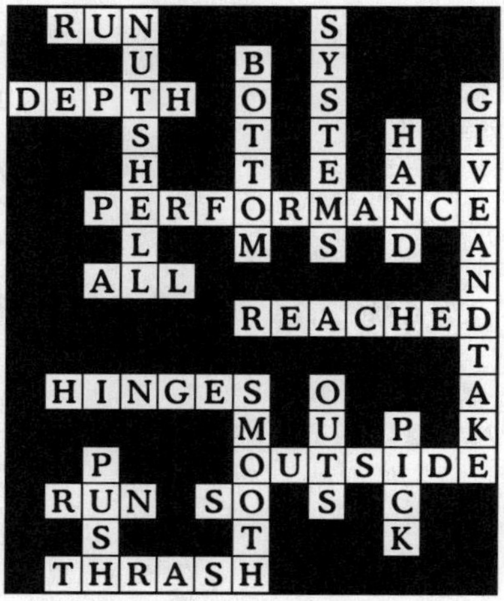

D.

1. smooth
2. bottom
3. sales
4. all
5. nutshell
6. depth
7. hand
8. hinges
9. push
10. take
11. forth
12. reached
13. so
14. thrash
15. loose
16. run
17. ins
18. go
19. smoothly
20. pick
21. outside

Practice Using General Business Slang & Jargon (p. 26)

A.

1. drawback
2. breakthrough
3. point
4. corners
5. dud
6. take
7. full
8. end

B.
1. a
2. b
3. c
4. a
5. c
6. c
7. b
8. a
9. c
10. c

LESSON TWO - *General Business Slang & Jargon (Part B)*

Practice the Vocabulary (p. 42)

A.
1. a
2. c
3. b
4. b
5. a
6. c
7. c
8. b
9. b
10. b

B.
1. record
2. booted
3. bumped
4. slacks
5. quits
6. crux
7. line
8. bend
9. snap
10. surface

FIND-THE-WORD GRID

N	A	R	K	O	W	T	O	W	S	A	S	A	A
B	E	N	D	U	B	B	L	T	B	T	L	B	K
U	U	C	S	R	C	H	C	A	S	N	A	P	I
M	C	O	U	X	D	A	R	W	C	D	C	D	S
P	K	R	R	W	T	E	U	I	E	A	K	E	S
E	L	E	F	N	Y	F	X	G	B	F	S	F	F
D	E	C	A	G	G	L	F	G	C	G	K	U	P
E	L	O	C	Q	U	I	T	S	H	K	E	E	L
F	P	R	E	C	J	N	T	B	O	O	T	E	D
E	R	D	J	P	U	E	H	E	R	J	L	P	J

C. 1. I
2. G
3. B
4. C
5. F
6. H
7. E
8. J
9. D
10. A

Practice Using General Business Slang & Jargon (*p. 52*)

A. 1. b
2. a
3. c
4. b
5. a
6. c
7. b
8. b
9. b
10. c
11. b

LESSON THREE - *International Trade (Part A)*

Practice the Vocabulary (*p. 63*)

A. 1. c
2. a
3. c
4. a
5. b
6. c
7. a
8. c

B. 1. control statement
2. certificate of inspection
3. clean bill of lading
4. container
5. collection papers
6. general export license
7. markings
8. dock receipt

C. 1. forwarder
2. container
3. export
4. control
5. markings
6. certificate
7. weight
8. net
9. bill
10. receipt
11. collection

Practice Using International Trade Slang & Jargon (p. 77)

A. 1. F
2. I
3. J
4. A
5. B
6. G
7. E
8. D
9. C
10. H

LESSON FOUR - *International Trade (Part B)*

Practice the Vocabulary (p. 88)

A. 1. barratry
2. at sight
3. customs
4. broker
5. booking
6. walloper
7. agent
8. purchasing
9. hard
10. irrevocable
11. marine
12. demand

B. 1. hard
2. marine
3. agent
4. barratry
5. customs
6. dock
7. demand
8. sight
9. credit
10. purchasing

C. 1. False
2. True
3. True
4. False
5. False
6. False
7. True
8. True
9. True
10. True

Practice Using International Trade Slang & Jargon *(p. 103)*

A. CROSSWORD PUZZLE

LESSON FIVE - *Initials Used in International Trade*

Practice the Vocabulary *(p. 116)*

A. CROSSWORD PUZZLE

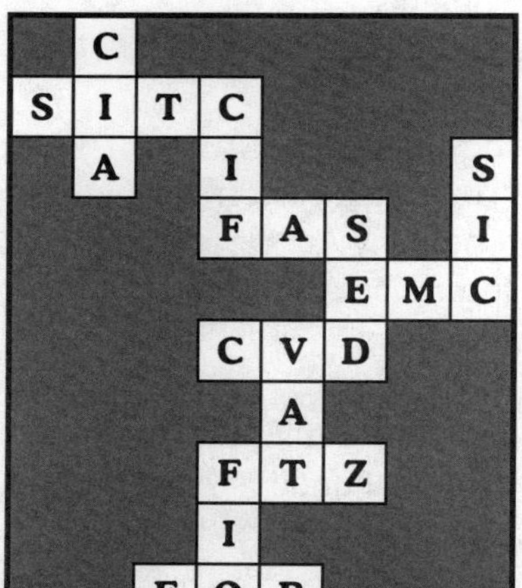

B. 1. b
2. a
3. b
4. b
5. b
6. a
7. b
8. a
9. b
10. b

C. 1. b
2. b
3. a
4. b
5. a
6. b
7. b
8. a
9. a
10. a

Practice Using Initials in International Trade (*p.* 132)

A. 1. cash against documents
2. cost and insurance
3. cost, insurance, freight
4. European currency unit
5. European Free Trade Association
6. Export Trading Company Act
7. Foreign Credit Insurance Association
8. foreign direct investment
9. free out
10. General Agreement and Tariffs and Trade
11. International Monetary Fund
12. multinational corporation

LESSON SIX - *MORE Computer Slang*

Practice the Vocabulary (p. 145)

A.
1. system
2. tech support
3. bug
4. sound board
5. plug-and-play
6. to access
7. up-and-running
8. app
9. multimedia
10. interrupt

B.
1. False
2. True
3. False
4. False
5. False
6. False
7. True
8. True
9. False
10. True

C.
1. ROM
2. tech
3. super
4. line
5. on
6. bug
7. up
8. hard
9. sound board
10. space

Practice MORE Computer Slang (p. 163)

A.
1. b
2. b
3. a
4. b
5. b
6. b
7. a
8. b
9. b
10. a

LESSON SEVEN - *Bureaucratese*

Practice the Vocabulary (p. 173)

A.
1. feedback
2. up-to-speed
3. pencil
4. doable, cost-prohibitive
5. revenue shortfall
6. whistle-blower
7. counterfactual
8. history
9. seed, implement
10. spearhead

B.
1. feedback
2. counterfactual
3. pencil
4. seed
5. cost-prohibitive
6. history
7. speed
8. doable
9. causal
10. task

C.
1. A
2. B
3. E
4. J
5. F
6. H
7. C
8. I
9. D
10. G

Practice Bureaucratese (p. 181)

A.
1. b
2. a
3. b
4. b
5. a
6. a
7. b
8. a
9. a
10. a
11. a
12. b

LESSON EIGHT - *Political Slang & Jargon*

Practice the Vocabulary (p. 195)

A. 1. junket
2. sitting
3. slinging
4. Hill
5. polls
6. out
7. up
8. flesh
9. run
10. waffling

B. CROSSWORD PUZZLE

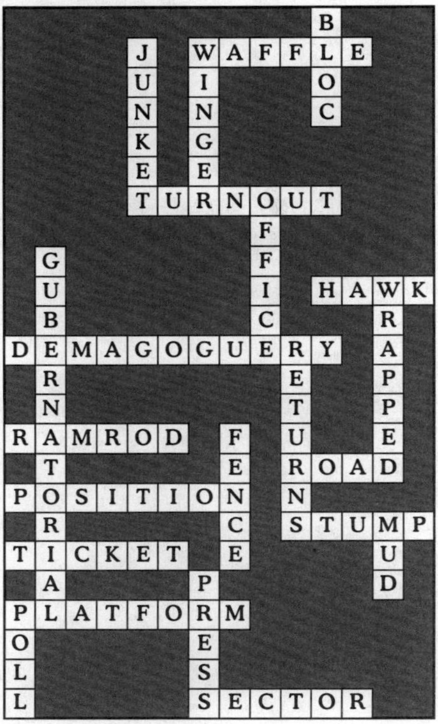

C. 1. False
2. True
3. True
4. True
5. False
6. True
7. False
8. False
9. True
10. False

Practice Political Slang & Jargon (p. 208)

A. 1. b
2. a
3. a
4. b
5. b
6. b
7. b
8. b
9. b
10. a

LESSON NINE - *Management Slang & Jargon (Part A)*

Practice the Vocabulary (p. 222)

A. 1. dirty
2. loop
3. power
4. spec
5. bolts
6. honchos
7. downsizing
8. sunrise
9. rainmaker

B. 1. b
2. b
3. a
4. b
5. b
6. b
7. b
8. b
9. b
10. a

C. 1. J
2. F
3. E
4. A
5. D
6. I
7. H
8. C
9. B
10. G

Practice Management Slang & Jargon (p. 235)

A.
1. bootstrapping
2. boiler
3. divest
4. partner
5. venture
6. housekeeping
7. governance
8. hands-on
9. entrepreneur
10. downtime

B.
1. analysis-paralysis
2. heuristics
3. DBA
4. camel
5. Filthy Five
6. functional management
7. competition analysis
8. audit trail
9. delphi technique
10. black magic
11. general partner
12. finder's fee
13. contract services
14. entrepreneur
15. corporate veil
16. know-how license

LESSON TEN - *Management Slang & Jargon (Part B)*

Practice the Vocabulary (p. 250)

A.
1. a
2. b
3. a
4. a
5. b
6. b
7. b
8. b
9. a
10. b

B. Earl: How do you like your new job?

Pete: Well, the **corporate culture** is pretty **buttoned-down**. The **COO**, who's a real **slave driver**, likes to run a **tight ship**. So at least there won't be the **Chinese fire drills** that there were in my last company, R&O Corporation, **aka** Rip 'em Off Inc. That **Mickey Mouse** company was **dead in the water**. All the **execs** were just **figureheads** and believed in the **MBI** approach. Fortunately, this new company is loaded with **heavy hitters**.

Earl: It sounds like your new employer has a pretty **deep bench**.

Pete: To tell you the truth, I wouldn't be surprised if we made **Fortune 500** next year. The **front end** of the company is full of **go-getters**. It's hard to believe that the company was a **greenfield** just two years ago. In fact, **Inc. 100** did a big **spread** on us just last month. They were really impressed by the managers' **MBWA** approach.

Earl: H'mm. With all those managers wandering around, I hope someone stays **behind the wheel**!

C.
1. wheel
2. buttoned
3. drill
4. water
5. figurehead
6. getters
7. hitter
8. Mickey Mouse
9. driver
10. ship

FIND-A-WORD CUBE

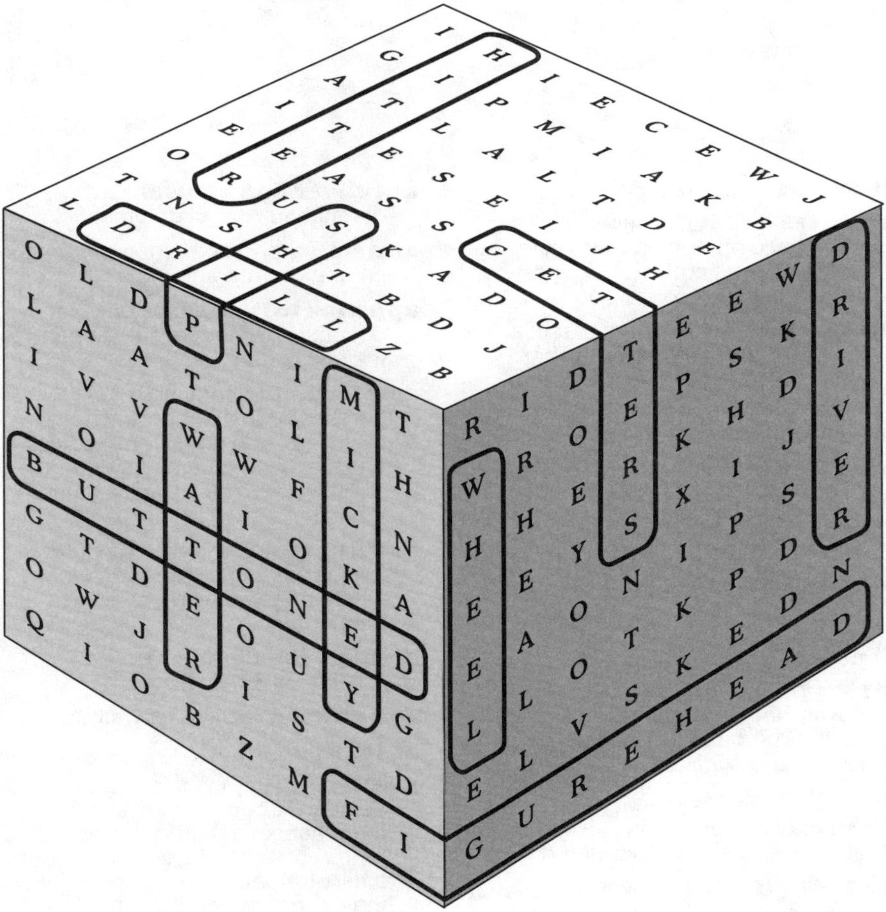

Practice Management Slang & Jargon (p. 266)

A.

1. learning
2. down
3. low
4. mouse
5. Law
6. collared
7. center
8. wheel
9. wheel
10. sweat

Glossary

above all *adj.* most importantly.

absentee ballot *n.* a ballot completed prior to an election by a voter who will not able to be present at the polling place.

access (to) *v.* to use some part of a computer system such as the hard drive, RAM, tape drive, CD-ROM, printer, etc.

affair *n.* a fund-raising event.

after hours *adj.* after the daily close of business.

agree up to a point (to) *exp.* to agree partially.

ahead of schedule (to be) *exp.* to complete or arrive earlier than planned (said of a product or a person).

air waybill *n.* a bill of lading which covers domestic and international air transportation of goods to a specified destination.

aka *exp.* also known as

all in all *exp.* considering all the elements, all things considered.

all sewn up *adj.* to be won.

all systems are go *exp.* everything is ready.

alongside *exp.* refers to goods which are to be delivered alongside a ship within reach of the transport ship's tackle.

America Online *n.* (also referred to as AOL) a popular computer on-line service which paid subscribers can use to transfer files and various information to their own computers through the telephone wire.

analysis-paralysis *exp.* all talk and no action.

antidiversion clause *n.* see destination control statement.

app *exp.* (application) another term for computer program.

append (to) *v.* to attach one document (or part of a document) to the end of another.

arbitrage *n.* the practice of purchasing stocks, bonds, foreign exchange, and other commodities in one market and immediately reselling them for a profit in another market.

archive (to) *v.* to store computer files on a diskette, tape, CD, etc. where they can be retrieved at a future date.

arrange for *exp.* to set up, to organize, to coordinate.

as a rule *exp.* usually, typically.

as to *prep.* in regard to.

ASCII *n.* (an acronym for American Standard Code for Information Interchange) a standard code for representing printable characters in binary format. It is understood by most computer systems and programs and includes certain control characters to indicate bell, carriage return, etc.

at sight *exp.* a term stipulating that payment on a draft or other negotiable instrument is due upon presentation.

at the outside *exp.* at the most.

audit trail *n.* the method of recording each step of a transaction.

authority to purchase *n.* authorization from a seller's bank to an importer's bank to draw a draft against the buyer's account to cover a specified shipment of merchandise.

ax (the) *exp.* to be dismissed from one's job, fired.

back down (to) *v.* to concede.

back-and-forth *n.* lengthy discussion.

barratry *n.* fraud or negligence on the part of ship's officers or crew resulting in loss or injury to the owners of the ship.

bean counter *n.* shortsighted accountant or bureaucrat.

behind-the-wheel *exp.* to be in control or in charge.

bend (to) *v.* to be flexible, to adjust.

better safe than sorry *exp.* better to be cautious than to regret being hasty.

big banana *n.* boss.

bilateral trade agreement *n.* a reciprocal commerce arrangement between two governments that specifies tradeable goods, categories, and quantities; and contains provisions for remittance of balances due.

bill of lading *n.* a document that specifies the terms of a shipping contract betweeen a shipper and transportation company. It serves three main functions: 1. a document of title; 2. a contract of carriage; 3. a receipt for goods.

bill *n.* a draft of a proposed law presented to a legislative body for enactment.

black magic *n.* used to refer to the skills of a technical specialist who is able to accomplish results no one else can.

bloc *n.* a group of people united by a commonality such as age, race, religion, etc.

Bloc *n.* the members of the European Monetary System, formed to stabilize exchange rate fluctuations. When the values of the bloc countries exceed an agreed upon value, there is a currency devaluation (The deutsche mark is the bloc's primary currency).

blocked currency *n.* a currency that a particular government prohibits from being converted on the foreign exchange market.

blocked exchange *n.* a currency that cannot be easily converted into other currencies.

boilerplate *n.* general structure of a contract's language that does not change from contract to contract.

bonded warehouse *n.* a facility approved by customs authorities for storage of goods upon which payment of duties is deferred until the goods are withdrawn.

booking *n.* a reservation with a sea freight company for the acceptance and transportation of cargo.

booted *exp.* to get fired.

bootstrapping *n.* using a company's own resources to start up a new product line.

boot-up (to) *v.* to start up a computer.

bottom line *n.* 1. the last line of an income or financial statement • 2. the basic issue in a discussion.

bottom-up *exp.* a management style in which low-level personnel are encouraged to make suggestions for business operations.

brainstorm (to) *v.* to gather in a group in order to contribute ideas for solving problems.

break new ground (to) *exp.* to make new discoveries (in medicine, science, product development, etc.).

breakthrough *n.* innovation.

bring about (to) *v.* to produce or generate, to facilitate.

btw *exp.* (by the way) used when chatting with someone on-line.

buffer *n.* a storage area used to hold information temporarily.

bug *n.* an error in a computer program that causes it to work incorrectly.

bulletize (to) *v.* to draw attention to important points in a document by the use of bullets (bold marks).

bumped up *exp.* to get promoted.

burn in (to) *v.* to run a computer (usually for a 48-72 hour period to test it for problems) before it is actually used for work. Most major failures occur during this time.

bus *n.* an electronic highway for carrying information from the microprocessor to other parts of the computer such as video display, hard drive, RAM, etc.

business plan *n.* a blueprint by which a new business lists its executive, financial, and product goals for the purpose of obtaining financing.

buttoned-down *adj.* formal, bureaucratic, executive style.

buying agent *n.* see purchasing agent

bypass *v.* use of a company's internal resources to accomplish tasks not normally performed by that company.

C & F *exp.* (cost and freight) a pricing term specifying that cost and freight are included in the quoted price.

C & I *exp.* (cost and insurance) a pricing term specifying that cost and insurance are included in the quoted price.

CAD *exp.* (cash against documents) payment for goods in which an intermediary transfers title documents to the buyer upon payment in cash.

call it quits (to) *exp.* to stop working for the day or to quit one's job permanently (depending on the context).

call report *n.* a report detailing a salesperson's calls/visits and customer responses to those calls/visits.

camel *exp.* ("a horse designed by committee") a project in which the elements are assembled by separate individuals without a clear picture of the final product. They intend to create a horse, but instead end up with a camel.

camp on the line (to) *exp.* to hold for a long time on the telephone.

Capitol Hill *n.* site of the United States Senate and House of Representatives (it is located on a hill in the nation's capital).

carpetbagger *n.* an arrogant politician who anticipates success in a new locality.

carry out (to) *v.* to follow, to implement.

catch (to) *v.* to understand or hear something.

caucus *n.* • 1. a group of people with similar political beliefs and goals • 2. a meeting.

causal factors *n.* reasons.

CCC *n.* (Commodity Credit Corporation) a government corporation that is controlled by the Department of Agriculture. Its purpose is to control the marketing and exporting of a particular agricultural commodity.

CCCN *n.* (Customs Cooperation Council Nomenclature) a tariff structure used by most European countries as well as others worldwide. It is also known as the Brussels Tariff Nomenclature.

CD or CD-ROM *n.* (compact disc read-only memory) a removable plastic disc that can hold over 600 megabytes of digital information and is accessed through a special drive. Because this type of disc is read only memory, the user cannot change any information on the disc.

censure (to) *v.* to reprimand, criticize.

CEO *n.* (chief executive officer) the person ultimately responsible for a company's success or failure.

certificate of inspection *n.* a document which certifies that goods or merchandise are in acceptable condition before being shipped.

check it over (to) *v.* to examine something (for errors or appropriateness).

Chinese fire drill *exp.* mass confusion.

CIA *exp.* (cash in advance) payment terms that specify that payment must be made in full before shipment of goods.

CIF & C *exp.* (cost, insurance, freight, and commission) a pricing term specifying that cost, insurance, freight, and commission are included in the quoted price.

CIF&E *exp.* (cost, insurance, freight, and [currency] exchange) a pricing term that specifies that cost, insurance, freight, and currency exchange are included in the quoted price.

CIF *exp.* (cost, insurance, freight) a pricing term specifying that cost, insurance, and freight are included in the quoted price.

class action *n.* a legal action started by a small group of people on behalf of a larger group.

clean bill of lading *n.* a declaration for goods issued by a common carrier indicating that all cargo accepted for transporation was in good condition when received.

coequal *adj.* to be equal.

collection papers *n.* any documents (including bills of lading, invoices, etc.) presented to a buyer to receive payment for a shipment.

come up with (to) *v.* 1. to gather information • 2. to invent.

Common Market *n.* (also referred to as The European Economic Community or EEC) an economic arrangement between Western and European nations that facilitates trade.

competition analysis *exp.* a euphemism for corporate spying.

computer superstore *n.* a store that sells computers, programs, games, accessories, printers, computer maintenance products, etc.

confirmed letter of credit *n.* a letter of credit that guarantees payment to the beneficiary, even if the buyer defaults and his bank fails to pay.

conglomerate *n.* a big corporation made up of smaller companies, generally in unrelated businesses.

consignment *n.* delivery of goods from the owner to a dealer. The owner retains title to the goods until the dealer has sold them. Upon sale of the goods, the dealer retains his commission, and sends the net proceeds to the owner.

consular declaration *n.* a formal statement describing goods to be shipped, made to the consul of a foreign country.

consular invoice *n.* a document describing a shipment of goods, listing such information as the consignor, consignee, and value of the shipment. It is verified by the consular official and used by the receiving country's customs officials to confirm the shipment specifications.

consultant *n.* an independent contractor (hired on a time or project basis) who gives professional or expert advice.

container *n.* a large rectangular shipping crate (usually made of steel) designed to be loaded and unloaded from transport vehicles without being unpacked.

contract services *n.* work performed by outside contractors with a formal agreement.

convene (to) *v.* to assemble (as in a meeting), to come together.

convertibility *n.* the ease with which a particular currency may be exchanged for another in foreign exchange markets.

COO *n.* (chief operating officer) one who reports to the chief executive officer.

coprocessor *n.* an additional processor optimized to perform specialized tasks more efficiently than the main processor.

corpocracy *exp.* duplicate or excessive corporate management caused by multiple companies having merged.

corporate culture *n.* a company's values and standards, represented through mission statement, dress code, style of management, and goals.

corporate veil *n.* a shield under which stockholders are immune from legal action resulting from business failure.

corporation *n.* a business entity composed of investors (or stockholders), each of whose liability is limited to the amount invested.

cost-prohibitive *adj.* too expensive.

counterfactual *adj.* false.

countertrade *n.* goods traded for other goods rather than for cash; also known as "barter."

country manager *n.* an individual in charge of a multinational company's operations in a particular foreign country.

crash • 1. *n.* a sudden computer failure where the entire system freezes or shuts down • 2. *v.* to fail suddenly (said of a computer).

credit risk insurance *n.* insurance designed to cover losses resulting from nonpayment of an obligation.

crux of the matter (the) *n.* the main issue or reason.

currency depreciation *n.* the process of a nation's money decreasing in value compared to the currency of other nations or compared to its own previous value. The reverse process is called currency appreciation.

currency devaluation *n.* the process that occurs when a government purposely reduces the value of its money relative to that of other countries.

currency exposure *n.* the amount of investments a country or business has placed overseas that is subject to changes in value as a result of fluctuations in currency valuations.

customs broker *n.* an individual or business licensed to enter and clear goods through customs.

customs *n.* • 1. a government agency responsible for collecting duties levied on imports and exports • 2. the actual tariff, tax, or duty levied on imports and exports.

cut corners (to) *v.* to use less expensive means to produce something.

cut one's losses (to) *exp.* to get out of a bad financial situation (before it gets worse).

CVD *n.* (countervailing duty) an extra duty imposed by the U.S. Secretary of Commerce on a particular product to counter the effects of a foreign government's subsidy.

CWO *exp.* (cash with order) payment terms that requires a buyer to pay when placing an order.

CYA *exp.*(cover your ass) vulgar expression meaning document everything so you can't be blamed later.

CYA memo *n.* (cover-your-ass memo) a memorandum used to document one's actions and avoid blame if something does not get done correctly.

cyberspace *n.* a term given to the "place" where computer users meet on-line • cyber = electronic / space = universe.

D/A *exp.* (Documents Against Acceptance) shipper's instructions to a bank specifying that title transfer documents will not be delivered to the buyer unless the buyer agrees to the terms of the attached draft.

D/P *exp.* (documents against payment) shipper's instructions to a bank specifying that title transfer documents will not be delivered to the buyer unless the buyer pays the attached draft.

DBA *exp.* (doing business as; also referred to as a "fictitious name") used when a person or business known by one name choses to do business under a different name.

dead-in-the-water *adj.* a company lacking direction or failing to succeed.

deadline *n.* the time when a project must be completed.

de-diversify *v.* to sell off individual companies or divisions of a corporation not compatible with its main line of business.

deep bench *exp.* (from sports) a company with a lot of management talent.

default • 1. *n.* the initial settings a computer uses unless given instructions to the contrary • ***2.*** *v.* to reset back to an initial setting.

delphi technique *n.* a method of using outside experts in an interactive fashion to make company forecasts.

delta *n.* Greek character depicted by a triangular symbol (Δ); used in mathematics to indicate "change in." Often used in business to represent a change.

demagoguery *n.* the use of popular prejudices and misleading claims to gain political power.

demand draft *n.* a draft payable upon presentation rather than on a specified date.

desktop publishing *n.* a type of word processing program where text, graphics, and photographs can be manipulated on the computer to create a professional looking product.

destination control statement *n.* a statement required by the U.S. government to prevent diversion of U.S. exports to unauthorized destinations.

detention center *n.* jail.

diagonal slice *n.* a randomly chosen employee cross-section (ranging from assembly line to middle management workers); the group is intended to meet with management as a way of improving communication.

dialog box *n.* a rectangular box that appears on the computer screen to: 1. request additional information from the user about a command just requested; 2. to give the user additional details.

dither (to) *v.* to combine two or more colors to simulate another color.

divest (to) *v.* said of a large company selling off certain lines of its business.

do lunch (to) *exp.* to have lunch (very popular, but pretentious. Originally coined by phoney Hollywood agents).

doable (to be) *adj.* to be achievable.

dock receipt *n.* a receipt issued by an ocean carrier to acknowledge arrival of cargo at the carrier's warehouse or dock facilities.

dock walloper *n.* a thief who steals cargo before it has received customs clearance or has been unloaded.

domicile *n.* • 1. the principle place of business, or where the governing power of an enterprise is exercised • 2. a place where a draft or acceptance is made payable.

dove *n.* one who believes in keeping peace at all costs.

download (to) *v.* to receive files from another computer or *BBS* (bulletin board system) through the telephone line.

downsizing *v.* reducing staff or personnel to minimize operating costs and improve efficiency.

downstream *v.* a movement of goods or funds from a parent company to a subsidiary company.

downtime *n.* an interval when no work can be performed due to equipment breakdown, power failure, employee breaks, etc.

draft *n.* an order, in writing, directing a person (other than the maker) to pay a specified sum to a named person.

drawback *n.* obstacle, problem, barrier.

drawee *n.* a firm or individual in whose name a draft is drawn and who is responsible for the specified amount.

drawer *n.* the firm or individual that signs or issues a draft and receives payment of the specified amount from the drawee.

dud *n.* failure.

dumping *n.* the practice of selling goods overseas below their cost of production as a means of competing with foreign producers.

duty drawback *n.* a customs law which refunds duties on imported components used to manufacture exports.

duty *n.* a tax imposed on the importation, exportation, or consumption of goods. Duties may be based on the value, weight, or quantity of goods, or a combination of value and other factors.

dysfunctional *adj.* ineffective.

ECU *n.* (European currency unit) the currency unit of the European Community (EC) that is based on a basket of Common Market currencies.

EEC *n.* (European Economic Community).

EFTA *n.* (European Free Trade Association) composed of Austria, Faeroe Islands, Finland, Iceland, Norway, Portugal, Sweden, and Switzerland.

EMC *n.* (export management company) a company, usually compensated on a commission basis, which arranges foreign sales for domestic manufacturing companies.

EMS *n.* (European Monetary System)

end product *n.* the final result.

end user *n.* the targeted customer.

entrepreneur *n.* one who starts a business; founder.

ETC *n.* (export trading company) a company doing business in the United States chiefly to export domestic goods or services, or to facilitate exports.

ETCA *n.* (Export Trading Company Act) a law passed on October 8, 1982 to promote export of U.S. goods and services.

etched in stone (not) *exp.* to be changeable.

exec *n.* (executive) director or controller of a company.

Eximbank *n.* (Export-Import Bank of the United States) a bank that promotes export trade by providing financial assistance to exporters and credits to their customers overseas.

export broker *n.* an individual or company, generally paid on a commission basis, who arranges contacts between sellers and importers.

export license *n.* a government permit which enables the holder to export certain goods to specific destinations.

export merchant *n.* a company which imports directly from an overseas manufacturer, then resells the merchandise under its own name.

export trade certificate of review *n.* a document which grants partial immunity from antitrust regulations. It is issued by the Justice Department in conjunction with the Department of Commerce and is based on ETCA (Export Trading Company Affairs) legislation.

export • 1. *n.* a domestic product or service sold in a foreign market • 2. *v.* to send or transport products or services out of the country for sale in a foreign market.

FAA *exp.* (free of all average) an insurance policy that excludes partial loss claims and covers only total loss claims.

FAS *exp.* (free alongside ship) a term used on a quote indicating that the price includes delivery of the goods alongside a specified ship.

FCIA *n.* (Foreign Credit Insurance Association) an association of commercial insurers who act as the insurance agent for the Export/Import Bank of the United States (also known as Eximbank).

FDI *n.* (foreign direct investment) a partial or total controlling investment in a foreign enterprise.

feedback *n.* reaction.

FI *exp.* (free in) a term of sale indicating that the shipper is responsible for the cost of loading cargo at the port of origin.

figurehead *n.* a person who is a chief or head in name only, and does not participate in the decision-making process.

filibuster • 1. *v.* to speak for a lengthy period of time, preventing legislative activity • 2. *n.* a tactic used to delay or prevent legislative activity.

Filthy Five *n.* a list of companies compiled annually by *Mother Jones* magazine based on their poor environmental record.

final analysis (in the) *exp.* when everything has been carefully examined.

finder's fee *n.* a commission paid to a third party who locates a buyer, property, personnel, etc. that leads to a business deal between two other parties.

FIO *exp.* (free in and out) a term of sale indicating that the shipper is responsible for the cost of loading and unloading cargo.

fixed disk *n.*

floor *n.* the main area of the Senate or the House of Representatives where debating and voting occurs.

floppy disk *n.* a thin circular piece of plastic which has been magnetically-coated in order to store data.

FO *exp.* (free out) a term of sale indicating that the shipper is responsible for the cost of unloading cargo at its destination.

FOB *exp.* (free on board) an international commercial term (INCOTERM). The seller pays for delivery and loading of cargo at a specified location.

focus (to) *v.* to direct one's energy toward; to concentrate.

foreign exchange *n.* (also known as FOREX or FX) in a given country, the currency of another country.

foreign sales agent *n.* an individual or firm which acts as the foreign representative of a domestic manufacturer and sells goods on a commission basis.

Fortune 500 *n.* annual list of the 500 largest U.S. industrial corporations compiled by *Fortune* magazine.

foul bill of lading *n.* a bill of lading indicating that goods were damaged when delivered to a carrier.

FPA *exp.* (free of particular average) the title of a marine insurance clause specifying that partial losses are covered if the salvage operation benefits all parties to a shipping transaction.

free port *n.* a port available to all traders in which imported goods may be held while awaiting re-export, without the need to pay duties.

free trade *n.* commerce without trade or tax barriers.

freight forwarder *n.* company that prepares shipping and insurance documents, and arranges cargo deliveries for domestic manufacturers.

freshman *n.* an elected official serving his/her first term.

from the outset *exp.* from the beginning.

front end *n.* the marketing division of a business, as opposed to the manufacturing division.

FSC *n.* (foreign sales corporation) an offshore company eligble for a preferential tax rate of 15-32%. To qualify for special tax treatment, the FSC must have a main office in a U.S. possession and at least one director resident outside of the U.S.

FTZ *n.* (free trade zone) a special port outside a nation's custom's territory. No duties are paid if the merchandise is re-exported, otherwise duties are collected when goods pass out of the zone into an area subject to Customs Authority.

functional management *n.* a management system based on a function, such as marketing or advertising, in contrast to being arranged around an end product.

fund (to) *v.* to pay for.

funding *n.* money.

futures market *n.* (also known as the forward market) the purchasing and selling of contracts for commodities at a price set at the time of purchase, but not to be delivered or paid for until a specified time in the future.

gag rule *n.* a ruling that forbids anyone from revealing information presented during an official meeting or hearing.

game plan *n.* strategy.

GATT *n.* (General Agreement on Tariffs and Trade) an agreement whose purpose is to lessen tariffs and reduce trade barriers among the participants.

gavel-to-gavel *adj.* a period from the opening session to the closing session of the Senate or the House of Representatives (also used in reference to a court trial).

general export license *n.* an export license covering certain export commodities when no formal or written application is needed.

general partner *n.* a partner who is generally responsible for the business and has unlimited liability.

get axed (to) *v.* to get fired.

get down to business (to) *exp.* to begin working, to concentrate on business matters.

get to the bottom (to) *exp.* to investigate, to begin an investigation.

give or take *exp.* approximately.

give-and-take *exp.* compromise.

glad-hand (to) *v.* said of a politician who goes around meeting people and shaking hands to stay in good favor with the public.

glitch *n.* a problem, bug, obstacle which prevents the completion of a project.

go-getter *n.* a highly ambitious person.

gold plating *n.* useful but unnecessary features.

GOP *n.* (Grand Old Party) also known as the Republican Party.

governance *n.* a method or system of management that must be followed by the officers of a company.

grandfather clause *n.* a provision in a new rule that exempts those already engaged in the activity affected by the rule.

grandstand (to) *v.* to try to impress an audience through speech or action.

grass roots *n.* having to do with the general public or the average person.

greek text (to) *v.* to display text on the computer screen randomly for purposes of position only.

greenfield *n.* a general business term referring to any business venture or project that is new.

gross weight *n.* the entire weight of a shipment, including packing and containers.

gubernatorial race *n.* a contest for the election of governor.

guest workers *n.* foreign laborers admitted to a country to work at certain jobs for a specific period of time.

hands-off *adj.* uninvolved.

hands-on *adj.* describes management style characterized by active personal involvement.

hard copy *n.* a printed version of a document created on a computer.

hard currency *n.* a currency that is stable and acceptable for international transactions.

hard drive *n.* a mass storage device made of a non-removable metal disc that spins at a high rate and is capable of storing large amounts of programs and data for execution and retrieval.

hard facts *exp.* the undisputable truths.

hardware *n.* the computer itself and any other equipment such as the hard drive, CD-ROM, RAM, printer, etc.

hawk *n.* one who supports aggressive military policy.

hearing *n.* a meeting held to investigate actions or behavior.

heavy hitter *n.* a powerful individual, someone with money, influence, or experience.

hedging *n.* the purchase of a foreign currency to sell at a future date as a means of protecting against variations in the exchange rate.

heuristics *n.* problem-solving by experimental or trial-and- error methods rather than formal mathematical techniques.

hinge (to) *v.* to depend on.

hit list *n.* a list of regulations or laws that a political group wishes to modify or eliminate.

honcho *n.* (from the Japanese term *hancho*) squad or group leader; person in charge of a work detail.

house-keeping *n.* the process of deleting, moving, and/or backing up files in order to keep a hard disk organized; routine management of any system such as an office filing system.

icon *n.* a small picture on the computer screen which represents a particular computer function.

IMF *n.* (International Monetary Fund) an organization which promotes international exchange of goods and capital and acts as a clearing agency for member nations to assist them in avoiding currency devaluations.

implement (to) *v.* to start.

import • 1. *n.* a good or service produced in one country and brought into another country for the purposes of sale • 2. *v.* to bring a good or service produced in one country into another country for the purposes of sale.

in accordance with *exp.* following the guidelines of.

in full *exp.* complete (in reference to a payment).

in order *exp.* said of something that is free of problems.

in terms of *exp.* in regard to.

in the long run *exp.* over a long period of time.

in the meantime *exp.* for the moment, for now.

in the running *exp.* to be under consideration for (a job, a government position, an appointment, etc.).

in time *exp.* during a scheduled period of time.

in touch (to be) *exp.* to be in contact .

in turn *exp.* in return.

Inc. 100 *n.* annual list of the 100 fastest-growing small public companies in the U.S. compiled by *Inc. Magazine.*

incumbent *n.* someone currently holding office.

in-depth • 1. *adv.* in detail • 2. *adj.* detailed.

inland bill of lading *n.* a bill of lading used when moving cargo via truck or train to an exporter's international shipper.

insofar as *conj.* to the extent that.

interface (to) *v.* to communicate or interact with (another person).

International Monetary Fund *n.* see IMF

interpersonal skills *n.* ability to get along with other people.

interrupt *n.* a signal sent to the computer to stop a program currently running so that another function may be executed.

inward investment *n.* a multinational corporation's investment in projects in its home country.

irrespective *prep.* regardless.

irrevocable letter of credit *n.* a letter of credit which guarantees a specified payment if the seller meets the stipulated terms. It cannot be revoked.

ITA *n.* (International Trade Administration) a division of the Department of Commerce which administers international trade agreements and domestic trade legislation.

joint venture *n.* an agreement between firms to share expenses, profits, and losses from a commercial undertaking.

junket *n.* a trip made at public expense by a politician to conduct official business or gather information.

keyboard buffer *n.* an area of memory in the computer which holds a certain number of keystrokes.

KISS *exp.* (an acronym for Keep It Simple, Stupid) general advice to focus on reliability rather than unncessary features.

knock-off *n.* a cheap imitation of an expensive product.

know-how license *n.* a contract for licensing a technology process to a vendor for commercial development.

L/C *n.* (letter of credit) a bank's letter instructing payment to a named payee. Payment is made when terms specified in the letter are met.

lame duck *n.* an elected official who is not eligible to run for another term.

land a contract (to) *exp.* to sign a contract with a client.

landscape [orientation] *adj.* said of a page which is printed horizontally or lengthwise (as opposed to portrait [orientation] which is vertically).

last, but not least *exp.* following all the rest, but not the least important.

LDC *n.* (less-developed country or least-developed country) an undeveloped country with limited natural resources and a poor supply of skilled labor. It is dependent on primary commodity exports for income.

learning experience *exp.* a euphemistic term for a business mistake.

left winger *n.* one who has liberal views.

legislation *n.* • 1. proposed law • 2. a law which has already been passed.

license (to) *v.* to authorize, for a royalty or fee, the right to use a patent, trademark, process, or other item of value.

lighter *n.* an open or covered flat-bottomed boat, motorized or towed by a tugboat, and used primarily on inland waterways and harbors.

limited partner *n.* a partner in a business whose liability is limited to his/her investment and who has no involvement in the management of the company.

linearity *adj.* said of a result which is directly proportional to its cause.

live with *exp.* to accept circumstances or consequences.

log on (to) *v.* to enter a name and password in a computer in order to gain access.

logical drive *n.* a partition of a single physical hard drive that has been created by the user for program and data storage.

long shot *n.* something that is not likely to succeed.

look into (to) *exp.* to investigate .

loop *n.* a process by which information travels inter- or intra-office.

loose ends *n.* unresolved issues, unfinished business.

lose one's shirt *exp.* to lose everything in a business deal.

lowball (to) *v.* to quote low prices early in a sales negotiation, then raise them once the customer appears committed.

make do (to) *v.* to make the best use of something that is not adequate.

make headway (to) *v.* to make progress.

make or break (to) *exp.* to allow no middle ground between

marine insurance *n.* insurance that covers loss or damage of a ship's cargo.

markings (or marks) *n.* letters, numbers, or symbols, attached to a bill of lading or cargo to expedite identification

mark-up *n.* a price increase attached to a piece of merchandise before it is sold, as a way of making a profit.

mature industries *n.* an industry producing a product no longer in demand.

MBI *exp.* (Management By Intimidation) a tactic by management to increase job performance through threats or coercion.

MBO *exp.* (Management By Objective) a set of mutually acceptable performance goals developed through collaboration between management and employees.

MBWA *exp.* (Management By Wandering Around) a system of visible management whereby executives "wander around" the work site in order to assess the work process and enable employee interaction.

meet halfway (to) *v.* to compromise.

MFN *n.* (most-favored nation) a foreign country granted the most favorable terms in its international trade with the United States.

Mickey Mouse *adj.* said of a business that is poorly organized, inadequately financed, and lacking management talent.

middle-of-the-road *adj.* politically neutral.

mini-merger *n.* a merger between a small high-tech, cash-starved company and a large company with substantial cash reserves.

MNC *n.* (multinational corporation) a firm which derives at least 25% of its annual sales income from its subsidiaries or branches located in other countries.

monochrome *adj.* referring to a computer screen, or monitor, which displays information in shades of one color (amber, green, or white) as opposed to a color monitor.

morph (to) *v.* to smoothly transform one image into another.

motherboard *n.* the main circuit board of the computer.

motivationally deficient *adj.* lazy.

mouse milking *n.* a project requiring substantial effort but producing minimal return.

mudslinging *n.* criticism and condemnation of an opponent.

mule *n.* low-level, often unsuspecting, smuggler of contraband.

multimedia *n.* the combination of graphics, text, and sound on the computer to create programs (such as computer games, music programs, television interfacing, etc.).

multinational corporation *n.* see MNC

multitasking *n.* the computer's ability to run more than one program (task) at the same time.

Murphy's Law *exp.* "Whatever can go wrong, will go wrong."

net weight *n.* the weight of the contents of a shipment excluding the weight of the container, pallet, skid, or crate.

NIH *exp.* (Not Invented Here) a close-minded view that if an idea was not created locally, it is not worth consideration.

NIMBY *exp.* (Not In My Back Yard) attitude of people who are opposed to anything undesirable in their community such as a factory, new prison, etc.

NTB *n.* (nontariff barriers) any obstacle to trade other than a tariff barrier such as quotas and VRAs.

nuts and bolts • 1. *n.* the working parts • 2. *adj.* (as an adjective, hyphens are used: nuts-and-bolts) experienced or well-trained in the fundamentals.

nutshell (in a) *n.* in summation.

ocean bill of lading *n.* a bill of lading indicating that an exporter transfers title of cargo to an ocean-going carrier for transportation to a specified foreign destination.

OECD *n.* (Organization for Economic Cooperation and Development) a group of twenty-four industrialized nations who meet to coordinate international, economic, and social policies.

offshore financing *n.* raising money in foreign countries for domestic business operations.

off-the-record *adj.* unofficially.

oil patch *n.* a descriptive term for the oil industry.

on behalf of *exp.* as a representative of.

on board (to) *exp.* hired, appointed.

on spec *exp.* work of a speculative nature; performing preliminary development for no fee hoping that the client will agree to a full contract.

on the surface *exp.* at first glance, apparently.

on-line service *n.* a digital service available using a modem and telephone line. It gives users access to reference information over a wide range of subjects, as well as enabling users to communicate with one another.

OPEC *n.* (Organization of Petroleum-Exporting Countries) a group of petroleum-producing countries, headquartered in Vienna, that attempts to influence the supply and price of oil.

open account *n.* a credit method for financing trade transactions in which goods are shipped to a buyer without guarantee of payment.

open insurance policy *n.* a marine insurance policy that covers all shipments made by an exporter during a specified period of time.

open-collared *adj.* a corporate culture characterized by an informal and relaxed atmosphere.

OPIC *n.* (Overseas Private Investment Corporation) a corporation (created by the Foreign Assistance Act of 1969) to finance and insure U.S. investment overseas.

opportunity *exp.* a euphemistic expression for a problem encountered in business.

or so *exp.* approximately.

order taker *n.* a salesperson who doesn't aggressively pursue potential business.

Organization for Economic Cooperation and Development *n.* see OECD

Organization of Petroleum-Exporting Countries *n.* see OPEC

outside directors *n.* individuals elected by share- holders to boards of public companies to protect investor interests.

over (someone's) head *exp.* to go to someone's superior to demand action, report behavior, or request that a decision be overruled.

over-budget *adj., adv.* said of a project whose costs exceed the allocated amount of spending-money.

Overseas Private Investment Corporation *n.* see OPIC

PAC *n.* (Political Action Committee) a group of politically active people who try to influence legislation.

panel *n.* a group of individuals assembled for a hearing.

Parkinson's law *exp.* a proverb coined by C. Orthcote Parkinson: "Work expands so as to fill the time available for its completion."

partnership *n.* a business entity composed of two or more individuals, corporations, or other partnerships. Each partner is fully liable for the debts of the partnership and the partnership is responsible for the acts of each partner.

past history *exp.* history.

pencil in (to) *exp.* to tentatively schedule (written in pencil so that it can be easily changed if necessary).

phase in (to) *v.* to begin an operation in phases.

phase out (to) *v.* to gradually discontinue .

phase zero *exp.* the planning stage of a project, usually before significant resources have been committed.

phytosanitary inspection certificate *n.* a certificate issued by the U.S. Department of Agriculture certifying that U.S. agricultural exports have been inspected and are free from insects or plant diseases.

pick up (to) *v.* to increase.

pigeonhole (to) *v.* to postpone voting on a bill by delaying its presentation to a voting body.

platform *n.* the plan presented by a person running for office.

play ball (to) *v.* cooperate.

plug (to) *v.* to work hard.

plug-and-play *adj.* said of a device (such as a printer, scanner, etc.) which can be plugged into the computer and does not require configuration.

point (to) *v.* to indicate, direct attention to.

point man *n.* a person appointed to a highly prominent lobbying position.

poll • 1. *n. & v.* survey; to survey • 2. *n.* the place where voting takes place (usually in the plural: polls).

pollster *n.* one who conducts a poll or survey.

pork barrel *n.* government funding that results in significant patronage benefits.

portrait [orientation] *adj.* said of a page which is printed vertically (as opposed to landscape [orientation] which is horizontally).

power down (to) *v.* to turn off an electrical applicance.

power lunch *n.* a midday meal where major business deals are discussed and confirmed.

power up (to) *v.* to turn on an electrical appliance.

precinct *n.* an election district of a city or town.

press the flesh (to) *v.* to mingle with the public and shake hands.

private sector *n.* the business community.

pro forma invoice *n.* a facsimile of an invoice describing the type, quantities, and value of the goods to be sent, specifications such as weight or size and shipping and/or handling costs. Payment terms of a pro forma invoice are generally "payment in advance" or "collect on delivery."

proactive *adj.* taking action in anticipation of future problems or needs; taking the initiative.

procuring agent *n.*

product life-cycle *n.* refers to the seven stages in the lifetime of a product: research and development, introduction, market development, exploitation, maturation, saturation, and decline.

profit center *n.* part of a company that maximizes revenue and minimizes costs.

prop *n.* (proposition) a proposed law presented directly to the voting public for enactement.

proprietary *adj.* exploited, produced, and sold only by the owner having the exclusive rights to a particular product or technology.

pros and cons *exp.* good points and bad points, pluses and minuses.

public sector *n.* the government, the people.

pull up (to) *v.* to retrieve a computer file.

pull-down menu *n.* a list of options displayed on a computer monitor and usually accessed with a mouse. This action resembles pulling down a window shade.

punch in (to) *v.* to insert one's timecard into a timeclock which stamps or punches the time and date.

purchasing agent *n.* an agent, either an individual or private firm, who purchases goods on behalf of an organization.

push (to) *v.* to promote.

put pressure on (to) *exp.* to be firm

put/set the record straight (to) *exp.* to correct a wrong impression, to establish the facts.

qualitative *adj.* relating to quality or certain other characteristics that have not been measured or specified.

queue *n.* (from the British term for a waiting line of persons or vehicles) documents that have been sent to a printer and are waiting in line to be printed.

quick-and-dirty *adj.* said of work performed rapidly and without careful planning, fast and simple.

quotation *n.* an offer to sell merchandise at a specified price and under named conditions.

QWL *exp.* (Quality of Work-Life) a term for actions taken to create a humane working environment.

rainmaker *n.* a successful salesperson, one who brings in a lot of business due to his/her influence.

ramrod (to) *v.* to push something through forcefully and quickly.

reach an agreement (to) *v.* to agree, to make a mutual arrangement.

reinvent the wheel (to) *v.* to start from the beginning, to develop something that already exists.

reserve assets *n.* a country's holdings in convertible foreign currencies or precious metals as a final means of making payment overseas.

reskill (to) *v.* to retrain.

restructure (to) *v.* to make significant and fundamental changes in a company's financial structure or operations.

returns *n.* election results.

revaluation *n.* see currency devaluation

revenue shortfall *n.* a smaller gross income than forecast or budgeted.

revocable letter of credit *n.* a letter of credit that can be modified or cancelled by the buyer after it has been issued by the buyer's bank.

ride one's coattails (to) *exp.* said of a successful candidate who identifies with a popular elected official.

right winger *n.* one who has conversative views.

role *n.* function, responsibility.

root cause *n.* fundamental cause.

root directory *n.* the main directory, created when the hard drive is formatted.

rule out (to) *v.* to eliminate.

run a tight ship *exp.* to operate a well-organized and structured company.

run for office (to) *exp.* to compete in an election for a position in government.

run out (to) *v.* to be depleted of one's merchandise.

run smoothly (to) *v.* to operate without problems.

run the risk (to) *exp.* to take a chance.

runaway *n.* a business that relocates or shuts down to avoid organized labor or compliance with local regulations.

running mate *n.* political companion in an election, especially president and vice president.

safe bet *n.* to be risk-free, assured, or "a sure thing."

sales performance *n.* rating of a salesperson's efficiency (such as good or bad).

SDR *n.* (special drawing right) a universal reserve currency created by the International Monetary Fund (also referred to as the IMF).

secrecy agreement *n.* an agreement authorizing a person or organization to evaluate or research a particular technology, but generally prohibiting its commercial development.

SED *n.* (shipper's export declaration) a form prepared by a shipper that indicates the value, weight, destination, and other basic information about the export shipment.

seed money *n.* funds used to start a project.

service business *n.* a company whose primary product is a service i.e. temporary office workers, typesetting, printing, etc.

shape up or ship out (to) *exp.* to improve one's job performance or lose his/her job.

SIC *n.* (Standard Industrial Code) a uniform classification system published by the U.S. Department of Commerce for identifying products and services.

sit on the fence (to) *exp.* to be indecisive.

SITC *n.* (Standard International Trade Classification) a uniform system of codes developed by the United Nations and used for collecting international trade data.

slack off (to) *exp.* to neglect one's responsibilities, to perform one's work in a substandard way.

slave driver *n.* an overly demanding employer who makes employees work like slaves without regard to their well-being.

sleep on it (to) *exp.* to get a good night's sleep to reach a clear decision about something.

slip (to) *v.* to decline.

smokestack America *n.* a descriptive term for automobiles, steel, and glass manufacturers (from a time when huge old-fashioned factories dominated American manufacturing).

smooth everything out (to) *v.* to rectify a situation.

snap decision *n.* an impulsive determination made without taking the time to consider all of the consequences.

soft currency *n.* a currency that cannot be easily converted into gold or other foreign currency.

solidify one's position (to) *exp.* to form a definite opinion, take a stand.

sound board *n.* a special circuit board in the computer that generates audio.

spearhead (to) *v.* to lead.

split hairs (to) *v.* to argue about something trivial.

spot exchange *n.* a foreign currency purchased or sold at its current market price.

spot market *n.* the market for cash purchases of foreign currencies or other commodities where delivery occurs within two days of the transaction.

spread *n.* a large newpaper or magazine article.

squeaky wheel *exp.* (from the expression "The squeaky wheel gets the grease") said of someone whose assertiveness gets results.

SRO *n*. (Self-Regulating Organization) an association of professionals who set industry standards to avoid government regulation.

stand (to) *v*. to be likely (to accomplish something).

state-controlled trading company *n*. an authorized trading monopoly; often a primary purchasing agent for basic commodities.

steamship conference *n*. a shipping association composed of several ocean carriers operating over the same trade routes and setting uniform freight and service standards for their members.

stem (to) *v*. to result from, to be caused by.

straw poll *v*. a random sampling of opinion.

stump (to) *v*. to travel from town to town making political speeches.

subdirectory *n*. a partition of a directory or subdirectory.

subsidiary *n*. a company completely controlled by another company through majority ownership.

Sullivan principles *n*. a code of conduct formulated by the Reverend Leon Sullivan of Philadelphia. It directs U.S. corporations who have dealings with South Africa to treat black and white workers equally.

sunrise industry *n*. a new potential growth industry (such as microcomputers in the 1970s.)

sunset industry *n*. a no-growth industry in decline.

surf (to) *v*. to explore cyberspace using an on-line service.

surviving spouse *n*. widow/widower.

sweat equity *n*. an investment of labor (rather than capital) in a business when cash is in short supply.

sweep *n*. an overwhelming election victory.

SWOT *exp*. (Strengths, Weaknesses, Opportunities, and Threats) information a company needs in order to perform strategic planning.

synergy *n*. combined action or operation, i.e. cooperation, leading to improved results.

sysop *n*. (an acronym for system operator) a term given to the person in charge of managing a BBS (bulletin board service) or website.

system *n*. a computer (an abbreviation for computer system).

table an issue (to) *v*. to postpone discussion on, or consideration of, a piece of legislation.

take a hard line (to) *exp*. to be uncompromising.

take a stand (to) *exp*. to be decisive.

take into account (to) *v*. to make allowance for, to consider.

take shape (to) *v*. to assume a definite form.

take steps (to) *exp*. to take appropriate action.

tare weight *n*. the weight of an empty shipping container or packing crate.

task force *n*. a small temporary committee.

team player *n*. one who works well with others.

tech support *n*. (technical support) a department composed of computer technicians who provide telephone assistance to customers experiencing trouble with their computers or programs.

term *n*. a period of time during which an elected official holds office.

that is [to say] *exp*. in other words.

the ball's in your court *exp*. It's up to you to decide how to continue.

the fact of the matter *exp*. the most important issue, the truth.

the facts speak for themselves *exp*. the facts are obvious and don't need explaining.

the ins and outs *n.* the particulars, the details.

think through (to) *exp.* to evaluate, strategize, plan.

third party ticket (run on a) *exp.* to enter an election campaign representing an independent party (other than the Democratic or Republican party).

thrash out (to) *exp.* to discuss in detail.

threshold company *n.* a business that has passed the entrepreneurial stage and is attempting to establish a solid financial footing and a pattern of long-term growth and prosperity.

through bill of lading *n.* a single bill of lading used when transporting cargo through intermediate domestic or foreign ports.

tin-cupping *exp.* interdivisional soliciting for resources and support for a new product or idea within a corporation.

tip of the iceberg (the) *n.* the seemingly small part of a larger situation, the beginning of something formidable and usually undesirable.

top dog *n.* boss.

tractor-feed *n.* a mechanism used for feeding continuous form paper into a dot-matrix printer.

tramp steamer *n.* a ship without regular routes or port schedules.

trigger (to) *v.* to cause, set off.

Trojan horse *n.* a highly destructive program created by irresponsible programmers. It is hidden inside a genuine program and intended to cause data damage or loss.

trust receipt *n.* a document used when financing by letter of credit in which a buyer pledges goods as collateral for the credit. After disposal of the goods, the buyer must place the sales proceeds in trust for the financing bank.

turnkey *n.* a method of construction or manufacturing in which a prime contractor assumes responsibility for all phases of the project.

turnout *n.* attendance.

twofold *adj.* that which contains two parts.

typeface *n.* a group of characters sharing a common design (whereas a font refers to the combination of typeface and point size).

unit price *exp.* cost for each item.

unsubstantiated rumor *exp.* rumor.

up to speed *exp.* to be up-to-date, current.

up-and-running *exp.* said of a computer or program which has been installed and operational.

upload (to) *v.* to send files from one computer to another computer or to a BBS through the telephone line.

upstream (to) *v.* to steer goods or funds from a subsidiary to its parent company.

utilize (to) *v.* to use, expend.

value-driven *adj.* said of a well-organized corporate culture that uses the values of a founder or top executives to motivate employees and improve the company's productivity.

VAT *n.* (value-added tax) a sales tax on the increase in the monetary value of a product or service that has been improved by the addition of materials and/or processes.

VER *n.* (voluntary export restraint) a voluntary reciprocal trade restraint agreement.

Vertical ETC *n.* (Vertical Export Trading Company) an ETC that sells a wide range of products not organized around a particular product line or specific industry.

vertical integration *exp.* corporate control of all major aspects of a business from collection of raw materials to distribution of finished products.

vertical supplier *n.* a company-owned supplier; or independent vendor of raw goods, components or services to a vertically integrated industry.

veto (to) *v.* to reject, cancel.

viable *adj.* possible, workable, practical.

visuals *n.* slides, illustrations, flip charts, graphs, videocassettes, etc. used in a presentation.

VRA *n.* (voluntary restraint agreement) a reciprocal restraint agreement between a foreign government and a private company or group.

WA *exp.* (with average) a term from marine insurance meaning that a shipment is covered for partial damage that exceeds a stipulated percentage of the value of the shipment.

waffle (to) *v.* to be vague and misleading, to evade an issue.

what's more *exp.* additionally.

whistle blower *n.* an informant.

whole ball of wax (the) *exp.* everything.

whole megillah (the) *exp.* everything

whole nine yards (the) *exp.* everything

whole shebang (the) *exp.* everything

wiggle room *exp.* flexibility, room to maneuver.

without further ado *exp.* without further bother or fuss.

without reserve *exp.* a term describing the unconditional authority granted to a shipper's agent to alter the terms of a transaction without consulting a principal.

work hand in hand (to) *exp.* to work together, as a team.

World Bank *n.* an autonomous agency composed of the International Bank for Reconstruction and Development and the International Development Association. The World Bank makes low-cost, long-term loans to limited-development countries for infrastructure projects (such as drinking water systems, irrigation systems, etc.).

WPA *exp.* (with particular average) a marine insurance policy that does not cover partial loss claims when the salvage operation aids only one party in the shipping arrangement.

wrapped up *adj.* to be won.

write-protect (to) *v.* to modify a disk or file so that the user cannot change or delete information.

written in sand *exp.* flexible.

WTDR *n.* (world traders' data report) a report issued by the U.S. Department of Commerce that contains information on foreign firms such as product line and business reputation.

zero fund *exp.* a process whereby a program receives no money for its operations.

ORDER FORM ON BACK

Prices subject to change

AMERICAN	BOOK	CASSETTE
STREET TALK -1 *How to Speak and Understand American Slang*	**$16.95**	**$12.50**
STREET TALK -2 *Slang Used in Popular American Television Shows*	**$16.95**	**$12.50**
STREET TALK -3 *The Best of American Idioms*	**$18.95**	**$12.50**
BIZ TALK -1 *American Business Slang & Jargon* (general office • finance • meetings & negotiations • business travel • "computerese" • marketing & advertising)	**$16.95**	**$12.50**
BIZ TALK -2 *More American Business Slang & Jargon* (more general office • international trade • commonly used initials in international trade • more "computerese" & on-line slang • management • "bureaucratese" • political slang & jargon)	**$16.95**	**N/A**
BLEEP! *A Guide to Popular American Obscenities*	**$14.95**	**$12.50**
FRENCH		
STREET FRENCH -1 *The Best of French Slang*	**$15.95**	**$12.50**
STREET FRENCH -2 *The Best of French Idioms*	**$15.95**	**$12.50**
STREET FRENCH -3 *The Best of Naughty French*	**$15.95**	**$12.50**
SPANISH		
STREET SPANISH -1 *How to Speak and Understand Spanish Slang*	**$15.95**	**N/A**
GERMAN		
STREET GERMAN -1 *The Best of German Idioms*	**$16.95**	**$12.50**

OPTIMA BOOKS Order Form

2820 Eighth Street · Berkeley, CA 94710

ORDER FAX line: 1-800-515-8737

International orders FAX line: 510-848-8737 · Publisher direct: 510-848-8708

www.optimabooks.com E-mail: stampy@optimabooks.com

Name ______________________________

Shipping Address ______________________________

____

City ______________ State/Province ______________ Postal Code ________

Country ______________ Phone ______________

Quantity	Title	Book or Cassette?	Price Each	Total Price

Total for Merchandise	
Sales Tax (California Residents Only)	
Shipping (See Below)	
ORDER TOTAL	

METHOD OF PAYMENT (check one)

☐ **Check or Money Order** ☐ **VISA** ☐ **Master Card** ☐ **American Express** ☐ **Discover**

(Money orders and personal checks must be in US funds and drawn on a US bank.)

Credit Card Number: ☐☐☐☐ ☐☐☐☐ ☐☐☐☐ ☐☐☐☐

Card Expires: ☐☐ ☐☐

Name on card (please print)

SHIPPING

Domestic Orders: SURFACE MAIL (delivery time 5-7 days).
Add $5 shipping/handling for the first item · $1 for each additional item.
RUSH SERVICE available at extra charge.

International Orders: OVERSEAS SURFACE (delivery time 6-8 weeks).
Add $6 shipping/handling for the first item · $2 for each additional item.
OVERSEAS AIRMAIL available at extra charge.